Thoughts to Ponder

from

GOD'S HEART

to

MY HEART TO YOURS

SHIRLEY BERTHOLF

Copyright © 2023 by Shirley Bertholf.
All rights reserved. This book or any portion thereof may not be reproduced or used in any manner whatsoever without the express written permission of the publisher except for the use of brief quotations in a book review.

Publishing Services provided by Paper Raven Books LLC
Printed in the United States of America
First Printing, 2023

Paperback ISBN 979-8-9882064-0-8
Hardback ISBN 979-8-9882064-1-5

Unless otherwise indicated, all Bible passages quoted are from the New Living Translation, copyright© ***1996, 2004, and 2015.***

Dear Reader:

I'm so glad you have decided to join me in this wonderful excursion through God's Word. Each of these thoughts has come out of my own spiritual journey, as I sought to "**listen**" for God's voice while reading my Bible each day. For the past 50 years, God has graciously challenged and taught me through Scripture, but it wasn't until late 2006 that this book began to take shape in its present form.

My husband and I were walking through some "deep" waters, and, as is so often true during those times, God's Word became especially precious to me. I found myself intensely listening for whatever God might want to say to my heart. When a question would arise or a thought would jump out at me, I would stop and ponder it, knowing this "interruption" was from Him.

Very often, the Lord would stir my heart with an insight that begged to be expressed. I would then go to my computer and begin to write, knowing full well that what was flowing out of my heart and through my fingers was not really my own wisdom, but His.

At that time, we were serving a church in Washington state, completing our 35th year in pastoral ministry. I began sending these thoughts as weekly email devotionals to the dear people in our church. As many of my readers began to express to me how God spoke very specifically and timely into their hearts through these words, I sensed that God was calling me to compile them someday into a volume of devotional thoughts that could be read over the course of a full year.

Here we are in 2023, and I continue to send my weekly thoughts. I have often prayed for whoever will read these words, so you see, my friend, I have actually prayed for YOU without knowing who you were or anything about you. But God knows you, and here you are, reading these words.

I believe God, in His infinite love and wisdom, knows how to orchestrate each of the influences necessary to draw us into deeper relationship with Himself. That's what He longs for. I trust this little book is part of His loving plan for you. I am praying that you will sense God speaking to your heart through the thoughts He has whispered into mine.

This book is not intended to be a "feel-good" devotional to give us one more thing to check off our religious "to-do list." In these pages, you will be invited to think deeply, to consider TRUTH and ponder whether or not you will allow that TRUTH to engage and transform your life, to decide whether you accept Who God says He is or embrace instead the version of Him that is currently circulating in our culture, and to open your heart and yield to whatever you sense God is saying to you.

At the end of each day's thoughts, I offer a suggested prayer. This is not designed to be "The End" of the devotional, but to stimulate an ongoing conversation with God concerning anything He has revealed during your time together.

I've been praying that every true believer will experience:

- a renewed passion for Jesus,
- a consuming hunger for God's Word,
- a deep longing for the transforming work of God's Spirit to make us like Jesus, and
- a broken heart and overwhelming love for the confused, hurting people who live and work around us every day without a clue what God is really like, how much He loves them, and the amazing LIFE He longs to give them.

I've also been praying for those who, like me in my first 21 years, have allowed themselves to settle for a religious lifestyle and Christian value system, rather than to pursue a personal relationship with the Living God through His Son, Jesus Christ. When I finally came to the end of all **my** efforts to obtain the approval of God and encountered the Living Christ as my ONLY way to the Father, my ONLY hope of abundant and eternal life, I wondered why in the world I had run from and resisted Him all those years.

The invitation of Jesus still stands for you, as it does for me and every human being who ever lived: *"Come to me, all of you who are weary and carry heavy burdens, and I will give you rest. Take my yoke upon you. Let me teach you, because I am humble and gentle at heart, and you will find rest for your souls…" (Matthew 11:28-30)*

I will continue to pray for you, Dear Reader, as you begin this year-long journey with me and with the God of the Universe, Who so passionately loves you. I am trusting that *"…God, who began the good work within you, will continue His Work until it is finally finished on the day when Jesus Christ returns." Philippians 1:6*

It would thrill me to learn how God uses these words to encourage and grow you in your faith. Please feel free to write and share your experience, so I can celebrate His goodness and faithfulness with you. For the joy of the journey, I offer these *Thoughts to Ponder From God's Heart to My Heart to Yours.*

Shirley Bertholf

Free Gift

Thank you for buying *From God's Heart to My Heart to Yours*.
I have a free gift that'll help you on your journey.
Just click below or scan the QR code to get it now:

https://www.shirleybertholf.com/bonus

Dedication

To my dear mother, Alice Thompson, who was the first person to show me the love of God. You are the one who made Jesus real to me as a child. It was you whose generous heart and sacrificial love made me want to know Him. You challenged me to be the best version of who God made me to be. Your beauty and grace inspired me to love being a woman with all its privileges and responsibilities. You saw potential in me and encouraged me to pursue music, drama, and writing, which have filled my life with rich meaning and joy.

You gave me the gift of music when I was just a baby in your arms. My favorite song was a sad folk melody about two little girls lost in the woods. You sang it with such feeling as we rocked back and forth that I would weep into your bosom, all the while begging you to, "Sing it again, Mama!"

Your beautiful harmony as I sat next to you in church called out the music within me as well. You eagerly helped me prepare little songs to sing at church and family gatherings, then solos for contests and school plays. After high school graduation, you designed the logo and became my "manager" and driver for a summer mini-tour of concerts we called "Teen Testimony in Sacred Song." Those concerts were among the first of many opportunities throughout my life to minister to others through music.

You were the one who encouraged me to do my first dramatic reading and showed me how to communicate with emotion and body language. It was in those early lessons that I caught your love for expressing yourself through words, both spoken and written. Little did I know, at that time, how God would use your passion to direct my life in service to Him.

Mother, you were my greatest cheerleader, always there for me, always sacrificing that I might have opportunities to grow and excel in whatever I set my heart on. You went without so many things, worked late into the night sewing lovely clothes for me to wear, and listened patiently for hours to my teenage "drama," always with wisdom and encouragement that gave me perspective and helped me grow in every difficult situation.

There are no words to express my gratitude to you and to the God who chose you to be my mother. A few years ago, you left us for Heaven, and I miss you every day. So much of who you were and what you instilled into my life has helped shape the pages of this book, and for that and so much more, I am forever grateful. I love and miss you, Mama, and I'm thrilled to dedicate this book to your memory.

January

January 1
Easier Said Than Done

"They spout empty words and make covenants they don't intend to keep." Hosea 10:4

The New Year inspires us. We feel we can hit the "reset" button, get a brand-new start. Hope fills our minds with possibilities, and we find ourselves making resolutions, many of them quite grandiose!

Unfortunately, we sometimes fail to take a realistic view of what will be required to follow through on our promises. When faced with the self-discipline and self-denial required, we, too, often "fold."

In this passage, God's people have been making promises, but their words are as empty as many of our New Year's resolutions. It's obvious there is no serious intention to follow through, because, when all is said and done, their promises don't change a thing.

Promises are not always easily kept, even for God. In Gethsemane, Jesus asked desperately if there was any way He could fulfill God's promise of redemption without going to the cross. But there wasn't! God had promised a deliverer down through the ages, and the time had come to make good on His Word.

PONDER: How many promises have I made to the Lord that I have not kept? ...to my spouse, my children, my boss?

PRAYER: Lord, I'm thankful you are a God Who <u>**keeps**</u> Your Word. I know I can count on <u>everything</u> You say! I want to be like You, so that, when **I** say something with **my** mouth, I'll follow through with my actions, <u>even</u> when it's not easy to do.

FROM GOD'S HEART TO MY HEART TO YOURS - 1

January 2
The Chance To Begin Again

"'Come now, let's settle this,' says the Lord. 'Though your sins are like scarlet, I will make them as white as snow...'" Isaiah 1:18

Talk about a "do-over!" No matter what my past looks like, the Lord is offering a brand-new start!

It's difficult for us, with all our sophisticated cleaning products, to understand how descriptive this passage was to the people of Israel. Back then, everyone knew that bright red stains just didn't come out, no matter how hard one scrubbed!

But God can do what we cannot. He offers us a "clean slate," a new beginning. We can be forgiven, cleansed of all unrighteousness! We can stand before God as if we had never sinned. How? By receiving the **GIFT** God provided through Christ's death and resurrection.

God did what no amount of "scrubbing" on our part could <u>ever</u> do.

"...He sent his own Son in a body like the bodies we sinners have. And in that body, God declared an end to sin's control over us by giving his Son as a sacrifice for our sins." Romans 8:3

"...anyone who belongs to Christ has become a new person. The old life is gone. A new life has begun!" II Corinthians 5:17

PONDER: Does having a "clean" heart sound too good to be true? Am I willing to trust that God **wants** to forgive me and make me brand new? Will I let Him?

PRAYER: Come, Lord Jesus, and do Your renewing, cleansing work in my heart!

January 3
God's Call To Worship

"Happy are those who hear the joyful call to worship, for they will walk in the light of your presence, Lord." Psalm 89:15

What is this **"call to worship"** the Psalmist refers to? Church bells clanging? ...the pastor's challenge to "prepare our hearts?" ...a feeling of obligation to set aside time for "devotions" each day?

Should worship be limited to certain times and places? Is that the sum total of what God desires from the human heart?

Ultimately, this joyful call to true worship issues from God Himself. Through His Spirit, God woos us into a constant <u>awareness</u> of His Presence. When we compartmentalize worship into particular days or times of the day, we close ourselves off to the moment-by-moment whispers of the Almighty.

Though encounters with God may happen at church, if we haven't heard and responded to His "call" in the mundane moments of every day, we've not yet comprehended His heart for each of us.

God wants to walk with us intimately, to be part of <u>every</u> moment. He wants to live **His** life through our bodies. When He does, the Light of His Presence will be unmistakable!

PONDER: Is worship something I practice only at church or during prescribed devotional times? Or is it the continual response of my heart to God throughout the variegated moments of each day?

PRAYER: Lord, sensitize my heart to hear and respond to Your *"joyful call to worship,"* so I may walk constantly *"in the light of Your presence."*

January 4
What Message Am I Sending?

"O, Lord, you alone are my hope, I've trusted you... from childhood... My life is an example to many because you have been my strength and protection. That is why I can never stop praising you..." Psalm 71: 5,7,8

The Lord wants our lives to be an example of the faithfulness and trustworthiness of our God!

Do those closest to me see me trusting God and praising Him, sure of His provision and protection, even in my darkest days?

What about those on the periphery of my life? What picture of God do they perceive as they observe my comings and goings? What might they conclude about Christ from my lifestyle, the way I talk, the attitudes I convey, the countenance I wear?

A peace-filled, joyful, hopeful, generous, loving, forgiving, patient, gracious, self-disciplined, kind person is the very best advertisement for Jesus Christ in this life.

When the rest of the world is filled with fear and finds little to smile about, with only temporary remedies and pleasures to dull the pain of their lives, I can assure you that smiling, confident, radiant Christ-followers will shine like stars against a black sky *(Philippians 2:15)*. Will you be one of those?

PONDER: What kind of message does my life portray about God?

PRAYER: Lord, I want to live in the power of Your Holy Spirit, Who alone can produce in me the qualities described above and cause them to spill out of my life as a radiant example of Who You are.

January 5
Facing My Personal Enemies

"He rescued me from my powerful enemies, from those who... were too strong for me." Psalm 18:17

Unlike David, most of us are not pursued by vengeful enemies, intent on killing us. When we read the Psalms, it's difficult to relate to David's cries of desperation, his frantic calls for God to deal mightily with those who sought his destruction.

We have our own "enemies," however, that "suck" the life out of us: bitterness, substance abuse, pride, depression, gossip, sexual impurity, lying, etc. What if we personalized the Psalms, identifying our own personal foe every time the word "enemy" is stated or implied?

"Only by Your power can [I] *push back* [my bitterness]; *only in Your name can* [I] *trample* [my resentment]." *Ps. 44:5*

"He rescued me from my powerful [alcohol, food, drug, nicotine addiction]." *Ps. 18:17*

"I trust in You, my God! Do not let...my [anger] *triumph over me." Ps. 25:2 NIV*

"It is You who [gives me] *victory over* [my gossip]." *Ps. 44:7*

"Oh, please help [me] *against* [my impure thoughts], *for all human help is useless. With God's help* [I] *will... trample down* [my lust]." *Ps. 60:11,12*

PONDER: What "foe" do I struggle with? Do I believe God is big enough to help me conquer it?

PRAYER: *"You are my strength; I wait for You to rescue me, for You, O God, are my place of safety. In* [Your] *unfailing love,* [You] *will come and help me.* [You] *will let me look down in triumph on all my enemies." Ps. 59:9,10*

January 6

Forgive? Are You Kidding Me?

"There will be no mercy for those who have not shown mercy to others. But if you have been merciful, God will be merciful when He judges you." James 2:13

This sounds a lot like the prayer Jesus taught us to pray, *"Forgive us our sins as we have forgiven those who sin against us." (Matthew 6:12)* We've all heard it, read it, and prayed it. But do we fully comprehend what we're really asking God to do?

Jesus is very clear: When we withhold forgiveness and harbor a bitter spirit, we effectively shut the door on God's mercy and forgiveness to us. Period!

In light of that reality, could there <u>ever</u> be <u>any</u> offense worth hanging onto? To say, in effect, *"God, I would rather burn in Hell than forgive this person,"* is a sobering thought.

Such a statement could only mean I have no comprehension of two things: (1) the absolute <u>horror</u> of eternity without God, and (2) the depth of my <u>own</u> sin against Him. Had I ever truly glimpsed my own heart through His eyes, I would forever understand how absolutely undeserving <u>I</u> am of **<u>His</u>** mercy.

PONDER: Do I see myself as <u>basically good</u>, therefore able to judge others? Or have I allowed God to reveal what He sees when He looks into <u>my</u> heart?

PRAYER: Lord, show me what I deserve, apart from Your love and mercy, so I can fully comprehend the <u>depth</u> of Your Amazing Grace. Change my life with that realization!

January 7
Don't Let The Fire Go Out!

"...the fire on the altar must be kept burning; it must never go out. Each morning the priest will add fresh wood to the fire and arrange the burnt offering on it... Remember, the fire must be kept burning on the altar at all times. It must never go out." Leviticus 6:12,13

Those of us who've heated our homes with wood know the importance of such a statement, especially on cold winter days. Maintaining the fire requires careful attention and diligence. Ironically, the times when it's most urgent to keep the flame burning are the very days when gathering the wood is the least convenient.

Each morning, by seeking Jesus first, acknowledging Him before running headlong into the day, spending time in His Presence and His Word, we "stoke the fire" He has ignited within our being. Once the flame is reinvigorated by the infusion of fresh "wood," we can arrange the parts of our day as a sweet-smelling sacrifice that will bring joy and glory to the Lord we love.

The days when that is most tedious are likely the times when it is also most critical.

PONDER: Has the "fire" of my passion for Jesus been allowed to cool or go out? How might I rekindle the flame? What "fresh wood" must be added to the fire every morning?

PRAYER: Lord, help me know how important it is to seek You first, each morning, each moment, in order to be the living sacrifice You can use.

January 8

What Joy!

"Though our hearts are filled with sins, you forgive them all. What joy for those you choose to bring near…" Psalm 65:3,4

Scripture declares God's desire to bring <u>every</u> person near to Himself. From Genesis to Revelation, God is revealed as moving to restore mankind's original relationship with Him.

He doesn't just randomly pick and choose those who will be saved or lost. Scripture makes it very clear: *"…<u>anyone</u> who calls on the name of the Lord <u>will</u> be saved!" (Acts 2:21)* (emphasis mine)

God "<u>chooses</u>" any who will call on Him. That's good news! It doesn't matter whether we're famous or infidel, rich or poor, religious or criminal. The only criterion is our humble cry to God for the salvation He's provided through Jesus.

It is **<u>Christ's</u>** merit, not ours, that satisfies the wrath of God against our sins! He was crucified so we might become children of God. No matter how many or what kind of sins we've committed, in God's grace, **<u>every</u>** transgression can be forgiven! Not one will be held against us. Though the rest of the world may write us off as worthless, even hopeless, God's grace offers a new start—power to be different from this day forward. That is truly cause for joy!

PONDER: Does God's extreme mercy, in the face of my unworthiness, evoke in me the kind of joy referred to by the Psalmist?

PRAYER: Lord, may Your name be praised forever! You have certainly done great things for me!

January 9
What Will It Take?

"I sank beneath the waves and the waters closed over me... As my life was slipping away, I remembered the Lord. And my earnest prayer went out to [him]..." Jonah 2:5a, 7a

How wonderful to know that even as we near the very end of life, God's Spirit is still striving with us, still ready to redeem, if we will but remember the Lord and earnestly cry out to Him.

In disobedience, Jonah ran away from God, willfully rejecting the Word of the Lord, choosing His own path instead.

Scripture warns there is a way that "seems" right to man, but leads to death *(Proverbs 14:12, 16:25)*. How like Jonah we are, thinking we know best for our lives, doubting the trustworthiness of God.

Though His Spirit continually strives with us, we tend to put our hands over our ears to block out the earnest pleadings of the Savior. For many of us, it's not until life slams us with the unthinkable that we come face-to-face with our own mortality.

Hopefully, we, like Jonah, will finally realize our total inability to rescue ourselves from the destiny we have chosen, and cry out to God. What will it take for <u>me</u> to finally acknowledge <u>my</u> need?

PONDER: Will I wait until my life hangs precariously in the balance? What if, in that moment, my heart has been dulled and my ears are too calloused to hear His voice?

PRAYER: Oh, God, I acknowledge **NOW** my desperate need of a Savior!

January 10

The Ball Is In Our Court

"I knew that you are a merciful and compassionate God, slow to get angry and filled with unfailing love. You are eager to turn back from destroying people." Jonah 4:2b

Just another glimpse into the true heart of God! If we search Scripture, we will see it over and over and over again.

God is holy. Sin cannot stand in His presence and must be dealt with justly. But God's heart is to invite sinners to repent and turn from their evil, selfish ways so that He may give them life.

He offers repeated warnings through His Word. He sends His Holy Spirit to convict us of the sin in our lives, the righteousness that His holiness requires, and the judgment that is to come. God "put on flesh" and was born as a man, because only as a man could He die, and only through His death could He pay for our sins and provide redemption for every person. *Hebrews 2:14*

God is so eager to turn back from destroying people that He has done <u>everything</u> necessary that no man, woman, boy or girl, would ever have to be separated from Himself, but could have eternal life, beginning right here, right now.

The ball is in our court! Now, we must make a choice.

PONDER: Why would I withhold myself from One who loves me so completely and has gone to such great lengths to win me back to Himself?

PRAYER: Forgive me, Lord, for ever doubting Your love and mercy!

January 11

Who Deserves God's Mercy?

"The Lord replied, 'Is it right for you to be angry about this?'" Jonah 4:4

Why are we so willing to accept the mercies and grace God pours out on us, yet so quick to demand justice for others we deem unworthy of it?

Jonah disobeyed a direct command of God. When a storm threatened his fleeing ship, Jonah admitted his disobedience to his shipmates. Thrown overboard, he describes the panic and desperation with which he sank to the bottom of the sea, knowing death was imminent.

Then… God, in His mercy, sent a great fish to swallow Jonah. Imagine as Jonah frantically sucks in the air provided for him within the belly of this whale. His life has been saved! God has had mercy! Jonah spends the next three days worshiping and praising God for His deliverance.

Once "released" from the whale's belly, Jonah heads straight for Nineveh to fulfill his mission. But what's this? When the wicked people of Nineveh repent, and God shows His mercy, Jonah is **angry**!

He had no trouble receiving God's compassion for himself. Why is he angered at God's kindness to the Ninevites? Does he think he deserved it, and they didn't?

PONDER: Do I feel I'm more deserving of God's kindness, or that I've somehow earned it?

PRAYER: Lord, may I never lose the awareness that it's **only** by Your mercy and amazing grace that I am saved. Help me offer Your compassion freely to any, and all, undeserving sinners—like me!

January 12
The Real Deal

"'Should we pull out the weeds?' '...No,' he replied, 'you'll uproot the wheat if you do. Let them grow together until the harvest. Then I will tell the harvesters to sort out the weeds, tie them into bundles, and burn them, and put the wheat in the barn.'" Matthew 13:29,30

Jesus explains to His disciples that the good seed represents the people of the Kingdom. The weeds are the people who belong to the evil one.

What surprises us, though, is that Jesus makes it clear that we humans shouldn't try to "pull out the weeds" because we won't always be able to tell them apart. They're going to grow up together, and someday, God will reveal the Truth.

To the human eye, "wheat" and "weeds" can, at times, look exactly alike. But God looks right into every heart. He **KNOWS**, even now, who is really His. He knows which of us has been born again and who is still hiding his/her spiritual nakedness, depending instead on the flimsy garments of "self-effort" and personal "acts of righteousness" to gain God's approval.

PONDER: Does it disturb me to know that God sees the truth about my heart? ...that He knows whether I've been changed by His Spirit deep within my Spirit, and have been infused with His own divine nature... or **NOT**?

PRAYER: Lord, am I a "weed" trying to pass myself off as "good seed" in Your Kingdom? Help me be honest with You. Do Your transforming work in my heart, O God.

January 13

Who's In Charge Here?

"I have been crucified with Christ; it is no longer I who live, but Christ lives in me; ...the life which I now live in the flesh I live by faith in the Son of God, who loved me and gave Himself for me."
Galatians 2:20 NKJV

My body is the "house" in which the real me resides. It often feels like I have no choice but to do what the real me dictates. Without Christ, that's true.

Once Christ comes to live in me, through His Spirit, my body becomes **His** dwelling place. However, my flesh still wars against His Spirit. We cannot both live our lives in this body. One of us will dominate. The other must yield.

When I'm in control of my life, the "stuff" that surfaces is self-serving and damaging to relationships. When Jesus Christ is in control, the fruit of His Spirit flows from my life.

I can choose, every day, every moment, to put Him in control, by saying, **"No,"** to the selfish part of me that wants my own way and **"Yes"** to His Spirit.

If I know Jesus really lives in me, and I choose to "do what Jesus would do" regardless of feelings, I can trust His life and power to "show up" and take it from there.

PONDER: What does the "stuff" flowing from my life say about who's in the driver's seat?

PRAYER: Lord, teach me what it means to let You live Your life in me.

January 14

What "Mercy" Is Not!

"Where are your accusers? Didn't even one of them condemn you? ...Neither do I. Go and sin no more." John 8:10,11

God is merciful. How glad we are for that truth. He asks us to be merciful in His Name. But, as with all beautiful truths of Scripture, the devil will do his best to pervert it. Sometimes the sincerest among us are the most vulnerable.

God's "mercy" can be twisted. We tell ourselves: *"God doesn't care what we do. He just wants us to be "happy" (however that word is defined in our vocabulary and lifestyle). If we break His commandments, it's okay. God understands. His wrath was Old Testament. Jesus changed things when He came, and now, anything goes. Now, because of Jesus, God is so merciful that he is willing to turn a blind eye to our sin, wink it away, so to speak, rather than deal with it. We're all going to be forgiven anyway, so what's the big deal, right?"*

The woman caught in the act of adultery was brought to Jesus for condemnation. He forgave her instead. But notice his next words, *"Go and sin no more."* Jesus didn't demonstrate His mercy to this woman so that she could continue to live in sin... but to change her life!

PONDER: Has my understanding of God's mercy turned into indulgence of sin in my life or the lives of others?

PRAYER: Help me see how much Jesus hates sin. That's why He went to the cross.

January 15

Dare I Approach God?

"'I will invite him to approach me,' says the Lord, 'for who would dare to come unless invited?'" Jeremiah 30:21b

Do we have any idea what would happen to one who dared approach God uninvited?

This is **GOD** we're talking about! …at Whose voice, when He spoke on Mt. Sinai, people shook in terror, fearing for their lives (*Ex. 20:18,19*).

This is **GOD**! …whose Holy Presence instantly consumed Uzzah as he reached out and touched the Ark of the Covenant on its return from Philistia. *II Sam. 6:6-8*

Yet <u>we</u> have been **invited** to approach Him! How can that be? Incredibly, God <u>Himself</u> has provided a *"new, life-giving way"* for us to boldly *"enter Heaven's Most Holy Place"* through the death of Jesus on our behalf. He invites us to *"go right into the presence of God, with true hearts fully trusting Him." Heb. 10:19-22*

If the evil in our lives has been washed clean by Christ's blood, we can boldly stand before God, faultless, clothed in Christ's righteousness! *Jude 1:24, Isaiah 61:10*

PONDER: Do I have any idea what a privilege I have been given? Have I neglected or, worse, have I been careless or flippant in my approach to prayer, which is the means by which I have access to this privilege? Do I have any idea what it cost God to provide this invitation for me into His presence?

PRAYER: Oh, Lord, I am humbled that <u>You</u> desire to be with <u>me</u>, and You invite <u>me</u> to be with <u>You</u>. I accept Your invitation with great gratitude!

January 16

How Impossible Is Impossible?

"They were totally amazed, for they still didn't understand the significance of the miracle of the loaves. Their hearts were too hard to take it in." Mark 6:51,52

Jesus has just fed 5000 men and their families with five loaves and two fish, after which His disciples gathered 12 baskets of leftovers. Later that same day, in the wee hours of the morning on the Sea of Galilee, the disciples are terrified by a huge storm that threatens to sink their ship.

Jesus comes walking on the water toward them. As He steps into the boat, the winds stop. Today's Scripture implies that, had they fully understood the miracle of the loaves, they wouldn't have been so shocked and amazed when Jesus calmed the storm.

So what was the lesson of the loaves?

We humans tend to qualify the impossible, as if some impossibilities are less feasible than others. Let's face it—each is equally hopeless for us, yet equally simple for God! If God has ever done <u>anything</u> for us, why not trust Him to do <u>everything</u>?

PONDER: Do I really believe nothing is impossible for God? Do I frantically struggle against life's difficulties in fear, or do I expectantly call on Jesus to help me accomplish what I cannot?

PRAYER: Lord, to You, <u>nothing</u> is too difficult! Help me learn from the ways You have helped in the past and trust that, though the impossible is always hopeless for me, it is a simple task for You.

January 17

Whom Do I Honor Most?

"…Why do you give your sons more honor than you give me…" I Samuel 2:29

Though the prophet Eli was mortified by the blasphemous actions of his sons, and even rebuked them, he stopped short of removing his sons from Levitical duties. Why, when Eli obviously loved and served God faithfully?

Whatever his motivation for failing to discipline his sons *(I Samuel 3:13),* God addressed the real issue with this probing question: *"…Why do you give your sons more honor than you give me…?"*
The truth God knew (to which Eli seemed oblivious) is this: Eli cared more about his sons' feelings than God's.

Jesus addressed this in *Matthew 10:37. "If you love your father or mother…son or daughter more than me, you are not worthy of being mine."* These are hard words.

Eli's sons would ultimately fall under God's judgment. In retrospect, was it really "love" that stayed Eli's hand?

Had he been willing to put God's honor ahead of his sons', might their hearts have turned away from their sin? Might the outcome have been different?

The wisest man who ever lived wrote under the Holy Spirit's inspiration, *"Those who spare the rod of discipline hate their children. Those who love their children care enough to discipline them." Proverbs 13:24*

Loving God <u>most</u> enables us to love others <u>best</u>.

PONDER: Who or what receives the highest place of honor in my heart?

PRAYER: Forgive me, Lord. Take your rightful place on the throne of my life!

January 18

Do We Argue With Our Maker?

"…Does a clay pot ever argue with its maker? Does the clay dispute with the one who shapes it, saying, 'Stop, you are doing it wrong!'" Isaiah 45:9

God paints a word picture here and wants us to use our imaginations to fully understand what He's saying. Most of us have probably not had the privilege of watching a potter spin and shape clay, but from the clay's perspective, it can't be much fun.

First, there's the shaping. It probably doesn't feel that good to be poked and prodded or spun into shape. And the clay doesn't even get to decide what shape it wants to become!

Thankfully, the decorating and glazing might be a little like putting on new clothes. Beautiful colors and patterns tend to make one feel attractive. But what if the potter chooses to make me just a plain ole jug for carrying water?

Finally, there's the firing. Believe it or not, the higher the temperature, the more durable the pottery. Just the thought makes me shudder! I'd be screaming, *"Don't put me in there. It's too hot! …Get me out of here! I can't bear it! I'll surely die!"*

PONDER: How like clay am I? Moldable? Yielding to the potter's fingers to be shaped as He sees fit? Willing to be used for <u>His</u> purposes? Laying aside my own ideas of how things should go?

PRAYER: Lord, please help me trust what You are doing in my life and use me for Your Glory.

January 19

Must Conflict Always Divide Us?

"Finally, Abram said to Lot, 'Let's not allow this conflict to come between us…'" Genesis 13:8

Nobody likes conflict, yet it is an inevitable facet of living together in community. Each person is unique and different. The varying personalities, priorities, and perspectives of us humans put us on a collision course with each other.

But according to this verse, conflict doesn't have to divide people. How we deal with our differences will make the difference. That seems so obvious, so simple! Then why is there so much division among people, even in the Church?

Scripture makes it clear: it's not our <u>differences</u> that make it difficult for us to get along. It's our <u>sinful nature</u>—that inner compulsion that demands things be done "my way or the highway!"

Selfish people find it difficult to yield. Even when social or religious pressure brings what appears to be a compromise, the self-centered individual will manipulate behind the scenes until he/she achieves the desired outcome.

PONDER: How do I react when I don't get what I want… in my marriage, in a board meeting, on vacation, at work? What happens in my thoughts, my actions, my conversations with others—after I "give in?"

PRAYER: Lord, I don't always recognize my selfishness. I just do what comes naturally. If anything is to change in my life, Your Spirit must reveal my true self to me. Give me grace to look honestly at my heart (my motives, my attitudes) and allow You to change me from within.

January 20

Making Myself God's Enemy?

"…Don't you realize that friendship with this world makes you an enemy of God? I say it again, that if your aim is to enjoy this world, you can't be a friend of God." James 4:4

Who would ever want to be considered God's enemy? Not I! Yet most of us don't realize that's exactly what happens when we get too "cozy" with the ways and thinking patterns of this world.

Jesus said the world hates Him and, therefore, <u>IF</u> we are <u>like</u> <u>Him</u>, it will hate us, too. Make no mistake. We cannot be "friends" with this world without compromising our desire for Christ, our pursuit of His mind, His will, His holiness, His likeness, and His heart.

Jesus declares, *"You must love the Lord your God with all your heart, all your soul, and all your mind." (Matthew 22:37); "If you try to hang on to your life, you will lose it…" Luke 9:24*

We can't have it both ways!

PONDER: How "friendly" am I with the values, the thinking, the ways of the world? Am I more comfortable with the things of this life than with the things of the Spirit? Who or what captures my loyalties, my time, my energy and money?

PRAYER: Forgive me, Lord. I don't want to be Your enemy. I choose to be Your friend. I renounce this world and all it offers. Disclose to me how to live every day in the awareness that this world is **not** my home.

January 21
Very Sincere, But Wrong!

"...I became very zealous to honor God in everything I did, just like all of you today. And I persecuted the followers of the Way, hounding some to death..." Acts 22:3,4

How is it possible to be zealous for God and, at the same time, deliberately hurt His sincere followers?

Paul is giving his testimony to the people of Jerusalem who had just mobbed and beaten him. His attackers were religious people who thought they were doing God a favor by persecuting him. Paul could understand that. He'd been on a similar mission when Jesus knocked Him off His horse and asked him, *"Saul, Saul, why are you persecuting me?"* Perhaps he'd been tempted to think there must be some mistake. After all, he had only been chasing Christians... not Jesus Himself!

So Paul identified with his attackers. He, too, had justified hurting others in the name of God. In the same way, we've all had times when we've mistaken our own agendas for God's and then been offended and/or acted offensively when others didn't concur.

God isn't impressed with what we do in His Name, unless it coincides with what He wants us to do in His Name.

PONDER: Have I ever acted unlike God while trying to do His Work? Do people and their feelings ever get trampled when I'm on a crusade for Him?

PRAYER: Lord, prick my conscience when, in my zeal for what I think is Your will, I fail to act with Your heart.

January 22
Hard To See In The Dark!

"If you are filled with light, with no dark corners, then your whole life will be radiant, as though a floodlight were filling you with light." Luke 11:36

In the dark corners of any room, dirt and other debris can safely hide from human eyes. Even in a well-lit room, unless that light is shone directly into the deepest crevices, and everything blocking its rays is removed, we may never know what is lurking in the shadows.

Jesus is inviting us here to allow His Light, with its pinpoint accuracy, to search every nook and cranny of our souls, exposing what we've kept hidden, even from ourselves. Once those secret things are brought to light, the choice is ours. Will we allow the Spirit of God to deal ruthlessly with the unwanted stuff of the shadows? Or will we dim the light just enough to remain comfortable with what we cannot bring ourselves to surrender?

Those who welcome God's Light into the deepest places of the soul, Jesus said, will be filled with radiance. When allowed to flood our whole self, God's Light beckons and enfolds all whose lives we intersect with its warmth and beauty. That pleases and glorifies Christ.

PONDER: Would anyone describe me as "radiant?" Are there secret, hidden things in my life that cower at the thought of exposure?

PRAYER: Flood me with Your Light, Lord. I yield the darkest corners of my life to Your scrutiny and to the cleansing power of Your Spirit.

January 23

Is There Such A Thing As "Good Grief?"

"Though He [the Lord] *brings grief, He also shows compassion because of the greatness of His unfailing love. For He does not enjoy hurting people or causing them sorrow." Lamentations 3:32,33*

Does it surprise you to read that God brings grief to those He loves? Somehow that cuts against the grain of our thinking! Yet, if we read Isaiah and Jeremiah, we see God bringing great trial upon His people. It was never capricious, never without intense warning and pleading, yet He did send great grief and sorrow upon them.

Verse 33 assures us that God gets no pleasure out of bringing us pain. So why does He do what gives Him no satisfaction and is so agonizing for those of us who must be its recipients?

Proverbs 13:24 gives us a clue: *"If you refuse to discipline your children, it proves you don't love them; if you love your children, you will be prompt to discipline them."* In other words, for God to stop disciplining and correcting us, He would have to quit loving us!

PONDER: What kind of person would I be today if I'd never encountered any difficulties in my life? If God removed all future trials, would that help or hinder my spiritual development?

PRAYER: Lord God, I want to be like Jesus, and I know everything You allow into my life can be used for that purpose, even painful circumstances and difficult people. Help me trust You and yield to the process You choose.

January 24

It's A Gift. Just Take It!

"…the free gift of God is eternal life through Christ Jesus our Lord." Romans 6:23

Salvation is not a result of anything you or I have ever done or ever will do. It is simply God's gift. A gift cannot be purchased or earned. To even suggest that we might pay for a gift given is a grave insult to the giver.

A gift is simply given out of the generosity and love of the giver's heart. It does not depend on our sense of worthiness, but on the worth the <u>giver</u> places upon us.

And a gift **must** be received. If we fail to reach out and take what is offered, it will <u>never</u> be ours, even though the giver paid a high price for the gift and wants so much for us to enjoy it!

"Can we boast then, that we have done anything to be accepted by God? No, because our acquittal is not based on our good deeds. It is based on our faith. So we are made right with God through faith and not by obeying the law." Romans 3:27,28

PONDER: Am I still trying to make myself worthy of, or somehow earn, God's gift of salvation?

PRAYER: Lord, I see that by continuing to live as if I must earn my salvation with good deeds, I have, in effect, refused Your free gift. Help me humbly acknowledge I will **never** be able to deserve or earn it, and simply receive this treasure you've offered me in love.

January 25

Peace Is My Choice

"Don't worry about anything; instead, pray about everything. Tell God what you need, and thank him... If you do this, you will experience God's peace, which is far more wonderful than the human mind can understand. His peace will guard your hearts and minds as you live in Christ Jesus." Philippians 4:6,7

"Lord, give me peace!" How many times have we prayed those exact words? Yet, in today's Scripture, God tells us that peace begins with a decision on our part: **"Don't worry... instead, pray... tell God what you need, and thank Him..."**

THEN, you will experience His peace.

Peace is a choice! I cannot <u>create</u> peace, but I can <u>choose</u> not to worry. I can deliberately move my focus from the problem/person who has filled my heart with anxiety to the God Who promises that nothing escapes His loving care. He works all things for my good.

God assures us that once that decision is made, we will experience something we could not even comprehend before. It seems utterly impossible that, with no change in our outward circumstances, our hearts—which moments earlier were racing with fear and turmoil—could find themselves quiet and at rest. That's the miracle of God's peace!

PONDER: When I'm anxious... upset... where is my focus? Am I willing to take God at His Word, make the <u>choice</u> not to worry?

PRAYER: Lord, I can't comprehend how this works, but I choose now to refocus, to stop worrying, to pray instead, and thank You for <u>**Your**</u> answers.

January 26

Love Deeply

"Most important of all, continue to show deep love for each other, for love covers a multitude of sins." I Peter 4:8

Perhaps the closest thing we have in our human experience to this kind of love is the love of a mother for her children. She remains their cheerleader/champion even when they fall flat on their faces, even when they disobey, even if they turn their backs on her and walk away.

A mother still hopes, still reaches out, still longs for reconciliation, still protects her children from the probing eyes of those whose only desire is to expose and destroy.

God asks us to love each other deeply, with the kind of love that would rather cover than expose, reconcile than cast aside. Too often, in our humanness, we prefer to confront and cut off. We feel justified in our castigations.

Thank God He didn't view **us** that way. Even at our best, we haven't lived up to His perfect standards. Yet He continues reaching out to us with mercy and forgiveness, offering a way back into relationship with Him. In return, He insists we pass on His gracious love.

PONDER: How do I react to the shortcomings and iniquities of others? Am I more concerned with being "right" than being reconciled?

PRAYER: Lord, in my humanness, I can't love deeply enough to overlook the sins and weaknesses of other people. Pour out Your love in my heart and give me the grace to pass it on.

January 27

Do I Misuse God's Name?

"You must not misuse the name of the Lord your God. The Lord will not let you go unpunished if you misuse his name." Exodus 20:7

When we think of taking God's Name "in vain," we typically think of swearing or saying God's Name in a casual, irreverent way.

What if God is more concerned with taking His Name—as in, "*I'm a Christian*"—and then living in a way that does not reflect Him, His heart, or His character?

In our culture, the word "Christian" is often used synonymously with words like "hypocrite, bigot, mean-spirited, etc." Why is that?

In any language, words have specific meanings. Whenever we use a word in a context that does not reflect its meaning, we have "misused" it, or used it "in vain." If misused often enough, its cultural meaning can be "hijacked" and changed, eventually even reflected in the dictionary (no doubt you can think of such words).

Aren't we misusing God's Name when we call ourselves Christians, but refuse to forgive, fail to be generous, kind, and gracious, or make life choices motivated by fear of what people think or love for the pleasures and thought processes of this world?

PONDER: Does my life accurately define or reflect God, as revealed in the Bible? Did I find myself having to justify my answer to that question?

PRAYER: Help me be honest, Lord, in Your presence. Point out anything in me that grieves You and misrepresents You to others.

January 28

Am I the "Older Brother?"

"… All these years I've slaved for you and never once refused to do a single thing you told me to…" Luke 15:29

God is a God of mercy, especially drawn to the weak and hopeless, those who are enslaved by their appetites and unable to break free from addictions, those paying the price for their decisions. He waits and watches for the day when one of His children will finally recognize, *"There is food in my father's house…"* and head back home.

The "older brother," the one who feels he's responsible for his <u>own</u> good fortune, can never appreciate the joy God feels and the party He throws for the wretched sinner who finally acknowledges he/she cannot fix what's wrong in his life.

It's actually very sad. The older brother doesn't really know his own father. He's worked for him faithfully, but not out of love and concern for his dad. The inheritance is his goal, and he believes he's earned it. His brother squandered his share and should have to pay the consequences. It's as simple as that!

But in the end, it's the older brother who is standing outside.

PONDER: Am I keeping track of all I do for God, measuring myself against the failures of others? Is my heart cold toward those who can't seem to get it together? Have I missed the heart of God?

PRAYER: Lord, may my relationship with You become my greatest passion. Help me LOVE and KNOW and FEEL Your heart.

January 29
What God Has Prepared for Us...

"...No eye has seen, no ear has heard... no mind has imagined what God has prepared for those who love him." I Corinthians 2:9

This morning, a beloved uncle went to be with the Lord. Some of my fondest memories of him center around his camera and tape recorder. In his younger years, Uncle Les was seldom without either. He loved life, thrilled to music, cherished family, relished beauty, and took great delight in capturing it all on film or tape.

As I think of him now, trying to take in all the glories of Heaven—colors that can't be described and sounds that no human ear has ever yet heard—I have a feeling that, if he could wish for any earthly thing, it would be the capacity to capture and record it all for us who are left behind.

Oh, what joy as he reunites with loved ones and friends who arrived before him, as his eyes adjust to the sparkle of Heaven's jeweled walls and golden streets, as he sees his Savior's face for the very first time!

Enraptured with this One who redeemed him and brought him safely to Glory, he won't know whether to hug first or simply fall down in worship. How could we ever wish him back?

PONDER: Do I have the hope and assurance of a home in Heaven when I die?

PRAYER: Thank you, Lord, for the hope of Heaven that makes our separation from believers we love only temporary.

January 30
God Isn't Impressed With Religion

"They love to make a show of coming to me and asking me to take action on their behalf. 'We have fasted before you!' they say. 'Why aren't you impressed?...' I will tell you why! It's because you are living for yourselves even while you are fasting." Isaiah 58:2b-3a

What is it inside the hearts of mankind that makes us want to "appear" righteous to others? For some, the appearance is even more important than the reality. Unfortunately, even the most Christlike among us is not free from this temptation.

We forget, don't we, that God isn't fooled by our religious façade. He's not impressed with the pious hoops we have learned to jump through. People may applaud our good deeds, but God is not impressed with the same things people take note of. God's eyes look all the way into the soul.

God knows! He knows the depth of my response to His love, His Word, His life in me. He knows who or what is presently enthroned at the center of my heart. He's aware of those times when even the good that I do is aimed more at people-pleasing than at honoring the Savior.

PONDER: When God looks through my religious talk and activity, what does He see and know about my heart? Am I willing to look honestly at what He already knows is true? How would that change me?

PRAYER: Lord, turn your searchlight on in my heart and reveal the truth about me.

January 31

Why Wasn't Jesus Afraid?

"He [Jesus] *saw that they were in serious trouble, rowing hard and struggling against the wind and waves... Jesus came toward them, walking on the water..." Mark 6:48*

The disciples are terrified, struggling to keep their little ship afloat. Meanwhile, the same tumultuous sea that threatens their craft also rages around Jesus as He walks the waves. His position is much more precarious and frightening than that of the disciples, who at least have a boat between them and the depths. Yet Jesus is at peace, unhurried, unafraid.

We might say, *"Jesus was God. No wonder He was at peace."*

It's true. Jesus is God. However, *Philippians 2:6,7* says He forfeited all His rights and privileges as God to empty Himself and become a man. Only by limiting Himself could Jesus fully identify with us.

So, when walking on that raging sea, Jesus did so as a mere man, but one who dared not depend on Himself. He'd come to know and trust His Heavenly Father utterly and completely.

How like the disciples we are as we face the storms in our lives. Even so, if we will listen, we, too, will hear His voice saying, *"Take courage! I am here!"*

PONDER: How well do I know God? Enough to trust Him in every situation?

PRAYER: Lord, You understand my human fears and frailties, but you call me to know and trust and depend on You, as You speak peace to my soul in the midst of life's storms.

February

February 1
I'm Strongest When I'm Weak

"...So now, I am glad to boast about my weaknesses, so the power of Christ may work through me..." II Corinthians 12:9

Most of us despise our weaknesses. We work hard to eliminate, minimize, or hide them. How is it that Paul could actually boast in his?

What if, as Paul says in this passage, God's power does actually show up best in weak people? What if God really does receive more glory through our weaknesses than our strengths? What if, in seeing God work through the least capable among us, others could actually be inspired to trust God to work through them as well?

Would that be cause enough for me to rejoice in my weakness?

I suppose it all depends on my primary motivation. If looking good and feeling "in control" are high priorities for me, then I'll probably never be comfortable admitting or exposing my weaknesses, let alone boasting about them.

If, however, bringing glory to God and seeing broken people forgiven and set free are among my deepest longings, then, "yes," whatever God can use to make that happen, I can rejoice in.

PONDER: Is my primary motivation one of self-preservation? Do I hide my weaknesses from others? For whose glory do I live?

PRAYER: Lord, give me the grace to humble myself and accept your purposes for making me a person with weaknesses and flaws. If you can receive glory in the midst of my worst stuff, I give it all to you now.

February 2

Gimme, Gimme, Gimme

"…I have calmed and quieted myself, like a weaned child who no longer cries for its mother's milk. Yes, like a weaned child is my soul within me." Psalm 131:2

Ever notice a nursing baby in its mother's arms? The mother's breast is not only his/her food supply, but a source of great comfort as well. Unless the baby has just eaten his fill or is asleep, he cannot seem to just lie still in Mother's embrace. His head turns toward her breast, and he begins to "root." Sometimes, he can be very insistent, punctuating his demands with cries, even temper tantrums as he gets older, until he gets what he wants.

It's only after that child is weaned that he can lie quietly in his mother's arms and just enjoy being with <u>her</u>. At that point, the mother's <u>presence</u> becomes the source of comfort, not just what she provides to fill his tummy.

PONDER: When I come to God, do I tend to "root," always wanting and/or demanding something from Him? If God were never to give me another thing, would I still be drawn to His presence? Would He be "enough" to satisfy the longings of my heart?

PRAYER: How often have I been like an un-weaned child, Lord? Always asking? Always evaluating Your love and Your goodness by what you <u>give</u> rather than who You <u>are</u>? Quiet my soul before You. Open my heart to the <u>thrill</u> of just being loved and enjoyed by Almighty God.

February 3

Me? Holy? Surely Not!

"...he [Christ] has brought you into the very presence of God, and you are holy and blameless as you stand before him without a single fault... you must continue to believe this truth and stand firmly in it. Don't drift away..." Colossians 1:22b,23

How can that be? I am far from holy! Absolutely not blameless! No one knows my faults better than I, except the Lord Himself. So how is it possible for God to say these things?

It's Christ's death and resurrection, not my performance, which guarantee God's assurance that He is <u>able</u> to keep us from stumbling and present us faultless before His throne. *Jude 24*

Sin is still ugly. God still hates it! But He has chosen to show kindness to us, instead of the judgment we deserve. He does this because of Christ's death on the cross. Our sin **has** been punished, our debt paid! God's wrath against sin has been poured out already, but not on us!

"...he [Jesus] was pierced for our rebellion, crushed for our sins... the Lord laid on him the sins of us all." Isaiah 53:5,6

PONDER: Have I ever fully comprehended the <u>gift</u> I've been given in Christ? Do I rest in and celebrate the assurance that <u>everything</u> has been forever accomplished on my behalf?

PRAYER: My sin—O the bliss of this glorious thought—my sin, not in part but the whole, is nailed to the cross and I bear it no more! Praise the Lord! Praise the Lord, O my soul!

February 4

How Big Is The God We Serve?

"In the first year of King Cyrus of Persia, the Lord fulfilled the prophecy he had given through Jeremiah. He stirred the heart of Cyrus..." II Chronicles 36:22; Ezra 1:1

Jeremiah's prophecy was proclaimed over a hundred years before this event. Even more remarkable is that, a century before Jeremiah spoke of it *(Jeremiah 25:11-12; 29:11)*, God had prophesied, through the prophet Isaiah, that He would use a Persian king named Cyrus, a man who wouldn't even acknowledge Him as God, to do His bidding and rebuild His temple.

WOW!

Cyrus hadn't even been thought of on earth, yet God already knew him! In spite of his disregard for the God of Heaven, Cyrus unwittingly fulfilled God's promise made to His people centuries earlier. *(Isaiah 44:28-45:1)*

These kinds of details, hidden in God's Word for our discovery, should cause us to fall on our faces before the God Who knows and sees us even before we are born. He is aware, before we even experience them, of the trials we will face. He is at work on our behalf, long before we ever get there, using even those who reject Him, to accomplish His purposes for us.

PONDER: How big is the God I serve? How intimately acquainted with my life? How faithful? From what source have I drawn <u>my</u> conclusions about God?

PRAYER: Oh, God, a resounding "Hallelujah" bursts from my heart! I am in awe that a God so big, so powerful, would be so intimately interested in me!

February 5

Worth Dying For

"...Others were tortured, refusing to turn from God in order to be set free. They placed their hope in a better life after the resurrection." Hebrews 11:35b

If threatened because of my faith, what would I do? Do I know? <u>Can</u> I know? The answer to that question should be settled long before we find ourselves face-to-face with our tormentors in that life-or-death moment.

The martyrs we read about in this passage had made their choice. They'd left all to follow Jesus because He offered what this world cannot.

Why would anyone give up eternity in Heaven with Christ for a few more days, or even years, here on this earth, only to be separated from God at death?

For the believer, to die is gain, the Bible says. To close our eyes here is to open them in the presence of Jesus, forever!

My persecutors, no matter how vicious, can only destroy this body. They cannot touch my eternal soul. That's why Jesus warns us to fear only God, Who has the power to condemn both body and soul to eternal damnation.

PONDER: If faced today with such a choice, which would I choose? Is my heart still wrapped around this world and its pleasures? Or is Heaven my clear aim, Jesus my dearest, most treasured love?

PRAYER: Lord, I shudder to think of eternity without You. I choose You <u>NOW</u> over every competing affection, and I know You'll give me grace to choose You <u>THEN</u>, no matter what!

February 6

A Bad Rap!

"Perhaps the people… will repent when they hear again all the terrible things I have planned for them. Then I will be able to forgive their sins and wrongdoings." Jeremiah 26:3

In this passage, we find God hoping He won't have to punish the sins of His people, hoping they'll repent instead, so He can have mercy on them.

Satan is the master of lies. Throughout history, he has slandered God, painting a picture of Him as capricious, One who delights in withholding pleasure, in confusing and hurting His creatures, a vindictive, harsh, and unyielding Sovereign.

Over and over in Scripture, God's compassion and mercy is revealed to those who search out His heart. Yet, sadly, because we have believed Satan's lie, we tend to view life through his distorted lens. Only as we seek to really know God's heart through His Word will we ever discover His true character.

The devil is the one who delights in destruction, not God. Satan is the cold, heartless one, willing to draw us with delightful images and skillfully crafted lies that mask his true intention: to rob, kill, and destroy those whom God cherishes *(John 10:10)*.

In this passage, we hear the pathos of God, the longing for people to wake up before it is too late.

PONDER: Who is it that arouses my suspicion—God or the devil?

PRAYER: Lord God, forgive me for believing the lies Satan has perpetrated on me and the human race. Transform my mind. Make known to me who You really are!

February 7

What Am I Planting?

"A troublemaker plants seeds of strife…" Proverbs 16:28a

Planting seeds of strife is not that hard to do. It usually happens when we get bent out of shape over something and don't follow the steps Christ gave us for resolving conflict. Instead of going straight to the person with whom we have a problem and talking it through with a sincere desire for understanding and reconciliation, we let it fester inside.

That, in itself, is damaging enough, but what most often happens is that we eventually find ourselves informing the ignorance of others regarding the 'true" nature of this person. We certainly wouldn't want our friends to get hurt or be disappointed like we were, right?

When others express similar feelings of disdain or frustration, we can certainly understand where they're coming from. And, secretly, we feel a certain amount of vindication as the words we speak add fuel to the fires of their discontent.

The seeds of strife have been planted. And, believe me, they will grow! Paul warns against *"…biting and devouring one another…!" (Galatians 5:15)* James, the Lord's half brother, decries the fact that *"…blessing and cursing come pouring out of the same mouth,"* and insists, *"Surely, my brothers and sisters, this is not right!" James 3:10*

PONDER: Have I ever been guilty of planting seeds of strife? What should I do about it now?

PRAYER: Lord, more than anything, You desire Your children to live in love and unity. Let them begin in my heart… here and now… today!

February 8
Christ Plus Nothing

"I do not treat the grace of God as meaningless. For if keeping the law could make us right with God, then there was no need for Christ to die." Galatians 2:21

A friend just died. I watched him walk confidently right up to the end, with the knowledge that his eternal destiny did not depend on him—his own goodness, his own ability to get things right. The peace that filled his heart in those last moments was possible only because he had discovered the grace of God and believed it to be absolutely true and sufficient.

That's why Jesus came. That's why He died: to take the fear out of death! To remove its sting! *"…He* [The Lord of Heaven's Armies] *will remove the cloud of gloom, the shadow of death that hangs over the earth. He will swallow up death forever!" Isaiah 25:7,8*

When Satan tells us we don't deserve Heaven, he's right. But God doesn't give us what we deserve! That's the miracle! When we place our trust in Christ's atonement, we receive, as a gift, what we could never be worthy of: God's grace and mercy.

PONDER: What am I depending on to get me into Heaven when I die? My own goodness? If so, how am I doing at being perfect?

PRAYER: Jesus, You alone are the Way, the Truth, and the Life. My only hope for relationship with God is through You. Thank You for the peace that comes from putting my trust in You alone!

February 9

Trusting Before Knowing

"May you experience the love of Christ, though it is too great to understand fully..." Ephesians 3:19

It is possible to know things we cannot fully understand... to experience things we cannot adequately explain in words.

That's where faith comes in. Faith, the writer of Hebrews says, is the *"substance of things hoped for, the <u>evidence</u> of things not seen." (Hebrews 11:1)* We believe FIRST; then we <u>know</u>. We trust <u>before</u> we experience.

God declares that our life with Him—every interaction, every encounter—is to be lived by faith. It's a choice we make when our longing for God and His Truth overwhelms all other desires.

Once we trust, then we experience Him. Once we experience Him, then we KNOW! Ask us to explain it, and we might not be able to find the words that would make sense to you, but we <u>know</u>! Oh, yes! We **<u>know</u>**!

This is not just some emotional or mental gymnastics without basis in reality. Our faith is in direct response to the Word and promises of God. We choose to trust what can't be fully explained or tangibly measured because **He said so**! And in our choosing, we find Him incredibly faithful, His Words absolutely true, His presence and power more real than the things we can see with our eyes.

PONDER: Am I still waiting to see before I believe?

PRAYER: Oh, God, may my desire for You so overwhelm all other passions that I'm driven into the Arms of Faith!

February 10

Why So Stubborn?

"Oh, that they would always have hearts like this, that they might fear me and obey all my commands! If they did, they and their descendants would prosper forever." Deuteronomy 5:29

Can you hear the longing in the heart of God to <u>bless</u> His people? Listen again from *Deuteronomy 6:24*, as we're told just why our obedience to God is so important: *"The Lord our God commanded us to obey all these decrees and to fear him <u>so he can continue to bless us and preserve our lives...</u>"* (emphasis mine).

Most perceive the making and enforcing of rules as an attempt to restrict their freedom, curb their enjoyment in life. God is declaring the very opposite! Our ability to fully experience the joys available to us in life is tied directly to our response to His commandments.

Why is that so difficult for us to absorb? Why the resistance to God's commands?

Deep within the heart of every person is a nature that stubbornly refuses to acknowledge any authority except itself. We want to be the captain of our own ship, the maker of our own destiny! We don't understand that our refusal to bow to our Creator automatically makes us a slave to our own desires, and, ultimately, to Satan, the enemy of our souls.

PONDER: When I think of yielding control of my life to God, what thoughts and feelings immediately surface?

PRAYER: Only You, Lord, can give what my heart yearns for. I won't fight you anymore. I surrender! Be Lord of my life.

February 11

Even Angels Worship Him

"Now Christ has gone to Heaven. He is seated in the place of honor next to God, and all the angels and authorities and powers are bowing before him." I Peter 3:22

Wait a minute! Doesn't the very first Commandment forbid worshiping anyone but God? This is amazing! In clear view of God the Father, angels, authorities, and powers are bowing before Christ! What a clear picture of Christ as God Himself, second person of the Godhead.

But this should not surprise us. *Philippians 2:10,11* declares, *"…at the name of Jesus every knee will bow, in Heaven and on earth and under the earth, and every tongue will confess that Jesus Christ is Lord, to the glory of God the Father."*

It actually glorifies the Father when we worship Jesus the Son. *John 5:23b* declares, *"…if you refuse to honor the Son, then you are certainly not honoring the Father who sent Him."* Within the Godhead, there's not a hint of competition, power-mongering, or jealousy—only love, honor, and mutual submission, flowing out of the perfect unity of the Three in One.

Any attempt to "honor" God the Father without acknowledging and worshiping God the Son and God the Holy Spirit actually dishonors the Father. They are One!

PONDER: What is my view of Jesus? Have I already chosen to bow before Him with the angels, authorities, and powers, kneeling at His throne?

PRAYER: Lord Jesus, God of the Universe, Lord of my life, I worship You now!

February 12

Not A Fickle Lover...

"They committed terrible blasphemies. But in your great mercy you did not abandon them... you sent your good Spirit to instruct them and you did not stop giving... you sustained them... they lacked nothing..." Nehemiah 9:18a-21

Israel's leaders are recounting their history in confession to God. It's not pretty! How often had they abandoned Him to worship idols? In spite of His miraculous provision, they'd complained bitterly. They'd sought human alliances rather than trusting His power to deliver. You and I would have <u>dumped</u> anyone who treated <u>us</u> with such disdain.

Yet, here is God, *"a God of forgiveness, gracious and merciful, slow to become angry, and rich in unfailing love." (v. 17)* He hung in there with them! Why?

Because even though <u>we</u> are fickle, He is not! Even if we're unfaithful, He remains faithful. These qualities are inherent in His nature. He cannot act contrary to who He is! Therefore, what He does, even when we don't understand it, is **always** consistent with His heart as revealed in Scripture.

Satan wants us to look at our circumstances and draw inaccurate conclusions about God. But the Lord has revealed what He is like through His Word. To live in Truth, I must interpret circumstances through what I've learned about God through His own revelation.

PONDER: Is my understanding of God based on my own conclusions and the world's suggestions? Or on the Truth of His Word?

PRAYER: Lord, help me know and trust who **You** say You are in Your Word.

February 13

Why Miss God's Best?

"...many of you have not given up your old sins. You have not repented of your impurity, sexual immorality, and eagerness for lustful pleasure." II Corinthians 12:21b

I am amazed at the number of "Christian" couples these days who are living together or having sex before marriage and don't seem to see the incongruity. Has God changed his mind about sexual immorality?

Concerning many questionable behaviors and habits, Scripture offers no specific directives, but when it comes to sexual sins, Scripture is consistent from Genesis to Revelation. God calls his people to a life of sexual purity. Sex was God's idea, planned for the pleasure of one man and one woman, committed to each other for life within the holy estate of marriage.

Could it be that God's laws are designed for our protection by One who knows full well what can damage and destroy our capacity to enjoy this amazing gift? His commands reflect His passionate longing that we experience to the fullest what He designed for our **pleasure**.

We cannot expect those who don't know Christ to care what God says about sexual sin, but those of us who claim the name of Jesus must ask ourselves why we don't take more seriously the consistent Word of the Lord concerning this issue. After all, Jesus said, *"All who love me will do what I say... Anyone who doesn't love me will not obey me." John 14:23a,24a*

PONDER: Do I care about God's commands? Do I even **know** them?

PRAYER: Lord Jesus, Help me love You and prove it with my trust and obedience.

February 14

Oh, Love, That Will Not Let Me Go

"The Lord says, 'I was ready to respond, but no one asked for help. I was ready to be found, but no one was looking for me. I said, 'Here I am, here I am!' to a nation that did not call on my name. All day long I opened my arms to a rebellious people. But they follow their own… paths…'" Isaiah 65:1,2

Can you hear the heart of God in this passage? How He longs for us to realize our need for Him, to **want** Him! Why didn't God give up on us long ago? Surely, He must have been disgusted and angry at the continual, stubborn, rebellious, and prideful independence of the humans He created.

"Only so many chances and you're gone!" That's how **we** tend to treat people. But not God! His compassionate heart cannot let go. He loves with an **everlasting** love, because He **is** love. To **not** love would slice against the grain of who He is. It is totally impossible for God to cease loving us!

In our love-starved world, why would anyone reject a love like that? Yet, every day, we humans say with our lives what most of us would never dare speak aloud: *"God, I don't need or want you. I'd rather do it myself!"*

PONDER: What about me? What is my life "saying" to God?

PRAYER: Dear Lord, open my ears to Your voice of love. Break my heart with Your longing for me and help me long for You.

February 15

God Wants Me For Himself

"You must worship no other gods, for the Lord, whose very name is jealous, is a God Who is jealous about his relationship with you." Exodus 34:14

Some folks get "bent out of shape" contemplating God's jealousy, as if God's being jealous makes Him selfish or mean. Yet, if we think about the most important relationships in our lives, jealousy is a healthy response to any person or outside influence that might jeopardize those relationships.

In my marriage, you'd better believe that any flirtation or dalliance between my husband and another woman would be perceived by me as a definite threat! If I failed to react with jealousy, it would demonstrate a callous, indifferent attitude toward my marriage and a lack of love and devotion to my mate!

God is deeply in love with you and me, desiring intimacy with us. He has told us just how important our relationship is to Him and how jealously He will defend it from all of Satan's efforts to sabotage it. Instead of invoking feelings of hostility, the awareness of God's jealous passion should wrap our hearts in the warmth and security of being truly treasured by the Lord of the Universe.

Ummmmmmm! That feels good to me!

PONDER: Have I perceived God's commands as restrictive and mean-spirited or as His way of protecting me and our relationship?

PRAYER: Thank You, Lord, that You cannot be indifferent or careless about our relationship because You passionately and unconditionally love me and desire what's best for me.

February 16

Can I Know My Own Heart?

"I don't even trust my own judgment on this point. My conscience is clear, but that doesn't prove I'm right. It is the Lord Himself who will examine me and decide." I Corinthians 4:3b,4

This is the Apostle Paul speaking, the one knocked off his horse, blinded, and then restored to sight by the Living Christ, the writer of two-thirds of the New Testament, the one *"caught up into paradise"* who *"heard things so astounding that they cannot be told." II Corinthians 12:4*

Paul, who, next to Christ, most influenced the world toward Christianity, doesn't trust his own judgment or the fact that, as far as he can tell, his conscience is clear!

You see, any of us can be easily deceived by the "flesh," and the Scriptures make it clear. *"There is nothing good in my flesh." (Romans 7:18)* The Lord knows my real intentions and motivations. *"…He will bring our darkest secrets to light and will reveal our private motives." (I Corinthians 3:5)* This verse refers to the final Judgment, but we may ask Him to do that <u>NOW</u>, humbly receiving His verdict and His power to change us.

PONDER: Do I arrogantly cling to my own impressions and judgments without recognizing how vulnerable I am to the deception of my "flesh?" Can I acknowledge that someone else may be more "right" than I? Am I constantly humbling myself under the penetrating gaze of God's Spirit?

PRAYER: Lord, protect me from my "flesh." Help me bring *"every thought captive and make it obey Christ." II Corinthians 10:5a*

February 17

What Makes God Gag?

"I <u>know</u> all the things you do, that you are neither hot nor cold. I wish that you were one or the other! But since you are like lukewarm water, neither hot nor cold, I will spit you out of my mouth! …be diligent and turn from your indifference." Revelation 3:15,16,19

Riding the fence is not an option with God. He says it's all or nothing!

At least if our choice is "nothing," He has opportunity to convict us of our sin and bring us to repentance. The indifference of those who "fence-sit" makes it difficult to hear the still, small voice of God's Spirit drawing them to humble themselves and seek His mercy.

Playing church doesn't impress God. If doing religious things, singing spiritual songs, and giving tithes and offerings aren't motivated by a deep and growing love for and trust in God, they become as repulsive to Him as lukewarm water in His mouth. No matter how noble they seem to us, any acts of "devotion" that don't stream from a fully devoted heart "gag" Him.

What can we do? *"Be diligent and turn from your indifference."* Continually seek the Lord until a compelling passion for Him becomes reality in our lives. He is able to give us new desires for what pleases Him *(Phil. 2:13).*

PONDER: What might God say He "<u>knows</u>" about me?

PRAYER: Lord, shine your searchlight into my heart. Help me look with You and acknowledge what You find there. Give me a longing to know and love You with <u>**all**</u> my heart and soul!

February 18

I Can't Help It!

"Oh, that my actions would consistently reflect Your principles! Then I will not be disgraced when I compare my life with your commands." Psalm 119: 5,6

This is David speaking, the man after God's own heart. It is obvious in his prayer that there were some things in his life that disturbed him and brought him great remorse and humiliation.

David refused to coddle the things in his life that didn't reflect his Lord. He didn't rationalize, as so many of us do today, *"It's just my personality. I can't help it. God made me this way, so you will just have to accept me the way I am."*

No, David's heart cried out to be **changed**, that his actions and attitudes **would** reflect the Lord's character. If, and when, his life was examined in the Light of God's Word, he wanted the two to match.

Even though God receives me by grace alone, He asks me to live a life worthy of all He has given and done for me, worthy of the Name He allows me to bear—"**Christ**ian."

PONDER: What areas of my life do not consistently reflect the Lord's principles? If God were to produce a chart right now of all the places where my life falls short of His known commands, would I be ashamed?

PRAYER: Lord, where do You want to start in rearranging my actions, attitudes, or motives? I'm willing to do <u>whatever</u> You show me, starting right now.

February 19

Does Power Corrupt?

"Saul replied, 'But I'm only from the tribe of Benjamin, the smallest tribe in Israel, and my family is the least important of all the families of that tribe! Why are you talking like this to me?'" I Samuel 9:21

Sounds like a humble man, wouldn't you say? Yet this same Saul, soon after being crowned king, took matters into his own hands rather than follow God's explicit instructions.

Later, he disobeyed another direct command of God regarding plunder from an Amalekite battle. And, when God withdrew His anointing, the king was filled with murderous rage against young David, whom he sensed had received the blessing Saul himself had forfeited.

What corrupted this man? Was it power? Wealth? Is there some inherent evil within these commodities?

It's the condition of the <u>heart</u> that determines how we're impacted by the influence or wealth entrusted to us. Until we have obtained a measure of power, or been blessed with wealth in abundance, we may not even be <u>aware</u> of what our hearts are <u>capable</u> of.

Power and riches, in themselves, cannot contaminate a person, But a life not yielded to Christ's lordship is vulnerable to deceit and corruption.

PONDER: What about <u>my</u> heart? Is it faithful? Loving? Generous? Or greedy? Ungrateful? Power-hungry? Can I rejoice over the blessings and successes of others? Is trusting and obeying God more important than anything else I might desire?

PRAYER: Lord, reveal the true condition of my heart. Make me like You.

February 20

An Anchor For My Soul

"…it is impossible for God to lie… we can hold on to His promise with confidence. This confidence is like a strong and trustworthy anchor for our souls…" Hebrews 6:18b-19a

Ever feel insecure about your salvation? Ever wonder if God is really there or if he cares about what you're going through?

Our emotions and intellect are such powerful determiners. An overwrought imagination, hormonal imbalance, stress, inadequate rest or nutrition, trauma, illness, or grief all have the potential to distort "reality." However, we seldom recognize the effect of their presence.

There is only one source of Truth! If and when **God** says something, we can "take it to the bank," because God cannot lie *(Titus 1:2)*.

Feelings are like the caboose of our spiritual "train." God's Word is its engine. If I trust my feelings to determine the truth of my relationship with God, it's like trying to pull a train by its caboose. It doesn't go anywhere!

However, when I put my trust in God's Word for assurance, hope, peace, etc., I not only move forward in my relationship with God, but my feelings **will** eventually, even if reluctantly, follow along behind.

PONDER: If the devil knows I will trust my "feelings" more than what God says in His Word, what advantage does that give him in his efforts to deceive me?

PRAYER: Lord, open my eyes to see the devil's schemes. Help me not lean on my ability to understand but trust solely and fully in the promises of your Word.

February 21

Slave Or Free?

"You will live by your sword, and you will serve your brother. But when you decide to break free, you will shake his yoke from your neck." Genesis 27:40

It appeared this prophecy regarding Esau's servitude went unfulfilled. Jacob ran away to a far country. The brothers wouldn't even see each other for many long years. Esau became wealthy and independent, a "free" man.

But what Esau didn't realize, as he nursed his fury, is that bitterness chains us to the ones we hate, enslaving our hearts and minds. His murderous hatred bound him unmercifully to Jacob.

How many otherwise happy occasions were spoiled, simply by the thought of his brother or the mere mention of his name? How many nights' sleep were lost because of the constant rehashing of the grievance, the plotting for revenge, the curdling of his spirit that refused to let go?

Many years later, when the brothers finally met again, Esau <u>chose</u> to forgive Jacob, and, to his amazement, the last words of his father's prophecy finally came true. *"...when you decide to break free, you will shake his yoke from your neck."*

So much wasted emotional, physical, and spiritual energy. If only he'd made that decision years earlier!

PONDER: Am I harboring bitterness toward someone, thus chaining myself to them?

PRAYER: Lord, help me! I **<u>choose</u>** today to forgive—to break free—in the **<u>power</u>** of **<u>Jesus</u>**.

February 22

No Matter How Hard I Try!

"...you are still controlled by your sinful nature. You are jealous of one another and quarrel with each other. Doesn't that prove you are controlled by your sinful nature? Aren't you living like people of the world?" I Corinthians 3:3

What does the "evidence" say about my life? Do my attitudes, actions, and words prove, as Paul suggests, that I really haven't surrendered to the power of the Holy Spirit, that I'm still allowing myself to be ruled by my old, selfish, sinful nature?

Even though I may be able to keep a tight lid on my words and actions <u>most</u> of the time, certain situations, certain people (usually those closest to me), just bring out the <u>worst</u> in me.

You and I will **NEVER** gain control of our sinful nature by trying harder. That's a recipe for failure and frustration. What we hold in and stuff down will find its way to the surface eventually and spill its ugliness all over those nearby when it does.

The **ONLY** answer is found in yielding to God's control, in humbly acknowledging I can't fix what's wrong inside me, where it really matters. I must "die" to self in each situation where I want to do it my way, deliberately crucifying my old inclinations, over and over.

PONDER: What does the evidence say about who's in control of my life?

PRAYER: Oh, God, I can't fix me. I've tried. You take over and do whatever it takes to make me like You.

February 23
When "Me First" Is Required

"...let all my words sink deep into your own heart first. Listen to them carefully for yourself. Then go to your people..." Ezekiel 3:10,11

There is such temptation to read the Word of God with someone else in mind.

This is especially true for those of us called to leadership positions within the Body of Christ. The weekly responsibility of teaching or preaching weighs heavy and keeps our minds and hearts on constant lookout for something to share with those to whom we minister.

Even those of us without a pulpit or other platform tend to see, in God's warnings, exhortations, and commands, the names and faces of specific persons for whom, in our minds, these Scriptures apply.

Our loving Creator knows our tendencies. How easy it is for us to miss a life-changing encounter with God's Spirit through His Word! That's why He warns in this passage—originally spoken to Ezekiel, but so appropriate for us today—to listen to and apply what God is saying to our own hearts **FIRST**. Then we can take the message to others.

PONDER: When I read God's Word, do I just "read," or do I "listen" to hear what God is saying to my own heart?

PRAYER: Forgive me, Lord, for my tendency to apply Your Word to everyone else, rather than to my own life. Give me the humility and the courage to allow You, first of all, to reveal what it is You want to me to know about "me."

February 24
Why Do I Even Ask?

"...King Zedekiah asked Jeremiah, 'Please pray to the Lord... for us.' But neither King Zedekiah... nor the people... listened to what the Lord said through Jeremiah..." Jeremiah 37:3,2

Why would the king ask Jeremiah to pray, if he had no intention of doing what God commanded? Good question! In the verses that follow, we're told the king asked Jeremiah at least twice more for a word from God *(37:17; 38:14),* but each time, he was not happy with God's answer and refused to obey.

Are we so unlike Zedekiah? How often do we pray to God, asking for His help, seeking His guidance, only to pick and choose, as in a smorgasbord, what we like, what fits our fancy at the moment, what we are willing to do or not?

We hate feeling frightened, weak, overwhelmed, or guilt-ridden, so we cry out to God. But are we really seeking <u>Him</u>—or only a band-aid, an aspirin to make the pain go away? Do we really intend to give up control, to yield our wills to His?

God is not in the business of making things "easier," more comfortable for us, so we can continue merrily down a road that leads to our destruction. Our pain could be His megaphone, warning that the path we have chosen leads to the wrong destination.

PONDER: Do I only want to "feel better," so I can continue running things myself?

PRAYER: Give me a heart that seeks to <u>know</u> You and longs to <u>obey</u> Your voice.

February 25
Crouching, Ready To Pounce

"...If you refuse to do what is right, then watch out! Sin is crouching at the door, eager to control you. But you must subdue it and be its master." Genesis 4:7b

The Lord is speaking to Cain, who had obviously chosen to do something he knew God would not be pleased with and then got angry when his brother's sacrifice was accepted by God and his was not.

In that moment, Cain had a choice to make. Would he humble himself and choose to listen and obey God's warning, or would he yield to sin's temptation toward bitterness and resentment, which would lead him down a treacherous road?

Though we may not hear the audible voice of God as Cain did that day, we, too, have a choice in every circumstance we face. Life is full of disappointments, hurts, and what we might call injustices. They may result from our own shortsighted choices, be totally random, or even caused by others, whether carelessly or maliciously.

Each situation offers us a choice. In those moments, the **only** thing we can **control** is our response. Will we seek God's wisdom to do the right thing, or will we harden our hearts, thus opening ourselves to sin's temptation?

Though sin makes a lot of promises, its satisfaction is short-lived. Ultimately, it **always** leads to death.

PONDER: Whose advice am I more likely to heed—God's or my own?

PRAYER: Lord, help me to choose Your wisdom over my own understanding!

February 26

Don't Believe The Lie

"'You won't die!' the serpent hissed. 'God knows that your eyes will be opened when you eat it. You will become just like God, knowing everything...'" Genesis 3:4,5

Before their sin, Adam and Eve had free rein of the garden, access to all the delicacies growing there, intimate relationship with God and each other, no weeds to make gardening difficult, no sickness or death, a perfect climate, freedom from worry and concern, only one choice to consider.

No doubt they'd both noticed and thought about the forbidden fruit with curiosity, perhaps even desire. Satan's enticements made so much sense. The fruit looked harmless enough. God <u>must</u> be <u>withholding</u> something from them!

Once the deed was done, however, they felt guilt and shame, were embarrassed by their nakedness, experienced pain, loss, hardship, and sorrow. The soil no longer cooperated with their efforts. Their bodies began the dying process.

Worst of all, they were expelled from the garden and the presence of God. There were suddenly way too many choices and no clear understanding of which decisions would be in their best interest.

PONDER: Like Adam and Eve, when I get what I <u>think</u> I want, am I really free? Satisfied? Happy? Better off?

PRAYER: Lord, it's really a matter of trust, isn't it? Help me not to lean on my own understanding or be governed by desires that insist on fulfillment. Give me the wisdom to trust that You are **always** in my corner, looking out for what's best for me.

February 27
The War Within

"What is causing quarrels and fights among you? Don't they come from the evil desires at war within you? But he gives us even more grace to stand against such evil desires..." James 4:1,6

Who would ever deny such a war exists within the human heart? From early childhood, we struggle with choices between right and wrong, obeying and disobeying, giving and taking.

Parental discipline and strong social pressure provide the impetus for a bit of self-control, but the war really only goes underground, where we learn to cloak our self-centeredness with pious-sounding words and good deeds. Though this ruse often looks impressive and very spiritual, even attracting a lot of favorable personal attention, nothing has really changed deep within.

True motives and attitudes eventually find expression, however. Gossip, backbiting, quarreling, and fighting are the natural responses of self-absorbed people who don't get their own way.

There is an answer, but we don't like it. Verse seven says we must humble ourselves. God opposes the proud but gives His grace to the humble.

It is God's grace that enables us to stand against the evil desires that war within our souls. It is His life in us that overcomes, His grace that secures our victory!

PONDER: What battles rage within me? What do my reactions reveal about the true motives of my heart?

PRAYER: Only in You, Lord, in Your life, in Your grace, will I ever receive power to win the battle against the selfish part of me.

February 28
It's Not About Me!

"The following day John was again standing with two of his disciples. As Jesus walked by, John looked at him and declared, 'Look! There is the Lamb of God!' When John's two disciples heard this, they followed Jesus." John 1:35-37

John the Baptist had two disciples. We aren't told whether, at this particular time in his ministry, John had other followers, but we do learn in this passage that John lost both these men as soon as he introduced them to Jesus.

Ask yourself what kind of thoughts ran through John's mind when he saw his friends leave him to pursue Jesus. Did he battle envy, jealousy, self-pity? In *John 3:29b,30*, we catch a glimpse of his heart: *"…I am filled with joy at his success. He must become greater and greater, and I must become less and less."*

Wow! Under the tutelage of the Holy Spirit who had filled him since conception, John had apparently discovered something that changed his life, something very important for all of us to learn: "It's not about me!" All of life is to be centered around another—Jesus Christ—and lived for His glory.

PONDER: Does my life revolve around me? My desires? My feelings? My interests and concerns? Do I seek FIRST the kingdom of God and His righteousness, or does my agenda have top priority?

PRAYER: Lord Jesus, take Your rightful place in my heart and life. May You become greater and greater and I become less and less.

February 29 – LEAP YEAR

God Can Use It All!

"…It was God Who sent me here ahead of you to preserve your lives… God has sent me ahead of you to keep you and your families alive… it was God Who sent me here, not you!" Genesis 45:5,7,8

Joseph is speaking to the very brothers who, years before, had spitefully sold him to Midianite slave traders. Their callousness had caused Joseph immense hardship and suffering, yet here he is, assuring them that it was actually God Who had orchestrated his trip to Egypt.

What Joseph affirms here goes against our sense of justice. How could a loving God ever endorse something like that? But Scripture declares that even *"the wrath of man shall praise Thee." (Psalm 76:10 KJV)*

God sees the beginning from the end. He knows His plans for us. They are good. But to move us from point A to point B, God sometimes uses even the wickedness of people to accomplish His purposes. What better evidence than the crucifixion of His own Son, so cruel and undeserved, yet so necessary for our salvation?

PONDER: What circumstances in my life seem impossible to reconcile with a loving God? Will I choose to trust Him, as Joseph did, with what I don't understand? Will I choose forgiveness and generosity toward those whose actions, no matter how mean-spirited, are being allowed by God to accomplish a purpose I don't yet know?

PRAYER: Oh, God. It's impossible for me. But with You, all things are possible. Your will be done!

March

March 1
The Good Ole Days

"...whenever the cloud lifted...the people of Israel would set out on their journey, following it. But if the cloud did not rise, they remained where they were until it lifted." Exodus 40:36,37

Do you think there were ever days the Israelites complained, *"Why can't we just keep things the way they are? We don't want to leave. God was right here, in this place, just yesterday! This is where we experienced Him in the past, and we're not moving!"*

Humans don't like change. We prefer routine—predictable and comfortable. Whatever "touches" us in our most tender moments is what we want God to do again tomorrow and the next day and the next and...

But whenever and however God decides to move, we must keep in step with Him, or risk living without His power and presence in our midst. No matter how God chose to work yesterday, or how close we felt to Him in times past, or how much we long for a return to things the way they were, God is doing a new thing today. He will not be contained in our traditions and expectations.

When the "cloud" moves, we'd better be traveling with Him.

PONDER: Am I guilty of "digging in" and insisting that God work according to my preferences? Do I watch for and celebrate evidence of His Spirit's work, no matter where I find it?

PRAYER: Open my heart, Lord, to the movement of Your Spirit, and help me follow!

March 2
A Brand-New Heart!

"I will put my laws in their minds, and I will write them on their hearts. I will be their God, and they will be my people." Hebrews 8:10b

Interesting! In *Jeremiah 17:9*, God declared the human heart most deceitful and desperately wicked, yet here, He promises to fix it. How does He propose to do that?

The secret? **Christ comes to live in us!** *(Colossians 1:27b)* When He takes up residence in our lives through His Spirit, we have access to all that He is! We are given the mind of Christ *(I Corinthians 2:16)*. We are filled with His character *(Galatians 5:22,23)*. It is Christ, then, who lives His perfect life in our bodies *(Galatians 2:20)* **if** we yield ourselves to His control instead of stubbornly insisting on our own way.

As we surrender the parts of our bodies to Christ as instruments of righteousness *(Romans 6:13)*, **He** speaks through **our** lips, looks at others through **our** eyes, touches through **our** hands, and pours out His love through **our** hearts.

Why don't I see this more often in my life? Because Christ is a gentleman. Only one of us, Christ or me, will live life in my body. The choice is mine!

PONDER: Who most often controls my life? Is it me? Or Christ?

PRAYER: Lord, help me know I can do nothing apart from Your life in me. I yield my body, mind, and soul to be fully inhabited by You and used for Your Glory.

March 3

They Didn't Want To See

"You search the Scriptures because you think they give you eternal life. But the Scriptures point to me! Yet you refuse to come to me to receive this life. No wonder you can't believe! For you gladly honor each other, but you don't care about the honor that comes from the one who alone is God." John 5:39,40,44

How can anyone read the Bible and miss Jesus? He is chastising the Pharisees here. They search the Scriptures, He says, looking for eternal life, yet settle for a "spirituality" that completely eliminates Him as its source.

The Pharisees were obviously more concerned about "looking" good than "being" good. They'd created a religious system they could navigate with confidence.

Those willing to conform to their spiritual "code" were honored, their opinions valued. Anyone, however, including Jesus Christ Himself, who called for radical departure from the spiritual patterns they'd established could not be trusted and had to be eliminated.

PONDER: Am I so different? Do I find it easier to conform to a set of rules than to answer a call to deny myself, take up my cross, and follow Christ down a road few others are willing to travel?

PRAYER: Lord, in Your mercy, convince me that I <u>dare</u> not rely on personal effort to make myself "fit" for God. Open my eyes to see how far short of the standards of a perfect and holy God I come, and that if I depend on anything or anyone besides You and You alone, I'm completely on my own…

March 4
Training To Endure

"I discipline my body like an athlete, training it to do what it should. Otherwise, I fear that after preaching to others, I myself might be disqualified." I Corinthians 9:27

Do I control my body, or does my body control me? Am I able to make my body obey my commands, or does my body, with its desires and drives, run the show?

This world has witnessed more Christians persecuted, tortured, and killed for their faith in this generation than any other time in history. Those of us in a free society can hardly imagine being forced to choose between Jesus Christ our Savior and physical agony or death.

Paul anticipated that crisis. Over time, with practice and with God's grace, he taught his body to obey his commands whether it "felt" like it or not. His body became his servant and not the other way around! We in the Western world can hardly imagine saying "no" to anything our body clamors for.

PONDER: Do I have power over my body to make it do what I want? If faced with the ultimate, life-and-death-question for Jesus's sake, would I embrace God's grace to walk through the fire, or would I recoil to the safety and comfort of self-preservation?

PRAYER: Lord Jesus, I am so weak. Strengthen my resolve to train my body into submission so that, through the power of Your Spirit, I may honor my desire to remain true to You no matter the cost.

March 5
A Dead Giveaway

"If you claim to be religious but don't control your tongue, you are fooling yourself, and your religion is worthless." James 1:26

Perhaps the ultimate test of a person who claims to belong to Jesus Christ is what comes out of his/her mouth.

Some of the cruelest things ever said were in the name of God or religion. Some of the most careless, pain-inflicting words have come from people who labeled themselves "Christians."

Does that mean true believers won't ever say anything unbecoming of the Savior? No. But those whose hearts have been humbled, purified, and changed by God cannot speak slanderous, wounding words without being immediately aware that they've grieved God's Holy Spirit.

When God is in control, His Spirit works within us to produce true repentance and genuine desire to make things right, to seek forgiveness and restoration with those we've wounded.

The "pain" of humbling ourselves, required in such obedience, works deeply to retrain our minds, hearts, and tongues to respond more Christlike in future opportunities.

As Christ is allowed to do His Work of refining us from the inside out, our tongues will reflect His character more and more in gracious, kind, encouraging words that minister His mercy and love.

PONDER: Is what comes out of my mouth a "dead giveaway" that my tongue is still not under the Spirit's control? ...that my heart is still far from Christlike?

PRAYER: "Prick" me each time my words bring grief to Your heart, Lord Jesus.

March 6

God Is God!

"They ask me [God] *to take action on their behalf, pretending they want to be near me." Isaiah 58:2b; "God understands all hearts, and he sees you…" Proverbs 24:12*

How can God know when I'm not really sincere? Among all the billions of people in the world, I must certainly escape His notice once in a while! Surely, He cannot see and know us all at the same time?

Fortunately (or unfortunately, depending on your perspective) God is God—all-knowing, all-powerful, and everywhere-present! To Him, limitations are unknown, except as He imposes them on Himself, and impossibilities don't exist!

The fact that I can't figure out how God does what He does in no way nullifies Who He is and what He can accomplish! If I could understand Him fully and anticipate His every move, I'd be God instead of Him, right?

Scripture is very clear in these verses. God looks straight into my heart. He knows what motivates me to do what I do, even as it relates to my worship and service in His Name. That's amazing because my heart and my motives are so convoluted that, at times, I'm not even sure what drives me to do and say the things I do.

PONDER: Am I willing to look at my motives through God's eyes? Do I have the courage to invite Him to expose the true condition of my heart?

PRAYER: Lord, reveal my true motives and give me new desires that really honor You!

March 7
Underneath Are The Everlasting Arms!

"The eternal God is your refuge, and his everlasting arms are under you." Deuteronomy 33:27

I love this verse. The thought of God's everlasting arms under me wraps my heart in a warm blanket of security. Close your eyes and picture it with me as best you can. Wow!

God's arms are everlasting! Unlike human limbs, they never tire or give way. They're always strong, always steady, always gently undergirding, supporting, and cradling His beloved children.

I once heard a circus performer say it was the net below him that gave him the confidence to perform with abandon on the trapeze and the courage to try new, more daring stunts.

Sometimes, what God asks of us seems daunting, too difficult, even impossible. The very thought is frightening and intimidating. Do we dare let the "net" of God's everlasting arms provide the comfort and security to try what would otherwise be too fearful?

Will we allow ourselves to step out in faith, knowing that to fall is but to land in the embrace of the One whose arms are always poised lovingly beneath us?

PONDER: When I think of saying "Yes" to what I know God wants, how does that make me feel? Do I really believe the promise of this verse? Will I trust the "safety net" of His loving presence?

PRAYER: Lord, You call me to trust You. Help me recognize I'm never outside the scope of your vision, nor beyond the reach of Your loving, everlasting arms.

March 8
Will I Let God Use My Story?

"My sanity returned, and I praised and worshiped the most High..."
Daniel 4:34b

King Nebuchadnezzar, one of the most powerful kings who ever lived, is writing to all his subjects, worldwide *(4:1)*, recounting his blatant disregard for a very specific warning from God concerning his arrogance.

One year after God had predicted it, Nebuchadnezzar lost his sanity. Apparently thinking he was a cow, he lived and ate with the cattle for seven years. Then one day, his sanity returned, and he acknowledged the One and Only True God.

What strikes me is how openly he recalls the humiliating details of his saga, with little or no regard for what people will think of him. His goal is obviously to highlight the undeserved mercy and grace of this amazing God Who has restored him.

Too many of us attempt to hide our past, rather than disclose it to showcase God's kindness and His power to change even the worst sinner. Our sense of shame keeps our focus on <u>us</u> and how we will be perceived rather than on <u>God</u> and how He could be glorified.

PONDER: Does God have complete access to my story? Am I willing to tell it if He prompts me to? What's holding me back?

PRAYER: Lord, take my eyes off myself. Help me care more about Your Glory than my reputation. If you can use my story, it's Yours. Help me know if, when, and how to share it appropriately for the glory of God.

March 9
Focusing On The Invisible

"...He [Moses] kept right on going because he kept his eyes on the one who is invisible." Hebrews 11:27b

Did you know Moses got <u>so</u> sick and tired of the Israelites' constant whining and complaining he wanted to give up?

"What did I do to deserve the burden of all these people?" he prayed. *"...The load is far too heavy! If this is how you intend to treat me, just go ahead and kill me. Do me a favor and spare me this misery!"* Numbers 11:10-15

This crisis occurred early in the journey, before the Lord pronounced His 40-year sentence in the desert. So, what enabled Moses to stay the course? Something changed, but it wasn't the Israelites.

Our Scripture explains that Moses was able to keep going because he took his eyes <u>off the problem</u> and fixed his gaze upon **"the ONE who is invisible."**

When his focus was on the Israelites, on the impossibility of his task, and what he did and didn't deserve, Moses felt the weight, the anger, and the self-pity such a situation can inspire. But when he fastened his eyes on God, Who is always with us even though we cannot "see" Him there, Moses could put one foot in front of the other again and move on in confidence.

PONDER: Are my prayers full of faith, or do I whine, whimper, and complain to the Lord?

PRAYER: Teach me, Father, to fix my eyes on <u>You</u> and trust <u>You</u> to do what I cannot.

March 10
There's More! Oh, Yes, There's More!

"As for you, go your way until the end. You will rest, and then at the end of the days, you will rise again to receive the inheritance set aside for you." Daniel 12:13

God makes this promise to Daniel at the end of several very disturbing, frightening visions concerning the end of time. Yet the Lord assures him the outcome is guaranteed. He can rest in God's amazing provision.

Christ had not yet conquered death when this promise was issued. Yet, even then, the resurrection was certain for <u>all</u> who <u>truly</u> believed. The Messiah was coming to suffer, die for sin, and rise again to offer new life to all who would believe.

Daniel was instructed to live out his life until "rest," in the form of death, would eventually come. However, death would not be the end of Daniel. God's promise is clear: *"you will rise again!"*

Because we live this side of the cross and Resurrection, we have the advantage of knowing more of the story than Daniel grasped, but the promise was no less secure for him. Anyone who has <u>ever</u> trusted in God, rather than his/her own ability to make themselves right with God, has been credited with righteousness (*Romans 4:3-5*) and given eternal life.

PONDER: Does the thought of death bring hope to <u>my</u> heart? Is resurrection a confident reality in <u>my</u> future?

PRAYER: Thank You, Jesus, for Your death and resurrection, which guarantee my hope of life after death with You forever and ever.

March 11
Never Assume To Know God's Mind

"Nathan replied to the king, 'Go ahead and do whatever you have in mind, for the Lord is with you...' But that same night, the Lord said..." II Samuel 7:3,4

The longer we walk with Jesus the easier it is to assume we know what God would want done in any given situation. Nine times out of ten, we might even be right. However, like the prophet Nathan, we cannot afford to speak on God's behalf unless we have taken time to ask—and then listen for—God's answer.

David was a man after God's own heart. God had blessed and prospered him. Nathan couldn't think of any reason why God would deny David's desire to build Him a temple. But God had other plans. It would **NOT** be David, but his son Solomon, to whom God would entrust that task.
God's ways are not our ways; His thoughts not our thoughts. *(Isaiah 55:8)* Romans 11:13 declares, *"How impossible it is for us to understand his decisions and his ways!"*

The **ONLY** way to stay in step with God is to spend time in His presence, seeking His wisdom and guidance, daring not to proceed into our agenda unless permeated with and controlled by His Spirit.

PONDER: How often do I get up and sprint through my schedule without a thought about God, assuming I already know what He wants?

PRAYER: Lord, help me be still and listen for **Your** voice. I dare not presume to know Your thoughts.

March 12
What More Could He Do?

"God chose him [Jesus] *as your ransom long before the world began..." I Peter 1:20*

As God created His beloved humans—beings He could shower His love and kindness upon—He also saw that they would spurn that love, reject His kindness, and follow a deceiver right into the pit of Hell!

So, before time began, God conceived a plan to buy back His cherished creation. Jesus, who had existed forever as the Second Person in the Godhead, would offer Himself as payment for the sins of God's wayward sons and daughters. He would leave the splendor of Heaven, empty Himself of all His prerogatives as God, and put on flesh—for one purpose and one purpose only—to become the ransom for our sin.

Sin had enslaved God's beloved, and, as a result, Satan legally ruled the earth. Mankind had forfeited their relationship with God to follow Satan's lies. The only way to buy us back was for One who knew no sin to become sin for us and offer Himself as our substitute.

No human could ever be perfect enough to accomplish this feat! God Himself would have to step into a human body!

PONDER: What else must God do to prove His love for me? Will I allow myself to trust Him?

PRAYER: Forgive me, Lord, for permitting myself to be deceived about who You are. You have forever settled the question of Your love for me through what You did in Christ. My life is Yours, now and forever!

March 13
The Father's Longing — Fulfilled!

"...Our father's life is bound up in the boy's life... how can I return to my father if the boy is not with me? I couldn't bear to see the anguish this would cause my father." Genesis 44:30,34

Judah offers himself in Benjamin's place, rather than return to Jacob without the boy, knowing how grieved his father would be.

Like Benjamin, we've been separated from our Heavenly Father, taken captive, made slaves to sin. To the Triune God, the thought of living without us, leaving us trapped in a Christ-less eternity, was so heart-wrenching, that the Son, like Judah, said, "Take me instead!"

So even before the foundations of the world were laid, He'd formed a plan. In the event mankind would choose against God, Satan would <u>not</u> go unchallenged. Clothing Himself in flesh, Christ became the ultimate sacrifice for sin—His death in exchange for our freedom—to redeem us back for the Father.

God is <u>not</u> a vindictive Sovereign, as often portrayed, who finds some perverted joy in sending people to a fiery Hell. Though we <u>deserve</u> such a destiny because of our sin, Jesus offered His own life to buy us back for God.

Our eternal destiny, then, is <u>our</u> choice, and ours alone!

PONDER: Have I believed Satan's devious implications that God is mean, vindictive, unreasonable? Or will I trust God's revelation of Himself as merciful, compassionate, and loving?

PRAYER: Lord, I acknowledge Your loving and gentle mercy. What more could You possibly do for me than You have already done?

March 14
Religion Or Relationship?

"Then the Lord said to Joshua, '...I have given you the king of Ai... and his land... but this time, you may keep the plunder...'" Joshua 8:1,2

Just days earlier, the Israelites had received marching orders for the battle of Jericho, where God had specifically forbidden them to take ANY plunder from that conquest. Now, however, He is inviting them to keep the spoils of victory.

Is God being wishy-washy? Can He not make up His mind what He wants them to do?

On the contrary. God is revealing here that, even in the Old Testament, He was interested in relationship. We humans tend to prefer "religion"—a prescribed list of predictable, measurable rules we can adhere to and feel good about. Then we can put our minds and hearts on "autopilot" and still "appear" quite spiritual.

Relationship is so much more demanding. It requires time and attention, caring about what is important to the other person, listening, and responding.

Being in relationship means that each situation may require a different response. God is always in the business of redeeming and transforming people, but He works very personally and specifically in each individual life and situation.

PONDER: Do I prefer the predictability of "religion" to the unquantifiable effort required to "abide" in relationship with Jesus Christ?

PRAYER: Lord, I don't easily live and move in relationship with You, but I want to. Help me focus my attention and energy on "abiding" in our relationship rather than fulfilling religious obligation.

March 15
Heaping Burning Coals Of Fire!

"Let my enemies be destroyed by the very evil they have planned for me. Let burning coals fall down on their heads…" Psalm 140:10

The Psalmist is crying out to God, detailing the abuse he is suffering at the hands of evil people. He begs God to help him, then offers <u>menacing</u> suggestions for what God could (and <u>should</u>) do to his enemies… heap burning coals on their heads, throw them into fiery or watery pits from which they can't escape….

Yes, that should do it!

Proverbs 25:21,22 and *Romans 12:19,20* give us God's answer to the Psalmist's prayer, in <u>no</u> <u>uncertain</u> <u>terms</u>: *"If your enemies are hungry, feed them. If they are thirsty, give them something to drink. In doing this, you will heap burning coals of shame on their heads."*

Jesus reiterated this in *Matthew 5:43-45:* *"…I say, love your enemies! Pray for those who persecute you. In that way, you will be acting as true children of your Father in heaven…"*

Romans 12:21 encapsulates the heart of God with these words: *"Don't let evil conquer you, but conquer evil by doing good."*

Everything God says is imperative, but when He repeats Himself, we'd best sit up and take notice!

PONDER: What's my typical response to people who wound or offend me? Am I more like the Psalmist in today's verse than I am like Jesus?

PRAYER: Loving and doing good to my enemies is <u>not</u> my gut response, but I **<u>want</u>** it to be. Lord, make me like **<u>You</u>**!

March 16
Whose Approval Is Most Important?

"Our purpose is to please God, not people. He is the one who examines the motives of our hearts." I Thessalonians 2:4b

The thought that anyone might see and know the motives of my heart makes me squirm. My motives are such a "mixed bag," sometimes pure, often self-serving, even when I do and say what others might consider to be spiritual and noteworthy.

Too often, I'd have to admit to being moved by my need to avoid criticism, to fix things, to manipulate circumstances, to control people, to be needed, to be appreciated, to be thought of as a good person.

There are times when I smile and speak words as smooth as honey while carefully concealing rancor and bitterness deep within.

How many of my good deeds, if never noticed or appreciated, would cease to find any motivation at all?

PONDER: Where do I most need the approval of others? Do my words and deeds match my motives and attitudes? Are there things I do or say in private that I'd be mortified if others knew? Is my heart's cry to please people or honor God?

PRAYER: *"Search me, O God, and know my heart. Try me and know my thoughts. Reveal any wicked way You see in me. Then let the words of my mouth and the meditations of my heart be pleasing in Your sight, O Lord, my Rock and my Redeemer." Psalm 139:23,24; 19:14*

March 17
Can Joy And Sorrow Coincide?

"Our hearts ache, but we always have joy." II Corinthians 6:10a

How is it possible to have heartache and joy in the same heart at the same time?

Joy is usually equated with good feelings that result from happy experiences in life. In reality, however, much of what happens to us would never make our "Top Ten Most Desirable" list.

There's no way to avoid heartache and disappointment. It's part of living with other humans in a less-than-perfect-world.

The Apostle Paul had more than his share of adversity *(II Cor. 4:8-12, 11:23-33)*. It is amazing that he could have experienced <u>any</u> joy at all in the midst of such suffering!

His secret? His life was anchored solidly in something that could never change or be taken away. Ours can be, too!

For believers, Jesus Christ—the same yesterday, today, and forever—lives within us, orders our steps, gives us hope, peace, and strength, promises to turn even life's worst circumstances into something good, and offers rewards that will make every experience on this planet pale in significance! And that's just the beginning!

PONDER: Who or what gives me "joy?" Can I count on my "source" to never let me down? Have I ever experienced joy in the midst of sorrow and difficulty? What made that possible?

PONDER: Dear Lord, Yours is the only Joy that can sing, praise, worship, and hope in the midst of whatever life might throw at me. That's what I want!

March 18

Do I Try To Manipulate God?

"Pray that the Lord your God will show us what to do and where to go. Whether we like it or not, we will obey… for if we obey Him, everything will turn out well for us." Jeremiah 42:3,6

When Jerusalem was overrun by Babylon and its people taken captive, those left behind asked Jeremiah to seek the Lord on their behalf to determine what their next step should be.

Their words in verse six are noble: *"Whether we like it or not, we will obey the Lord."* Sounds a lot like Jesus's prayer in the garden, doesn't it? *"Not my will but Thine be done."* Luke 22:42

Later in this same chapter, however, we learn that these people were actually using their pious-sounding words to manipulate and bargain with God, hoping He would make things turn out "well" for them. Unfortunately, they weren't willing to accept God's definition of that term.

PONDER: Do I ever "obey" God with the express purpose of trying to manipulate His blessings in my life? When things don't go the way I'd hoped, how do I react? Can I say in complete honesty, "Whether I like the outcome or not, I will obey the Lord?"

PRAYER: Lord, forgive me for not believing You enough to let You determine what is best for me. Help me take my hands off and simply trust. Help me rest in Your unfailing love and wisdom and say with all my heart, *"Not my will but Thine be done!"*

March 19
Even When Things Are Good...

"When I was prosperous, I said, 'Nothing can stop me now!' Your favor, O Lord, made me as secure as a mountain. Then you turned away from me, and I was shattered." Psalm 30:6,7

How easily we forget who we really are!

When things go well… when life runs smoothly… when we enjoy abundance, we tend to forget we are hopelessly finite creatures who depend on God for our very next breath, for the opportunity to wake up each morning, for health and strength to make it through another day. How quickly that realization returns, however, when "the rug is pulled out from under us!"

Just because we can't "feel" His presence when life comes tumbling around us, does that mean God has turned away? No! Absolutely not! In those moments, we find ourselves crying out to God as the Psalmist did. When we do, we discover that, like a loving parent whose independent child breaks free from his grasp, God hovers near enough to reach for us at our first cry for help.

PONDER: Is life good for me right now, or am I walking through a dark and lonely valley? How deep is my awareness that my entire life depends on God's mercy and grace towards me?

PRAYER: Lord, never let me forget what a fragile being I am. Apart from You, I can do nothing. *(John 15:5)* Help me cling desperately to You in the good and prosperous times, as well as the difficult seasons of my life.

March 20
How "like God" Am I?

"The wicked borrow and never repay, but the godly are generous givers." Psalm 37:21; "Some people are always greedy for more, but the godly love to give." Proverbs 21:26

To be "godly" is to be "like" God. God is generous! Look at the earth He created. He could have made it totally functional—black-and-white, without "frills," without the beauty that squeezes our souls with awe.

Instead, He filled the earth with color, fragrance, music—a plethora of things to hear, see, smell, taste, and touch—all designed to thrill our senses. Extravagant sunsets, majestic, snow-covered peaks, quiet meadows, peaceful streams, crashing waterfalls, twinkling stars in the black night, moonlight on shimmering water, a delicate rose…!

It was generosity that prompted God to hide beautiful lakes and streams in the middle of deep forests and at the top of rugged mountains, and to paint extravagant color at the bottom of the ocean floor where only a determined few would see it.

Only a gracious, generous God would go to all the trouble to make wildflowers, whose brief splash of elegance, often trampled underfoot by careless humans, can "stop the heart" of one who examines them closely.

PONDER: How like God am I? Could I be described as generous? How far does my generosity extend? To family? Friends? People I don't know? Enemies? How like God am I?

PRAYER: O God, make me like You. Give me Your generous, gracious heart and show me where to pour it out.

March 21

Can God Be Trusted?

"'As surely as I live,' says the Sovereign Lord, 'I take no pleasure in the death of wicked people. I only want them to turn from their wicked ways so they can live. Turn! Turn from your wickedness, O people…! Why should you die?'" Ezekiel 33:11

Does this sound like the cry of a capricious, vindictive God, whose heart is indifferent to the suffering of mankind?

The lie of the ages, first perpetrated by God's archenemy, Satan himself, as he instigated a revolt among one-third of Heaven's angels, is that God cannot be trusted.

Again, in the Garden of Eden, to the beloved and treasured beings newly created by God, Satan intimated that God was selfishly withholding something special from them.

Throughout time, this same lie has gained momentum. God has so often been portrayed as harsh, vindictive, volatile, detached, uncaring, self-serving, etc.

In the devil's attempts to rob, kill, and destroy those God loves so dearly, he unashamedly slanders the reputation of the God of the Universe in such a way that we humans "swallow the bait, hook, line, and sinker."

PONDER: Would the God, Who designed this incredible world for our pleasure, Who gave us the choice to love Him or not, then came in the person of Jesus Christ to be condemned and crucified, to rescue us from the deadly, eternal consequences of that fateful choice, be Someone I cannot trust? Really?

PRAYER: Open my eyes, Lord, that I might see the Truth!

March 22
All Or Nothing!

"But you must continue to believe this truth and stand in it firmly. Don't drift away from the assurance you received when you heard the Good News." Colossians 1:23

All God has planned for us has been fully accomplished. *"It is finished,"* *(John 19:30)* Jesus cried on the cross. He knew He'd fulfilled everything necessary to reconcile mankind back to God.

There is nothing you or I can do that could add to, or take away from, the atonement He has provided. We must simply believe... and receive. However, there is a qualifier in today's verse: *"You must continue to believe this truth and stand in it firmly."* Believing is not just a passing fancy, here today and gone tomorrow.

It is casting my life, my hopes, my eternal existence <u>completely</u> on the mercy of God in Christ Jesus. It is setting my course for the long haul, in effect saying, "Christ is my <u>only</u> hope. There is <u>no</u> other!"

As long as I maintain even a shred of confidence in my own righteousness or harbor the slightest hope that anyone, or anything, else could ever satisfy my deepest longings, my salvation will remain unclaimed, never enjoyed or experienced. In effect, I've rejected what Christ has thoroughly accomplished on my behalf.

PONDER: Is Christ <u>my</u> only hope? Do I cling to Him as to a lifeline, or is my heart still grasping for something or someone else?

PRAYER: In Your mercy, Lord, bring me to the place where it's "all" or "nothing."

March 23
Trusting God Pleases God

"The Lord is good… he knows everyone who trusts in him." Nahum 1:7

He knows! Those of us counting on Him to be our salvation, our righteousness, our strength, and our provision should be greatly encouraged. The Lord knows who we are, and He can't help responding to our believing hearts.

God is keenly aware when even the tiniest glimmer of trust begins to flicker in the heart of one of His creatures. Scripture declares that His eyes roam to and fro throughout the whole earth to show Himself strong on behalf of anyone who is committed to trusting Him. *(II Chronicles 16:9)*

Only in trusting God can we ever fully please Him. *(Hebrews 11:6)* The good news is—it is not about our performance! That will always fall short because we are human.

But those who trust in Christ are automatically considered righteous through what Christ did on the cross. He was made sin for us so we might be made righteous through Him. *(II Corinthians 5:23)* It doesn't depend on me!

PONDER: Have I rested my full "weight" on Jesus, trusting Him as God's only provision for my salvation and sanctification? Or do I feel there is still some part of this whole process that depends on me?

PRAYER: Lord, open my eyes to the many times You've declared in your Word that I am made right with You by trusting in what Jesus has done for me. It's a gift! It cannot be earned—only received.

March 24
Will I Bear His Disgrace?

"So let us go out to him, outside the camp, and bear the disgrace he bore." Hebrews 13:13

None of us likes to be misunderstood. When others speak against us, mistreat us, put us down, dismiss us without even bothering to listen to our point of view, it hurts, and we are NOT happy about it.

That and more is what Jesus endured for us. It cost Him dearly, more than we could ever imagine, to secure eternal life for us and to give us power over sin and the futility of this world!

He promised, because the world hates Him so much, it is going to hate us as well, simply because we align ourselves with Him and His Word. Jesus spelled it out very clearly: *"If the world hates you, remember that it hated me first… I chose you to come out of the world, so it hates you… They will do all this because of me, for they have rejected the one who sent me." (John 15: 18-21)* And God promises in *II Timothy 3:12, "…everyone who wants to live a godly life in Christ Jesus will suffer persecution."*

We must make up our minds whether we will *"bear the disgrace he bore"* or look for a way to avoid it.

PONDER: Does the thought of persecution frighten me? Is there anything or anyone I would choose over Christ? Could anything cause me to relinquish Christ?

PRAYER: Oh, Lord, nothing I desire on earth compares to You! *(Psalm 73:25)*

March 25
What Do I Expect?

"...once you were slaves of sin... you let yourselves be slaves of impurity and lawlessness... in those days... you weren't concerned with doing what was right." Romans 6:17,19,20

Let's face it! Without Christ, human beings don't concern themselves with what is right! Why would we ever expect otherwise? Jesus certainly didn't.

He saw people as they were: lost, in need of being found, sick, in need of a physician. Until a person comes into relationship with God through Christ, he/she is incapable of producing a morality or righteousness that's not somehow tainted by self-interest.

Jesus first accepted people where they were, then loved them to where He wanted them to be.

Even on the cross, Christ begged God's forgiveness for his persecutors, because He perceived they had no clue as to the spiritual pawns they'd become. *"Father, forgive these people, because they don't know what they are doing." Luke 23:34*

Surely they knew! They were murdering an innocent man! Yet Jesus understood that, until His Spirit opens people's eyes and hearts, we humans can look at evil and call it good because we're held captive to the father of lies. Only in Christ can that change!

PONDER: Do the expectations I place on unbelievers make it impossible for me to accept and love them as Jesus does?

PRAYER: Lord, help me accept people where they are, so my love can play a part in moving them toward where You want them to be. Use me to shine Your Light, spread Your sweet fragrance, and awaken their hearts to You.

March 26
Quit Hiding!

"The Lord's light penetrates the human spirit, exposing every hidden motive." Proverbs 20:27

How many hours have I spent justifying—to myself first, then to others—why I did or said certain things? We all do it. The energy required to "spin" things in our favor is enormous! And such a waste, too, because all along, there is One who sees and knows the truth, whose desire is to expose what we're trying to hide.

Why does God want to expose us? Because everything we keep hidden has **power** over us! Those things we bring out into the open can be conquered in the strength of His Spirit.

This is nothing new. Adam and Eve first hid from God in the Garden. Mankind has been hiding ever since. The first couple sewed together feeble, fig-leaf garments and cowered behind bushes, supposing they could hide their nakedness. But the all-knowing, everywhere-present God had been there all along. He'd seen everything!

It was only as they came into the Light of God's presence that God could clothe them in garments of His own making and gave them a hope-filled promise of deliverance.

Deliverance would come through God's Son JESUS—the Light of the world, the Way out of bondage, the Truth that sets us free, and the Abundant Life we all long for.

PONDER: What actions, attitudes, or motives am I trying to keep hidden?

PRAYER: Lord Jesus, help me walk into Your Light and live in the freedom of the Truth.

March 27

Do I Even Care?

"They do not see your punishment awaiting them... They think, 'nothing bad will ever happen to us!' ... They think, 'God will never call us to account.'" Psalm 10:5b,6,13b

As I read this passage this morning, names and faces of beloved friends who do not know the Lord flashed before me, and my heart was suddenly and profoundly broken for them.

Until a few years ago, most of my friends, acquaintances, and social contacts were believers. Then, through a series of painful events outside my control, I was thrust into situations in which I met and built relationships with outsiders to the faith, many of them blatantly atheistic or agnostic in their beliefs.

I've read these Scriptures before, but as long as I could keep my distance from the "wicked," something in me secretly agreed with the Psalmist, *"...Punish the wicked, O God! ...Go after them until the last one is destroyed." Psalm 10:12a,15b*

Now, however, they have become **real** people, whom I **know** and **love**. And suddenly, my cry is that God will have **mercy** on them, that He will somehow **use me** to show them the Truth about Himself.

PONDER: Does my circle of friends, my day-to-day schedule, my social life, allow for meaningful interactions with unbelievers?

PRAYER: Lord, I admit, I prefer spending time with believers, whom I love and with whom I have so much in common. Help me deliberately make time to get acquainted with, and **love**, the "outsiders" you have strategically placed around my life.

March 28
Like Fine Gold Jewelry

"To one who listens, valid criticism is like a gold earring or other gold jewelry." Proverbs 25:12

Can any of us really imagine getting as excited over a word of criticism as we would over fine gold jewelry? I don't think so!

Most often, we find ourselves offended by criticism, no matter how valid it might be. We typically respond defensively, sometimes with tears. Too often, the relationship between those involved is damaged as a result.

What if we would open our hearts and minds, instead, to **receive** criticism and **listen**? What if we could choose to look for **value** in what is being said? Instead of viewing criticism as an indictment of all the ways we fall short, what if we could view it as an invitation, a way to become better?

Of course, not all criticism is equal… not all of it is valid. How can we determine whether the criticism directed at us is valid or not?

Perhaps the only way is to listen with a **desire** to know. Let's never dismiss criticism without prayerful consideration. God will inform a heart that is humble and willing to learn. Look for "nuggets" of truth, as if panning for gold, and discard everything else.

PONDER: What is my "default" reaction when criticized? Am I willing to let God reprogram my responses?

PRAYER: Lord, Jesus, I know this is Your Word, and it is wise. Make me secure enough in who I am in You to open my heart to this advice.

March 29
How Can I Not Love Him?

"Don't you realize that I could ask my Father for thousands of angels to protect us, and he would send them instantly? But if I did, how would the Scriptures be fulfilled that describe what must happen now?" Matthew 26:53,54

Jesus had agonized in the Garden of Gethsemane over what He knew was ahead of Him. His whole being recoiled at the horror, the torture, scorn, and humiliation, the pain, abandonment, and death He was about to endure.

Knowing that one word from Him would scrap the whole plan—that though He had chosen this path, He could "un-choose" it at any time—made it even more difficult to follow through.

No one took His life. He laid it down freely *(John 10:18; 19:11)*. The battle that must have raged within Him, as He anticipated the agony such a choice would entail, cannot be overstated. Jesus cried out in anguish, *"Father, if there is any other way, I don't want to do this!"*

But there was <u>NO OTHER WAY</u>! *(John 14:6)* If there had been, Jesus would not have kept going to the cross.

Christ **chose** to move steadfastly toward Calvary's cross because of His unfailing love and the knowledge that the **only** provision for our forgiveness, freedom, and reconciliation with God was through His becoming the scapegoat for our transgressions, the atonement for our sins.

PONDER: How can I not trust, worship, and serve One who endured such suffering on my behalf?

PRAYER: Hallelujah! What a Savior!

March 30
Thoughts That Delight The Lord

"May he [God] *be pleased by all these thoughts about him, for I rejoice in the Lord." Psalm 104:34*

The Psalmist has been rehearsing in his mind all the incredible things God has done and how dependent every creature on earth is upon Him. It thrills him to realize that his thoughts could bring delight to the heart of God.

Does God feel pleasure when we just sit and contemplate Him with a sense of awe and wonder? Does the Lord enjoy knowing that His creation, His power, and His provision stir our hearts with worship and adoration for Him? The answer is obvious.

In our feverish, frenetic, fast-paced lives, it's a challenge to carve out a healthy chunk of time to spend with God and just be quiet. Our days are typically filled to overflowing with noise and activity.

Getting alone with God will require deliberately shutting the door on all competing voices and images to marvel at His creation, to think thoughts about Him, to acknowledge His love, His presence and His power!

PONDER: When was the last time I just sat—quietly, unhurriedly—and contemplated the beauty around me, the intricate design, detail, and order of all God has made?

PRAYER: Lord, free me from the tendency to fill my life with so much activity and noise that I never get the chance to sit and think thoughts about You. Help me <u>choose</u> to take time to be still and know that You are God.

March 31

Death Is Broken

"He broke the power of death and illuminated the way to life and immortality..." II Timothy 1:10b

When something is broken, it no longer works as originally intended. It may continue to function to some degree but can no longer produce as designed.

Death is Satan's "baby," a tool he's used against us since that fateful moment in the Garden when he talked Eve into second-guessing God. It has worked well for him over the centuries, as the most hated and feared aspect of human life.

Then God entered history as a man. He faced death head-on, conquered it, and <u>forever</u> broke its power!

Death still functions to some degree, however, and will until its ultimate destruction at the Judgment. We encounter it each and every day. So what about death did Jesus break? What gave death so much power? Fear.

The sting of death lay in its ability to enslave us in fear. Jesus rose from the dead with the keys to death and Hell in His hands, offering LIFE eternal to any and all who will look to Him in faith.

Yes, death still disrupts and grieves us deeply, but its <u>sting</u> is gone. For we who are "in Christ," fear has been replaced with vibrant **HOPE** of life to come.

PONDER: Am I still caught in the fear of death?

PRAYER: Lord, thank You that, through faith in Christ, death no longer has power over me. I am forever alive in Jesus. Praise His Name!

April

April 1

Which Tastes Better, New Wine Or Old?

"But no one who drinks the old wine seems to want the new wine. 'The old is just fine,' they say." Luke 5:39

We are such creatures of habit. The old is comfortable, familiar. It gives a semblance of control. No surprises.

That's why "religion" seems to work for folks who want to feel good about themselves. It gives us a list of things to do that promote feelings of spirituality, while protecting our pride and sense of control. It's measurable, predictable, and doable. We like that!

The religious leaders of Jesus's day hated Him because He challenged their religious systems, exposing their manipulative, prideful masquerade, their self-centered efforts to "appear" spiritual before men.

The Pharisees loved "old wine." But Jesus came, offering "new wine"— not religion, but a vital relationship with God in which love and trust are the hallmarks.

It's sometimes easier for those who have no "wine" at all, whose thirst is obvious and demanding, to recognize their need, than for folks who've become content with the taste of the old wine of religion and self-effort.

However, as at the wedding in Cana, the new wine Jesus offers is always the best wine of all!

PONDER: Am I content with religion, with going through the motions, just having a "form" of godliness? Or do I long for real relationship with God, the abundant life Jesus promised, and the power to be like Christ?

PRAYER: Give me new wine, Lord. I'm tired of the old!

April 2

No Condemnation — For Real!

"There is therefore now no condemnation for those who are in Christ Jesus…" Romans 8:1 (KJV)

According to the first seven chapters of Romans, God has a new way of making people right with Him, and it is NOT by trying to be good enough. Faith in Jesus Christ ALONE is what is required.

As a result, God does not condemn me. Christ absorbed the condemnation I deserved and died in my place. Because He did, God took the goodness of <u>Christ</u> and credited it to <u>my</u> account!

Jesus did what no amount of effort on my part could ever do. He lived a perfect life and satisfied the wrath of God against all sin, including mine, through his death on Calvary.

For many of us, that is too much to hope for. We cannot forgive ourselves. How can we believe God could forgive us?

Are we more righteous than God? Are our standards higher than His? Isn't it rather arrogant to continue condemning one whom God has declared to be righteous?

PONDER: God blamed and punished Christ for all I've done. I can either <u>receive</u> that or <u>reject</u> it. If I reject it, I have no one to lean on but myself. If I choose Christ, I can REST in what **<u>He</u>** has done.

PRAYER: Lord, I'd be a fool to trust in my own ability to make myself good enough to satisfy the perfect standards of a holy God. Thank you for being condemned in my place! Thank you for taking my sin and giving me Your own righteousness instead.

April 3

Mere Remorse Or True Repentance?

"'I have sinned... for I have betrayed an innocent man.' Then Judas threw the money onto the floor of the Temple and went out and hanged himself." Matthew 27:4a,5

Judas felt genuine remorse for what he'd done. Guilt was weighing heavily on his heart. On the surface, his confession "sounds" like true repentance, but Judas didn't find the peace he sought because he failed to identify his real crime. He refused to acknowledge and expose the true motivation of his heart.

After all, Judas wasn't the only one who betrayed Jesus. Peter, too, turned his back on Christ, swearing he'd never even met Him, yet he was restored to fellowship with Christ and entrusted with leadership in His church.

The difference is that Judas failed to identify the true source of his heart's condemnation. Sadly, he had chosen his own agenda over Christ's. He'd stiffened His heart against the denial-of-self required to make Jesus Lord of all. And though he deeply regretted having betrayed innocent blood, he only sought relief from his mental anguish, not the transformation of a life totally yielded to God.

PONDER: How often do I approach God or others with confessions stemming from my need to relieve my sense of guilt, but without the intention of bowing the knee to Christ's Lordship or owning honestly the true condition of my heart?

PRAYER: Holy Spirit, search me. Expose the truth about me that only You are aware of. Then help me obey Your promptings.

April 4
Now Is All We Have!

"…you did not accept your opportunity for salvation." Luke 19:44b

Jesus spoke these words as He rode into Jerusalem, in the midst of a triumphant procession, with people shouting praises to God, declaring Him their promised King.

As He looked out over the city, He began to weep. He grasped what no one else could see, and it broke His heart. He'd come to bring salvation, not from the Romans, but from the vise-grip of sin that'd plagued the world since mankind's fall in the Garden.

In spite of their enthusiastic celebration that day, the people of Jerusalem were not open to what God was doing in their midst and would miss their hour of opportunity.

So, when is the time of salvation? Is it a specific date and hour? How will I recognize it? How will I know if and when it has passed?

The Lord has told us <u>exactly</u> when it is. He was very specific and abundantly clear. *"I tell you, <u>NOW</u> is the time of God's favor, <u>NOW</u> is the day of salvation." II Corinthians 6:2 NIV (emphasis mine)*

As long as it is still "today," we have opportunity for salvation. When **NOW** is gone for good, it's over.

PONDER: Do I presume there'll always be another day, another moment, another opportunity? How can I possibly know which breath will be my last?

PRAYER: Bring me face-to-face with my own mortality, Lord—the fleetingness of my life. Help me seize my opportunity **<u>NOW</u>**.

April 5

The Truth About Myself?

"Keep me from lying to myself..." Psalm 119:29a

The Bible makes it very clear that without God's Word and His Spirit, we will have a difficult time recognizing the true condition of our heart. *"The human heart is most deceitful and desperately wicked. Who really knows how bad it is? But I, the Lord, search all hearts and examine secret motives..." Jeremiah 17:9,10*

Only God knows "the truth, the whole truth, and nothing but the truth" about our hearts, our lives, our motives, and our attitudes.

We are masters at convincing ourselves of what we <u>want</u> to believe, especially when it comes to our true motives. We're aided by the enemy of our souls, Satan himself, whose primary agenda is to blind our eyes to our true spiritual condition, distort our view of God, cast doubt as to God's trustworthiness, love, and goodness, and rob us of the abundant life that is ours in Christ Jesus.

For us to escape the trap of self-deception, we must allow God to reveal to us what <u>He</u> sees when <u>He</u> looks into our hearts. We cringe at the very thought, yet only in seeing ourselves through <u>God's</u> eyes will we finally experience His peace, deliverance, freedom, and power to change.

PONDER: How desperate am I to know the truth? ...desperate enough to ask God to reveal what He sees in my heart?

PRAYER: Get me to the place, Lord, where I am willing to look at my heart through Your eyes.

April 6

Does God Have Access To My "Stuff?"

"…just say, 'The Lord needs them,' and he will immediately let you take them.'" Matthew 21:3b

Jesus sent his disciples into a nearby village to get a donkey and colt for his triumphant ride into Jerusalem. I am struck by the willingness of the owner to release them to these two strangers upon hearing simply that "the Lord" needed them.

How did Jesus <u>know</u> this man would freely give his donkeys for the Master's use?

The donkeys' owner apparently didn't argue with the disciples. We aren't told whether he even knew how long they would be gone, what purpose they would serve, or whether he would ever get them back.

In those days, donkeys were critically important to one's livelihood and transportation. To part with one's donkeys might be similar to losing your job or totaling your car!

How did he let go of them so easily? Had he already determined in his heart that no matter what the Lord might ask for, he would give it freely?

PONDER: Am I as free with <u>MY</u> possessions as this man was? How about my <u>time</u>? My <u>thoughts</u>? What is my response to God's claim on them?

PRAYER: Lord, expose right now those areas of my life I've placed "off-limits" to Your Spirit, those things which, if you asked for them, I could not give without an incredible struggle. Help me determine <u>now</u>, ahead of time, that they are Yours, at Your disposal, and ready for Your use.

April 7
Worst of All!

"He told them, '...My soul is crushed with grief to the point of death...'" Mark 14:34

What was it that weighed so heavily on Jesus's heart and mind that He felt He might not live through it? Was it the anticipation of torture, humiliation, and shame that would accompany His trial and crucifixion?

How He must have agonized at the very thought of the excruciating pain and suffering He would soon endure at the hands of His Roman executioners. Their reputation for inventing the worst kinds of torture was widely known.

But imagine with me something that, for Jesus, was <u>even</u> <u>worse</u>! The blameless Son of God—pure, holy, and incapable of evil—would soon experience the full force of sin's alienation, condemnation, and horror as He took upon Himself the sinfulness of every human being who has ever lived, or ever will live.

Though He had <u>**never**</u> sinned, He allowed Himself to be blamed for the sins we had committed. Though not guilty of <u>**anything**</u>, He took our punishment.

He died the death meant for us, then rose from the dead to open a "New and Living Way" back into relationship with God. It's a gift! It cannot be earned... just gratefully received!

PONDER: What made Him do it? What kind of love would motivate such sacrifice? In view of such mercy, what should my response be?

PRAYER: O Love that will not let me go, I dare not hide myself from You! How can I not trust One who loves me like that?

April 8
Jesus Paid It All!

"...God's will was for us to be made holy by the sacrifice of the body of Jesus Christ, once for all time. ...by that one offering he forever made perfect those who are being made holy... there is no need to offer any more sacrifices." Hebrews 10:10,14,18

Jesus declared on the cross, *"Father, forgive them! It is finished!"* What needed to be done has been accomplished. Jesus paid it all. All to Him I owe.

Why is that so difficult for us to wrap our minds around? Why do our proud hearts insist on paying our own way? Why is it so hard to admit I can't do **<u>anything</u>** to earn God's approval—that without Him, I am lost?

My forgiveness is His **<u>gift</u>**! My holiness is His Work in me. The only thing I bring to the table is **<u>trust</u>** in what He's already accomplished and **<u>obedience</u>** that springs, not from any attempt to earn His love, but out of sheer gratitude, rising from a heart fully aware of having received undeserved mercy and grace.

PONDER: Am I trusting solely in Christ's sacrifice for my sins? Or is there something in me that still believes it's, at least partly, up to me to make myself more acceptable to God?

PRAYER: I choose to reject all my own efforts at right living as worthless and throw them aside. The righteousness I will depend on from now on is by faith in Christ's provision for my soul.

April 9

A Gift... Unopened?

"This is the new covenant I will make... I will forgive their wickedness, and I will never again remember their sins." Jeremiah 31:33a,34b

This is Good News that must be declared! When Jesus made atonement for sin on the cross, His blood covered ALL sin for ALL time! Sin would never again keep man from relationship with God.

God invites everyone, no matter who we are or what we've done, to come home... without condemnation! Be reconciled to God! Receive His forgiveness and His eternal presence in your life. God loves you and wants you back!

What will our response be to God's invitation? Many of us, too stubborn to admit we are sinners who <u>need</u> a Savior, send our RSVP, *"No, thank you! Not interested!"* or *"I'll take care of this myself."*

Perhaps others have never heard that, because <u>Christ</u> was punished for <u>their</u> sin, God will never hold it against them. They don't yet know that it's safe to come "home" because their loving Father waits eagerly to celebrate their return.

Salvation is a **gift**, but as with any present, it can be left unopened. No matter how intense the Giver's feelings or how costly the offering, unless we receive it and make it ours, we will never enjoy and experience it.

PONDER: What's my response to this amazing and priceless gift? Does it remain unopened or have I received it with gratitude and dedication?

PRAYER: Thanks be to God for His unspeakable Gift! I embrace and receive all that Jesus provided for me.

April 10

What If He'd Stayed Dead?

"I pray that you will begin to understand the incredible greatness of his power for us who believe him. This is the same mighty power that raised Christ from the dead…" Ephesians 1:19,20a

This time of year, Christians everywhere gratefully remember the crucifixion of our Lord Jesus Christ, which freed us from the penalty of our sins! But think for a moment what would have happened had Christ stayed in the grave.

Without His Resurrection, we'd still be in slavery to the power of sin, doomed to keep repeating our sins, no matter how sorry we were, or how much we hated ourselves for committing them.

I don't know about you, but I remember those days of spiritual bondage, and I don't want to go back there. Glory to God, we don't have to, but it's because of the Resurrection! When Christ burst through that tomb on Easter morning, He forever broke sin's power over us, conquering not only death, but sin itself!

For you and me, that means the ability, IN CHRIST, to say "No!" to sin. We are no longer obligated to obey its evil desires. Now we can live free, if we choose to, by the power of Christ's Resurrection Life at work in us. Hallelujah! Praise the Lord!

PONDER: Am I living free of sin's domination over me, or have I allowed myself to remain in its shackles?

PRAYER: Lord Jesus, thank You for conquering sin so I'm not forced to live in it any longer!

April 11
Do I Need A "Talkin' To?"

"Why am I discouraged? Why so sad? I will put my hope in God! I will praise him again—my Savior and my God. Praise the Lord, I tell myself; with my whole heart, I will praise his holy name. Praise the Lord, I tell myself, and never forget the good things he does for me." Psalm 42:5,11; 43:5; Psalm 103:1,2

Ever notice that the Psalmist talks to himself on occasion? He asks himself questions and issues commands.

Sometimes, we just "need a good 'talkin' to,'" don't we? Our eyes get focused on the wrong things. Our hearts slip into discouragement and despair. We begin listening to voices contrary to the Word of the Living God.

Sometimes I must become my own counselor and call myself back to the Truth, back to the basics. What is it I really believe? Is God real? Is He good? Do I believe His Word?

If my answer is "yes," then I must call myself to praise, trust, and hope again, just as the Psalmist did.

PONDER: Do I need a good "talkin' to?" Will I choose to stand on what God's Word declares about Himself? Will I fasten my eyes on Jesus, the Author and Finisher of my faith? Will I take every thought captive and make it obey Christ? *(II Cor.10:13)*

PRAYER: Lord, forgive me for allowing myself to lose perspective and give way to discouragement. I <u>know</u> I will praise You again. Help me <u>choose</u> to praise You **NOW!**

April 12
Belief Is A Choice!

"Then the 11 disciples left for Galilee... where Jesus had told them to go. When they saw him, they worshiped him, but some of them doubted!" Matthew 28:17

How do we "doubt" what we've just seen with our own eyes? These disciples had witnessed Christ's crucifixion. They'd spent three agonizing days afraid and dejected. The women's tale of Christ's Resurrection may have been confusing, but they'd still headed for Galilee as He'd instructed.

Now, Jesus appears before them, and yet some still doubt. Do they question His resurrection? Surely not! He's standing in their midst, after all.

The Message puts it this way: *"...The moment they saw him, they worshiped him. Some, though, held back, not sure about <u>worship</u>, about risking themselves totally."*

So much of what we call "doubt" is actually a "choice" we make, whether conscious or unconscious. The truth is, if we **choose** belief, there is only one response that makes any sense: to fall on our faces in worship.

But that would require that we acknowledge Jesus is God, that we crown Him King of Kings and Lord of Lords in our <u>lives</u>, that we forsake all we have previously clung to, depended on, and believed in—all that rivals Him—and give Him absolute reign and control. Are we ready and willing to do that?

PONDER: Question: is it really **"doubt"** I struggle with, or **"surrender?"**

PRAYER: Lord, I'm done fighting Your Spirit. I **choose** to believe. I crown You Lord of my life!

April 13
Where He Leads Me...

"The Lord is my shepherd... He lets me rest in green meadows... He leads me beside peaceful streams... I walk through the dark valley of death... You prepare a feast... in the presence of my enemies..."
Psalm 23:1-5

How easy it is to proclaim the goodness of our Shepherd while resting in green meadows or walking beside peaceful streams, when our souls are being restored, and our hearts are able to understand and rejoice in the paths He has chosen.

How differently we react, however, when this same Shepherd leads us through the dark valley of death, when He guides and corrects us with His rod and staff, or when He allows us to be surrounded and taunted by enemies.

If He really loves us, why would our Shepherd ever lead us through painful, difficult situations?

Because it is in the valleys, when surrounded by enemies, that we experience the intimacy of His comfort, the "feast" he prepares in the midst of our troubles, the anointing that overflows our "cup." Without these times in our lives, we'd never come to **know** and **experience** the Shepherd's most precious attributes.

PONDER: Am I a "fair-weather friend," celebrating God's love and care only when things go according to my desires, my understanding?

PRAYER: Dear Lord, forgive me for receiving blessings from Your Hand while rejecting all that eludes my ability to comprehend what You're doing and why. Help me <u>choose</u> to trust You, even in those times when trusting will be the most difficult thing of all.

April 14
How Do I Treat "Sinners?"

"Or do you show contempt for the riches of his kindness, tolerance and patience, not realizing that God's kindness leads you toward repentance?" Romans 2:4

We tend to think it's judgment, not kindness, that causes people to confess and repent of sin. But look at the life of Jesus.

Although "religious people" of His day hated Him and plotted His death, outcasts loved Him. He was kind to them. Rather than judging or condemning them, Jesus accepted them for who they were: SINNERS... in desperate need of the mercy of God.

Prostitutes, tax cheats, and reprobates couldn't figure out why this good and holy man would have anything to do with them. Yet, in spite of their sinfulness, Jesus treated them with <u>love</u> and <u>respect</u>. He sat at their dinner tables, attended their parties, ministered to their needs! And, as they were touched by such kindness, their hearts opened to the Truth of the Gospel.

PONDER: What's my approach to sinners? Am I more likely to judge and distance myself from them than to reach out with kindness and love? Do I fully comprehend that, apart from Christ, I, too, am a wretched sinner, completely undeserving of God's tender mercy and compassion? Yet He offers grace and kindness to me anyway! How should that realization inform my view of people around me?

PRAYER: Thank You, Lord, for your incredible mercy to lost and wounded people, including me. May Your kindness motivate me to treat sinners like You do.

April 15
Tired Of Hiding

"You spread out our sins before you—our secret sins—and you see them all." Psalm 90:8

No matter how impressed others may be with us—our accomplishments, the way we live, raise our kids, volunteer in church/community, give to charity—God looks past it all and sees straight into our hearts, where our real motives are exposed before His all-seeing eyes.

For those trying to hide their sins, this verse holds no comfort at all. *"Where can I go from Your Spirit?"* asks the Psalmist in *Psalm 139*.

We feel exposed, uncomfortable. We know our thoughts and motives condemn us, and we don't like the idea that God is so keenly aware of what we've worked so hard to hide.

We hide for fear our attitudes and motives, if exposed and truly known, would keep folks from loving us. We fear if people knew what we're really like, they would reject us.

But God is not like us humans. This God, who's always been totally aware of all our secret sins, passionately declares His love for us throughout Scripture. This love is undeserved, unconditional, everlasting, and unfailing! It has the power to transform our hearts.

PONDER: Can I trust God with my deepest, most secret self? Will I allow His healing love to wash and bathe and heal those hidden areas I'm so ashamed of?

PRAYER: Lord, I'm tired of hiding. You are the only One who can transform my heart. Please begin that work in me now.

April 16

What Wondrous Love Is This?

"...[Jesus] told them, 'My soul is crushed with grief to the point of death.'" Mark 14:34; "...He was in such agony of spirit that His sweat fell to the ground like great drops of blood." Luke 22:44b

Yet He prayed, *"I want Your will, not mine."* Why? Jesus didn't have to suffer on Calvary's cross! More than once, He declared that no one took His life—He laid it down *freely (John 10:18)*. If He'd chosen, He could have called 10,000 angels to destroy the world and set Him free. *(Matthew 26:53)*

You and I are the reasons Jesus kept going—*"...because of the joy He knew would be his afterward..."* when He would present us to God as reconciled children, forgiven and purified through His atoning sacrifice. *(Hebrews 12:2)* Was it worth it? Jesus thought so!

Nothing in our human experience compares to that kind of love. It's inconceivable that anyone should ever care that much for us. *"But God demonstrates His own love for us in this: while we were still sinners, Christ died for us." Romans 5:8*

PONDER: What kind of response does Christ's sacrifice evoke in my heart? Have I allowed myself to be stirred to the depths of my being by the thought of such intense longing and love for me? Has anything in my life been changed as a result?

PRAYER: Lord, I worship You and surrender to You, because *"love so amazing, so divine, demands my soul, my life, my all!"*

April 17

Does My Pain Hurt God?

"In all their suffering He also suffered…" Isaiah 63:9a

Have you ever watched someone you love go through intense suffering? A child? A spouse? A friend?

There is no pain quite like it. So often, the misery inflicted seems totally unjust, entirely random and arbitrary, with no possible explanation. Other times, pain is the direct consequence of their own unwise choices, perhaps even arising from some disciplinary measure we ourselves felt it necessary to impose as a result. Even <u>then</u>, the anguish we feel can be intense.

In those raw, emotional moments, we'd be willing to do most anything to relieve their pain. If only we could somehow absorb it into our own selves rather than watch our loved ones endure it! Since that's impossible, we've no choice but to stand helplessly by, our love and support the only consolation we can offer.

If we humans, sinful and weak as we are, are capable of such empathy *(Matthew 7:11)*, how much more our Father in Heaven?

Unlike us, however, God <u>did</u> make a way to enter into <u>our</u> torment and take it onto Himself through His suffering and death on the cross. Now, through His Spirit, He is an intimately present burden-bearer in our time of need.

PONDER: Am I feeling all alone in a painful place in my life? What proof has God offered that He knows and cares?

PRAYER: Thank You, Lord, for going all the way to the cross to take my sin and sorrow upon Yourself.

April 18
Once For All Time

"And when sins have been forgiven, there is no need to offer any more sacrifices." Hebrews 10:18

We humans find it so difficult to give up atoning for our sins. The Bible makes it clear, when Jesus allowed Himself to be crucified on Calvary's cross, His sacrifice was completely adequate, totally sufficient—once for all time!

"For God's will was for us to be made holy by the sacrifice of the body of Jesus Christ, once for all time. …by that one offering, he forever made perfect those who are being made holy." Hebrews 10:10,14

So why do I still feel like it's up to me? Why this inner "compulsion" to make amends for my sins? Do I not really trust God's Word?

Satan's defeat on Calvary left him with only one weapon in his arsenal: deception. If he can't block our salvation, his next strategy is to rob us of its joy through accusation and condemnation.

His suggestions sound true enough, but God's Word declares otherwise: *"Whoever believes in him is not condemned, but whoever does not believe stands condemned already…" John 3:18 NIV*

PONDER: To whose voice am I listening? Do I dare trust that God means it when He says, *"With his own blood… he entered the Most Holy Place once for all time and secured our redemption forever?" Hebrews 9:12*

PRAYER: Oh, God, help me totally and completely give up my own efforts at righteousness. Help me trust Your provision for my salvation, which is both abundant and sufficient.

April 19
Not On Passover!

"The leading priests and the teachers of religious law were still looking for an opportunity to capture Jesus secretly and kill him. 'But not during the Passover celebration,' they agreed, 'or the people may riot.'" Mark 14:1,2

In this passage, as Jesus's enemies lay out their plans to kill Him, they make a very emphatic declaration, and with good reason. It will definitely **not** happen during Passover because the people might riot!

Little do they know that God has a different plan. Jesus Christ came to this earth with one purpose: to die as God's Passover Lamb, so His blood might be sprinkled over the "doorposts" of our hearts, freeing us from spiritual death, allowing us to walk free from all that has enslaved us.

Centuries earlier, as the Israelites prepared to leave Egypt, God instituted the Passover Celebration, not just for that night, but as a yearly remembrance of their deliverance. He also detailed, very specifically, the lamb was to be sacrificed on a specific day of the year—Passover.

Sadly, the religious leaders think they are on a mission from God. They're too in love with their own plans to reexamine or abandon them, even for God Himself.

PONDER: How often do I make plans, then ask God to bless them, without first seeking to know what God wants, and when?

PRAYER: Lord, teach me to search Your Word, to wait upon You and seek Your heart, so You may direct my steps.

April 20
Dying Is Never Easy!

"I command you to love each other in the same way that I love you. And here is how to measure it—the greatest love is shown when people lay down their lives for their friends." John 15:12,13

What does it mean to lay down our lives? Is Jesus referring to sacrificing ourselves, as in physically dying? Or does he have something else in mind, something that is, perhaps, even more difficult to do?

If we are to fulfill Christ's command, what must die is that part of us that cherishes itself and its plans and looks out for its own interests. Christ asks us to relinquish our rights to our time, energy, and the comforts we hold dear. Other people have a nasty way of interfering with those things, needing us when we don't want to be needed.

Jesus Himself showed us how, and, thankfully, He also comes to live within us through His Spirit, to do in us what we could not otherwise accomplish.

Through His power, we **can** lay down our lives for those God asks us to serve. We **can**, but the real question is—are we **willing**?

PONDER: Do I dig in and hang onto my rights, my pleasures, my plans, etc., refusing to lay them down in the interest of people around me?

PRAYER: Lord, my natural tendencies are so self-centered. Forgive me. Right now, I pray You'll help me relinquish claim to myself, so I can lay my life down as You command.

April 21
Grace—When We Need It

"Jesus fully realized all that was going to happen to him, so he stepped forward to meet them..." John 18:4

This verse describes a scene in the Garden of Gethsemane, when temple guards came to arrest Jesus. He is fully aware of all that will take place in the coming hours and has agonized over it, to the point of sweating drops of blood, as He battled intense temptation to abandon God's plan.

Now the soldiers are upon Him. He doesn't run. He doesn't fight. He simply steps forward to meet them. He has received the grace to do what, moments earlier, He struggled to even imagine.

That's how God's grace works. We receive it when we <u>need</u> it and not a moment before.

Perhaps that's why Jesus warned his followers not to worry about things in the future. While we're worrying and fretting about them, we have not yet received God's grace to deal with them.

But, when the time comes to walk through those trials, God abundantly pours out His grace. Then, if we will <u>receive</u> it, we'll find ourselves more than able to endure.

PONDER: What do I dread? Am I running away in fear or moving ahead in confidence that, when the moment arrives, God will give me all the grace I need to triumph?

PRAYER: Lord, help me trust Your promises to strengthen and uphold me, to make everything turn out for my good. Help me know Your grace is truly sufficient for me.

April 22
Surely Not, Lord!

"Jesus turned around and… reprimanded Peter, 'Get away from me, Satan!' he said. 'You are seeing things merely from a human point of view, not from God's.'" Mark 8:33

How like Peter we are! Jesus is describing the cruel suffering and death He will soon be called upon to endure. Peter, no doubt speaking with compassion and with a "keen sense" of what <u>must</u> surely be God's will, immediately scolds Jesus for such talk. *"Surely, something like that would <u>never</u> happen to <u>You</u>, Lord. You are good and God's beloved Son. God just wouldn't allow it!"*

In our humanness, we, too, find it difficult to imagine that such suffering could **<u>ever</u>** be part of God's plan. But, like Peter, we see with human eyes! Most often, our point of view lacks God's perspective. And then, when life blindsides us, whether via the self-centeredness and cruelty of others or the seeming randomness of nature, we find it almost impossible to reconcile with our assumptions about how God works.

Jesus's words are just as true for us as they were for Peter. *"You are seeing things merely from a human point of view, not from God's."*

PONDER: Is there a person or situation against which my mind and heart recoil, crying out, *"Surely not, Lord!"* Can I trust God and thank Him for His purpose in allowing me to walk this road?

PRAYER: Heavenly Father, help me to pray, like Jesus, with a sincere heart, *"No matter what, I <u>**CHOOSE**</u> Your will."*

April 23

When "Bad" Is Actually "Good!"

"But while in deep distress, Manasseh sought the Lord his God and sincerely humbled himself before the God of his ancestors." II Chronicles 33:12

Why is it that deep distress is so often necessary for stubborn humans to humble themselves and cry out to God?

When we feel "in control" and life is moving "according to plan," God seldom gets much attention. However, when life takes a turn, and we feel vulnerable, thoughts of God crowd the surface of our minds and demand a response.

The beautiful thing about trouble is it can soften even the hardest heart. Manasseh was one of the most wicked kings in Israel's history. God sent repeated warnings of disaster. Manasseh ignored them all *(v. 10)*. So the Lord sent <u>severe</u> trouble into Manasseh's life. Only in the midst of <u>deep</u> distress did Manasseh finally seek the Lord.

Those of us who've come to know God look back at the difficulties that brought us to our knees with <u>grateful</u> hearts. We view those trials as merciful expressions of God's love, which motivated and enabled us to humble ourselves.

PONDER: When people I love experience distress, do I pray God will <u>relieve</u> it or that He will <u>use</u> it? Do I try to <u>rescue</u> my loved ones or <u>trust</u> that God is at work in the midst of their pain?

PONDER: Thank You, Lord, for the circumstances that brought me to my knees. Help me trust You to deal as mercifully with those I love.

April 24

How Did You Make Yourself Do It, Jesus?

"…My soul is crushed with grief to the point of death… My Father! If it is possible, let this cup of suffering be taken away from me… if this cup cannot be taken away unless I drink it, your will be done." Matthew 26: 38,39,42

Contemplating Christ's anguish as He prepared to lay down His life for us, my heart cries out, *"How did you do it, Jesus? How did you* **MAKE** *yourself do what You absolutely did* **NOT** *want to do?*

"You knew You didn't **HAVE** *to go to the cross, to become sin for us, to die the cruel death we deserve. One word from You, and all of Heaven would have come to Your rescue! (Matthew 26:53) Why didn't You just leave us to pay our* **OWN** *penalty for sin?*

"My heart already knows the answer, Lord. It's because Your everlasting love simply would not let us go. You couldn't stand the thought of living without us and, quite simply, there was **NO OTHER WAY** *to bring us back into relationship with You."*

Before Creation, God the Father, Son, and Holy Spirit had known this would be necessary. They'd understood Satan would manipulate and deceive mankind into mistrusting and disobeying God and going their own way.

Though some would try with all their might, no mere human would <u>ever</u> be able to repair this breach. Only God could do it. And He would!

PONDER: What should be my response to Christ's sacrifice on my behalf? Can I turn my back on love like this?

PRAYER: Lord, I receive what You did for me and gratefully give You my life in return!

April 25
A Defeated And Humiliated Foe!

"...he [Christ] disarmed the spiritual rulers and authorities. He shamed them publicly by his victory over them on the cross." Colossians 2:15

Good News! The enemy of our souls has been disarmed, publicly shamed, and thoroughly vanquished by Jesus Christ! It happened through Christ's death on the cross and His resurrection over death and Hell.

What does that mean for us now? It means Satan has absolutely NO power over us who are in Christ Jesus. Those of us who have *"died with Christ and been raised to new life with Him" (Romans 6:13)* by trusting what He accomplished on our behalf don't <u>ever</u> have to give in to Satan's temptations again!

If that's true, why does temptation <u>feel</u> so overwhelming? Because, though Satan's been "creamed," he still awaits his doom. <u>He</u> knows he's defeated, but he's hoping <u>we</u> don't! Stripped of his power at the cross, his <u>only</u> weapon now is the lie.

If he can <u>convince</u> us that he has power over us, we will succumb to his enticements. If we **<u>know</u>** that we *"can do all things through Christ" (Philippians 4:13)* who strengthens us, and that the devil can never again **make** us do anything, we will recognize and refuse his bait, in the power of the risen Lord Jesus Christ, Who lives within us.

PONDER: Do I know—really **<u>know</u>**—Satan has <u>no</u> power over me? How does that affect my response to his temptations?

PRAYER: Thank You, Lord Jesus, for <u>soundly</u> defeating the enemy of my soul!

April 26
When I Feel Strong...

"These men had a great reputation as mighty warriors and leaders... They were all skilled... and armed... They cried out to God during the battle and He answered their prayer because they trusted in Him..." I Chronicles 5:24,18,20

We are all familiar with the sense of need that comes when we feel totally inadequate for the task ahead. However, when we feel skilled, capable, and gifted, that sense of desperate dependence isn't always there.

The men in today's Scripture passage, though mighty warriors, skilled and highly armed, understood that to accomplish God's objective in God's way, <u>God</u> must do the fighting <u>for</u> them and <u>through</u> them. Sure enough, verse 22 says they won the battle, *"because God was fighting against"* their enemy.

We, too, are in the middle of a continual, spiritual battle, raging for the hearts and lives of people around us. As we serve and interact with others, our skills, talents and gifts may <u>impress</u> them, even <u>help</u> them. However, without **God's anointing**, nothing of <u>eternal</u> value will <u>ever</u> take place. No <u>spiritual</u> battles will be won.

PONDER: When I feel strong and adequate, how inclined am I to earnestly seek God's help and anointing? How often have I relied on personal abilities and strengths, completely oblivious to the spiritual battle waged in unseen places?

PRAYER: Lord Jesus, help me realize if anything of <u>eternal</u> significance is to take place through my life, every word, deed, and service must be consecrated to You, anointed by Your Spirit, for Your Glory.

April 27
What is Obedience—Really?

"'How foolish!' Samuel exclaimed. 'You have not kept the command the Lord your God gave you.'" I Samuel 13:13

True obedience honors not only what God <u>says</u>, but what we <u>know</u> He <u>means</u>.

King Saul was told to wait seven days for the prophet Samuel to arrive before going to battle against the Philistines. In the meantime, the Philistines made ready to march against them.

When Samuel did not come as anticipated, the Israelite soldiers started to panic, and Saul decided to proceed without the prophet's blessing. He prepared a sacrifice, thinking God would surely be pleased and go with them into the conflict.

That's when Samuel showed up. Saul insisted he <u>had</u> done what God asked, that he <u>had</u> waited seven days as instructed. But God wasn't pleased. He is not simply interested in a particular time sequence or some sacrifice designed to appease Him.

God was, and is, looking for hearts tuned to His—men and women who will trust and fully obey rather than take matters into their own hands, even when it doesn't make any sense to them.

PONDER: Do I settle for the "<u>letter</u> of the <u>law</u>" rather than seeking to understand and respond to God's <u>heart</u>, as revealed in His Word? Do I ever take matters into my own hands when I can't see what God is up to?

PRAYER: Lord, trusting is not easy for me. Help the part of me that struggles to obey when I can't see what You're doing.

April 28

Do I Need A Bath?

"...Christ loved the church. He gave up his life for her to make her holy and clean, washed by the cleansing of God's Word." Ephesians 5:25,26

This morning, as I was standing in the shower, feeling the warm water rush through my hair and over my body, I suddenly felt such gratefulness for the ability to wash and be clean. "Clean" smells and feels <u>so</u> good!

Bathing or showering brings a sense of refreshment, provides more confidence in life's intimate moments, and makes it easier for other people to be around us.

However, just as soap and water must be applied if offensive odors, dirt, and grime are to be washed away, we must intentionally open our hearts to the cleansing work of the Word of God. Simply reading, even memorizing it, will have no effect.

Children are usually oblivious to the fact that they need a bath. Bath time is often met with great resistance. "I'm not even dirty!" the child vigorously declares.

Not until the child becomes attracted to the opposite sex does personal hygiene become important in his/her life. The possibility of loving and being loved suddenly makes cleanliness a much higher priority! And so it is with God and His Word. The love relationship makes all the difference!

PONDER: How motivated am I for God? …for His Word in my life?

PRAYER: Lord, may my love for You cause me to hunger for the Scriptures and to open my heart to Your Spirit's deep cleansing.

April 29

What Is My Soul Worth?

"...what do you benefit if you gain the whole world but lose your own soul? Is anything worth more than your soul?" Matthew 16:26

Let's face it! We love this world. It is familiar, tangible, and visible. Its values and ideas make sense to us, because we humans tend to think alike. We like this world's trinkets and treasures and are forever tempted to just get comfortable and settle down, surrounded by the pleasures it offers.

Choosing to value the "soul" that we cannot see or fully understand, over the very real offerings of this world, is not a decision arrived at without struggle, especially because Jesus makes it clear that protecting my soul means letting go of my rights, giving up my life for His sake, denying "self" to follow Him.

His question, *"Is anything worth more than your soul?"* must be answered. We can answer it now and discover the abundant life that paradoxically comes only with the relinquishing of self. Or we can continue our love affair with this earthly life and take our chances.

PONDER: Is anything—anything at all—worth more than my soul? What is it I'm clinging to? What or who do I love more than Christ?

PRAYER: Lord, open the "eyes" of my heart to see that which is eternal. Through the power of Your Holy Spirit, strengthen my resolve to pursue Christ, His Kingdom, and His righteousness, at the expense of all else in this world, even that which is most dear and familiar.

April 30

Guard Your Affections

"Dear children, keep away from anything that might take God's place in your hearts." I John 5:21

We'd prefer the <u>literal</u> translation, *"Keep yourselves from <u>idols</u>,"* because few of us actually worship images of wood, gold or silver. No conflict there!

But carefully scrutinizing our hearts—discerning whether there is anything, including our own selves, usurping God's rightful place in our affections—is a much more difficult and convicting experience.

The thought of bowing to an "idol," even purchasing one as an ornament, would appall most Christians. But Satan is far too clever to be so obvious. His temptations take the form of legitimate loves, drawn out of proportion. Subtlety is his game, often playing on our fear of losing what seems rightfully ours.

An intense devotion to treasured persons or things in our lives <u>feels</u> justified, sometimes even holy. We seldom recognize when we've relegated God to second place.

PONDER: Who or what is sitting on the throne of my affections? Have I allowed anything to wrap itself around my heart in such a way that I'm no longer able to trust God with it? Or perhaps I'm so preoccupied with myself that there's no room for enthroning Christ as Lord of my life?

PRAYER: Lord, help me discern whether <u>You</u> are truly the passion of my life. Help me give you more than just "lip service." I yield all of me, and all the loves of my life, to You. Take Your rightful place in my heart.

May

May 1
Phony Bologna

"Prove by the way you live that you have really turned from your sins and turned to God." Matthew 3:8

John the Baptist is talking here to people who are trying to make sure they don't go to Hell. These are Pharisees, very "religious" people. They have come to be baptized by John to make sure all their spiritual "bases" are covered.

John knows their desire is more to please and impress people than to humble themselves before God. John is calling them to "get real." He knows they will resist Jesus's teaching and authority and eventually have Him crucified, because He will ask more of them than they're willing to give: humility of heart, acknowledgement of sin, and surrender to the Lordship of Jesus Christ.

They've focused only on outward behaviors and appearances. They'd like to keep it that way, but Jesus will expose what's in their hearts (greed, self-centeredness, temporal values, etc.), because God looks past our pious, religious show. He's not impressed when we parade our "goodness" before Him.

PONDER: Does my inner life (motives, attitudes, thoughts) match my spiritual words and religious activities? If people could glimpse the real me, would they see I'm a phony?

PRAYER: God, You gaze straight into my heart. You're aware of all I have carefully hidden from the eyes of others. Forgive me for settling for "religious appearances." I commit myself right now to the cleansing, refining process of Your Holy Spirit and ask You to make me like Christ, inside and out.

May 2
Who Will I Believe?

"What are you trusting in that makes you so confident?" II Kings 18:19b

These words, defiantly shouted at the people of Jerusalem by Assyria's field commander, were designed to frighten them into submission. Over and over, he reminded them that none of the gods of other nations had succeeded in protecting them from Assyria's power.

But Assyria's army didn't realize that the God in whom the Israelites trusted was not a mere idol like those of other nations. This time, they were actually defying the Holy One of Israel, the Only True God!

Judah's King Hezekiah instructed the people not to answer him. Instead, they chose to trust in their God.

How often do we, like they, hear the enemy's voice insinuating that our trust in God is misplaced, that He's either uninterested or unable to help us? Everything Satan whispers <u>feels</u> true, so we cower in fear and contemplate surrender in the face of his onslaught.

God reminds us that He alone is God over all the kingdoms of the earth. *"I will defend this city and protect it…"* he declared to Jerusalem. *(v. 34)* And, sure enough, just as God had predicted, the Assyrian army was decimated by the angel of the Lord and King Sennacherib assassinated by his own sons.

PONDER: What voices have my attention right now? In whom/what do I trust? What is it that makes me afraid?

PRAYER: Lord, help me trust what Your Word tells me about You and stand confidently against Satan's lies.

May 3

What Kind of God Is This?

"He [God] alone can never die, and he lives in light so brilliant that no human can approach him. No human eye has ever seen him, nor ever will. All honor and power to him forever! Amen!" I Timothy 6:16

What kind of God is this? Certainly not just "the man upstairs!" We're talking about a fearsome, terrifying Being, One whom we dare not approach. If we flagrantly saunter into His glorious, Holy Presence, we will surely, and immediately, perish!

Yet He graciously extends an invitation for us to approach Him, but **only** through the New and Living Way that He Himself has provided *(Hebrews 10:19,20)*. That "Way" is Jesus Christ. There is no other! *(John 14:6)* Without Jesus, we'll never have access to the Father.

In our culture, we've all but lost any sense of the fear of God, any dread of His displeasure. We've declared Him dead, ignoring the soft whispers of His Spirit that indicate otherwise, crafting our own ways to God, assuming that, when our time comes, we'll strut right into His presence and receive audience on the basis of our own merits.

We are in for a rude awakening! Scripture declares unequivocally: God is absolutely unapproachable, <u>except</u> through His Son!

PONDER: How do I view God? What do I trust in for access into His presence?

PRAYER: Lord God. I stand in awe of You! I humbly bow in worship, profoundly and gratefully aware that I am received into Your presence by Your mercy alone.

May 4
He Feels My Grief

"...the Lord replied, '...it is me they are rejecting, not you. They don't want me to be their king any longer. Ever since I brought them from Egypt, they have continually abandoned me... And now they are giving you the same treatment.'" I Samuel 8:7b,8

The Lord is speaking here to Samuel, one of Israel's greatest judges. God's people have announced they want to be ruled by a king, like the nations around them, not by Samuel and his sons.

After serving the Israelites faithfully all his life, this news is very difficult for Samuel to receive. It feels extremely personal—rejection of his leadership and little or no appreciation for all the years of sacrifice and dedication.

God's chosen people, recipients of the law, who've watched God do incredible miracles in their midst, apparently can't bring themselves to admit they are turning on God, so they reject His servant instead. And it hurts!

God assures Samuel, however, that the rejection and lack of gratitude he's sensing is really directed toward the Lord. It has been going on for a long time, but, despite their rebuff, God loves them deeply and will not abandon them.

PONDER: How does it make God feel when people misunderstand, malign, or reject Him? Dare I believe He identifies intimately with what I'm going through?

PRAYER: Lord, You're the *"Man of Sorrows, acquainted with grief."* You know the full extent of my pain, and You alone can bring healing to my heart.

May 5
"Ho-Hum..."

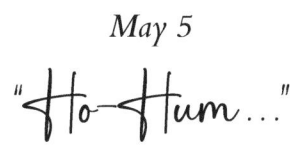

"O my people, what have I done to you? What have I done to make you tired of me? Answer me!" Micah 6:3

Why would God ask such questions of people who were called by His Name? The Israelites had been delivered out of slavery in Egypt. They'd witnessed God's mighty power and amazing provision. Surely God is mistaken here! Surely these people have not grown weary of this One, Whom to know is life eternal!

For the careless of heart, even life's greatest treasures can become commonplace and lose their power to inspire awe. Familiarity <u>does</u> tend to breed contempt.

The stories of the Bible—we've heard them all, more times than we can count—provoke little more than a yawn. "Been there, done that!" Our brains kick into "neutral," shift into "autopilot," and we're off to something more exciting, more stimulating.

We assume we know as much as we need to about the unfathomable, mysterious, unapproachable God of the Universe.

Our knowledge of the Scriptures produces, as Paul warned it would, a pride that glosses over our own spiritual bankruptcy. Thinking ourselves to be rich, we don't recognize our immense spiritual poverty.

PONDER: Does my heart thrill at the thought of God? Do I marvel at the intricacies of God's love and care? Or does Scripture bore me?

PRAYER: O Lord, restore unto me the JOY of Your salvation. Open my eyes to see and my ears to hear. May Your Word become a delight to my Soul.

May 6
Remember Who You Are

"Whatever you do or say, do it as a representative of the Lord Jesus…" Colossians 3:17

I grew up in a small community, well aware that what I did would <u>not</u> go unnoticed or unreported. My parents were good people. They taught us kids well, but our behavior could easily have called that into question.

We realized quickly that people drew conclusions about "The Thompsons" by how their kids behaved when Mom and Dad weren't around. Our love for them, and respect for what they taught us, and how they lived, kept us anxious to make choices that honored them.

Not that all our choices were the best, mind you, but we were grieved when we knew we'd brought them sorrow, and we accepted the necessary discipline to help us make better decisions in the future.

Even then, however, honoring our parents wasn't something we felt we <u>had</u> to do just to avoid punishment. We <u>loved</u> our parents, respected them, and <u>wanted</u> to make them happy. Because of that, anything important to them became important to us.

Even when no specific rules concerning certain situations existed, we evaluated our options in light of what we <u>did</u> know about our parents' ultimate priorities.

PONDER: Do the different facets of my life reflect well on God? Am I familiar enough with God's Word to know what honors Him and what grieves Him?

PRAYER: Lord, make it the desire of my heart to accurately represent You to others and so to honor You.

May 7
Accommodating My Desires

"This is what the Lord says, 'You have defied the word of the Lord and have disobeyed the command the Lord your God gave you.'"
I Kings 13:21

This is one of the strangest stories in the Bible. A man of God travels from Judah to give God's Word to wicked King Jeroboam. Twice, he is invited to eat and drink before returning home, but he is very clear about his mission *(13:9,17), "...the Lord gave me this command: 'You must not eat or drink anything while you are there...'"*

Then the strangest thing happens. A prophet of God tells him an angel said he should stop, mid-journey, and be refreshed at the prophet's home. It wasn't true, but the man believed him. The rest of the story reveals the sad result.

What could make a man of God disobey the <u>direct</u> Word of God that he knew well enough to quote verbatim? Could it be, in his heart, he thought God's request was unreasonable and hoped God would change His mind? Wicked King Jeroboam hadn't dissuaded him, but the words of another "believer" were welcomed as if from God Himself.

How often do we squirm under the clear commands in God's Word? How often do we use what other believers say or do as "permission" to disobey what we <u>know</u> God has already revealed to us?

PONDER: Am I committed to God's Word or looking for a way to accommodate my own desires?

PRAYER: Search me, O God!

May 8
Just Give Me Something To DO!

"I am the Vine, you are the branches... apart from me, you can do nothing." John 15:5

Jesus gives an analogy of a grapevine whose branches automatically produce delicious fruit every year without fail, as long as they are not severed from their source of life and nourishment—the vine.

In horticulture, that makes sense. Staying connected to the vine is the only thing branches must "concentrate" on, and if that happens, fruit will routinely grow without their effort. Whoever heard of a branch huffing and puffing to produce grapes?

Our primary responsibility as believers is to stay connected to Jesus. Our job is not to work at loving or producing self-discipline, etc. Our assignment is simply to stay in relationship with Him, seeking Him in prayer and Scripture, surrendering to His Lordship.

Our "job" is to make sure there is nothing choking off the Life of the "Vine" as it flows through the "branches." Fruit will be the unconscious result of His Life flowing through ours.

Unfortunately, we'd rather work at it. Activity is visible and obvious to the human eye. It's easier to "feel" spiritual if we have something spiritual to "do."

PONDER: How about me? Do I long for more of God? Am I pursuing relationship with Him, or do I prefer a list of things to do that make me "feel" more spiritual and appear that way to others?

PRAYER: Lord Jesus, don't let me settle for "doing" rather than "being." Help me recognize the difference!

May 9
Giving Christ A Bad Reputation

"Work willingly at whatever you do, as though you were working for the Lord rather than for people. Remember... the Master you are serving is Christ." Colossians 3:23,24

No matter who signs our paychecks, Scripture makes it very clear: if we are believers, our boss is the Lord Jesus Christ. Unlike our earthly "masters," Christ sees us when no one else is in the room.

He hears whispered conversations around the drinking fountain and behind closed doors. Whether it's stamped on a timecard or not, He is very aware of the exact time we slip in and out of the workplace.

He recognizes who owns the calculator, stapler, or ink pen that makes its way home with us. He tracks not only what we accomplish, but whether we even come close to what we are <u>capable</u> of accomplishing.

Why should He care? It's no skin off His nose, right? Wrong! The way we conduct ourselves on the job is one of the <u>surest</u> ways to either glorify or defame Him. When we, who have taken His Name, act in ways that He never would, we give Him a bad reputation.

PONDER: Would anything change if I could see Christ standing over my shoulder every moment of the day—even at work? What would I do differently?

PRAYER: Lord, help me practice the presence of Jesus <u>every</u> moment of <u>every</u> day. Make me aware that You are the One I work for. My work represents You. Help me reflect You accurately.

May 10

It's Just Not Fair!

"Joshua... protested, 'Master, make them stop!' Moses replied, 'Are you jealous...?'" Numbers 11:28,29

Joshua, Moses's assistant, was looking out for his leader. God had asked 70 of Israel's elders to meet Him at the tabernacle, where He would give them the same Spirit that rested upon Moses.

Two of those 70 missed the meeting, choosing rather to stay back in the camp. Yet God's Spirit came upon them as well. Joshua didn't think it fair that those two men received the same blessing and authority as the others, who did what God asked.

We aren't told why these two stayed behind. Joshua's first inclination was to assume they were being lazy, indifferent, or rebellious. His sense of justice and loyalty rose up to decry what he considered an obvious inequity.

Aren't we like that? What we are sure we would never do becomes the basis of our judgment of others. "I would never treat someone that way! I would never be so lazy, live like that, waste so much money, do those things!" So... we look down on those who do.

However, receiving God's mercy depends on our need, not our worthiness! It isn't "fair," but it's unbelievably wonderful for anyone willing to swallow their pride and simply receive it!

PONDER: Do I judge others by the self-righteous standards I hold for myself, demanding that God deal with them according to my sense of fairness?

PRAYER: Lord, help me focus on my <u>own</u> need for mercy and give up being "judge."

May 11
Where ~~Does~~ My Help Come From?

"...look up to the mountains—does my help come from there? My help comes from the Lord, who made Heaven and earth!" Psalm 121:1,2

The Psalmist had often fled to the mountains, hidden in its caves, and fought behind its boulders. When things got difficult, he would again flee to the mountains 'til the danger had passed.

In today's passage, David is looking at those mountains and asking himself what His **true** source of help is. Is it really the mountains that protect him?

"NO!" he reminds himself. *"My help comes from the <u>Lord</u>,"* the One who made those mountains!

We, like David, find ourselves tempted to trust the bulwarks of strength available in our lives. We look to our military for protection, our presidents for leadership, our doctors/hospitals/pharmaceuticals for health, our jobs/careers for provision, etc… These are all good gifts from His Hand, but not our real source of help.

Let's read this verse again and substitute whatever it is we are trusting in for the word "mountain." Follow that with this question: *"Is that what I'm counting on as my source of help?"* Then wait, in brutal honesty, in the presence of Almighty God, Who already knows the answer to that question.

PONDER: Who or what am I trusting in for help, for life's answers?

PRAYER: Lord, help me be honest with myself and You. Help me acknowledge You and trust in You as the **true** and **only** source of all I need!

May 12

A Hate-Love Relationship

"For Herod respected John; and, knowing he was a good and holy man, he protected him. Herod was greatly disturbed whenever he talked with John, but even so, he liked to listen to him." Mark 6:20

There is often a strange contradiction within those who are rejecting our Lord. On the one hand, they hate the Lord we love. They're afraid of God's claim on their lives. They don't want to listen to truth for fear it will expose the empty, vain persons they really are.

Yet, at the same time, they are often drawn, almost irresistibly, to us for reasons totally unbeknownst to them. Perhaps they can only handle so much "exposure" before the need to retreat overcomes their hunger, but they find themselves back again, not even knowing why.

To our knowledge, King Herod never allowed his heart to be changed by God's Spirit, but many others, equally wicked and perverse, including the Apostle Paul, were finally won over by God's love and mercy.

You and I can only see the outward "show." Only God can look into their hearts and know what motivates the things they do and say. God perceives the longings inside.

PONDER: What is my attitude toward those who show obvious disinterest or disdain for my faith?

PRAYER: Lord, even when people hate what I stand for, may my life, and my genuine love for them, ignite a deep hunger to know what (and Who) makes me the way I am.

May 13

Shhh! Can You Hear It?

"The heavens tell of the glory of God. The skies display His marvelous craftsmanship. Day after day, they continue to speak; night after night, they make Him known." Psalm 19:1,2

The sun is coming up. What a breathtaking, spectacular display of God's handiwork! If you missed it, you can look for another quite like it this evening.

We're surrounded with such incredible beauty! Wild flowers carpeting a hillside, lakes and rivers shimmering their reflections of the sun, trees silhouetted against the night sky, blue heavens and white fluffy clouds outlining the broad expanse of an eagle's wings as he soars easily on the wind.

God, You are such an artist!

Why, when so few stop to notice, does God continue the extravagant display of His artistry? To prove He exists? To delight my senses? To speak peace to my troubled mind, healing to my aching heart?

PONDER: How many times do I rush past the incredible pictures God paints in the sky and the world around me? Has the enemy of my soul succeeded in crowding out of my life the moments I so desperately need in order to, *"Be still,"* as the Scriptures say, and know that He is God?

PRAYER: Creator God, open my eyes that I may see! Help me pause, enjoy, and breathe in the wonder of your creation. Unstop my ears to hear the stillness of Your presence… to know, deep within my spirit where worship springs forth, that You <u>are</u> an awesome God!

May 14
Hanging On In The Dark

"The Lord was with Joseph, so he succeeded in everything he did..." Genesis 39:2a

Hundreds of miles from home, sold as a slave to a powerful Egyptian officer, Joseph probably didn't feel much like singing the doxology. But the Lord **was** with him. The Lord **was** blessing him, whether he **felt** like it or not!

Joseph served the best he knew how, with integrity, yet was falsely accused and thrown into prison. What was he to think? What would you and I think? *"I trusted You and served you faithfully, and this is what I got?"*

"But the Lord was with Joseph in the prison..." Genesis 39:21

How long Joseph was in that dungeon, we don't know. Long enough for the warden to notice and put him in charge, then for at least two years after that. No doubt everything in him was tempted to rail at God, *"Where are You! Why did You let this happen?"* But somehow he trusted and stayed faithful.

Unbeknownst to Joseph, God **was** at work. The day would come when Joseph would see how God had used it **all**, every difficult detail, to produce an amazing outcome!

PONDER: How do I determine whether or not God is with me? By the way I feel? By my circumstances?

PRAYER: Lord, forgive me for evaluating You and Your faithfulness through the lens of my circumstances and feelings. Help me **trust** You, even when I don't **feel** You, even when I can't **see** what You're doing.

May 15
Such A Heavy Burden!

"For the person who keeps all of the laws except one is as guilty as a person who has broken all of God's laws." James 2:10

How utterly discouraging! What a weight! What a burden!

That's the exact response the law was designed to produce in <u>my</u> heart and yours. Because of our sinful nature, no matter how hard we try, how well we clean up certain facets of our lives, we will **NEVER** be perfect, **NEVER** keep God's laws without failure at <u>some</u> point.

For those who "feel" that's what God expects, it's like forever running on a treadmill that just keeps going faster and faster and faster.

It's tiring... debilitating... suffocating!

Jesus offered Himself as a sacrifice to pay for every sin that has ever been committed or ever will be, to give us, in its place, His own perfect righteousness. What I could not do, no matter how hard I tried, has been accomplished <u>for</u> me. That, my friend, should invoke within our hearts a tremendous sigh of relief!

Humanity should have <u>run</u> to embrace such a gift! Yet we've rejected Christ and His offering of salvation. Why?

Because we <u>hate</u> the feeling of "need." We keep <u>trying</u> because we think somehow, with enough effort, we'll accomplish our goal.

PONDER: Am I still on the spiritual treadmill, too afraid (or proud) to let up, to let down, or to let go?

PRAYER: Lord God, I humble myself now and receive by **faith** what <u>cannot</u> be accomplished through effort.

May 16

The Safest Place In All The World

"Saul hunted him day after day, but God didn't let Saul find him."
I Samuel 23:14b

Right in the very center of God's will may not be the <u>easiest</u> place to reside, but it will <u>always</u> be the safest! Everything taking place around David made it "seem" like God had surely forgotten him.

<u>Confusion</u>. God had told David he would be king. Yet present circumstances seemed to contradict that promise.

<u>Difficulty</u>. Hiding in caves, moving from place to place, wondering where the next meal would come from… surely, if God cared, it wouldn't be so hard!

<u>Betrayal</u>. Even after all David had done to deliver Israel, many valued King Saul's approval more than loyalty to David and his men.

<u>Collateral Damage</u>. 85 priests and their families were killed for helping David. That awareness filled him with guilt and remorse.

And yet… *"Even when… chased by those who seek to kill you, your life is safe in the care of the Lord your God, secure in his treasure pouch!" I Samuel 25:29a*

Perhaps, if I really knew God like David did, as He has revealed Himself in Scripture, I could trust what He says is true, even when everything around me speaks to the contrary.

PONDER: Do I <u>know</u> God? Really? Do I <u>trust</u> Him?

PRAYER: Lord, I confess my understanding of You is so distorted. I don't know who You really are and therefore don't fully trust You. I want that to change. Help me pursue You with all my heart!

May 17

Does Father Really Know Best?

"So Sarai said to Abram, 'The Lord has prevented me from having children. Go and sleep with my servant. Perhaps I can have children through her.'" Genesis 16:2

Listen <u>carefully</u> to what Sarai is <u>actually</u> saying: *"The <u>Lord</u> has prevented me... <u>but</u>... Perhaps <u>I</u> can..."* Oh, what familiar words! Who of us has not said, or at least thought, them?

God had promised Abram and Sarai a son. They were old when the promise was made. They'd already waited for years. Time was running out! What were they supposed to do?

How like them we are! When God doesn't do what we think He should, at a time, or in a way that makes sense to us, we set out to accomplish it on our own.

It's all part of Satan's lie from the beginning. God cannot be trusted with our happiness. He's withholding something. Therefore, He must be cruel and unkind. If anything is to get done, I'll have to do it myself!

Does it ever occur to us that, if the All-knowing, All-wise, All-loving God of the Universe is preventing something from occurring, either it must not be good for us, or it's not the right time for its fulfillment?

PONDER: When God doesn't meet my expectations, am I guilty of pushing through anyway? Do I feel I am better qualified to know and accomplish what's best for my life than He?

PRAYER: Forgive me, Lord, for arrogantly assuming I know, better than You, what will make me happy and fulfilled.

May 18
Blessings In Disguise

"...some of the wise will fall victim to persecution. In this way, they will be refined and cleansed and made pure..." Daniel 11:35

We find it difficult to conceive that God allows bad things to happen to good people. Yet, in this verse, good people are enduring intense hardships. Not only is God allowing it, He's using it to refine their lives.

We humans hate persecution! We rail against our tormentors, begging God to remove them. Rarely do we entertain the thought that painful circumstances might be useful in perfecting the life and character of Jesus within us.

A careful look at God's creation reveals numerous illustrations of beauty, wrought through difficulties: an exquisite pearl, produced by the irritation of a grain of sand inside an oyster... the majestic butterfly, unable to fly without the struggle to break free from its cocoon...

From God's vantage point, our troubles may well be our best friends in disguise.

God will eliminate trial and hardship <u>only</u> when they cease to be constructive in building character or shaping destiny. When <u>that</u> day comes, we'll be in Heaven with Him!

PONDER: Have I ever learned, after the fact, that something I struggled against was actually a blessing in disguise? If I could somehow eliminate every painful experience from my past, what kind of person would I be right now?

PRAYER: Lord, I will trust Your purposes in each of the circumstances and persons you allow into my life. I want to be more like Jesus!

May 19

Living Outside My Comfort Zone

"Live wisely among those who are not believers, and make the most of every opportunity. Let your conversation be gracious and attractive..." Colossians 4:5,6

The assumption is that we are <u>out</u> <u>there</u>, living our lives among those who are still strangers to the faith. God wants us to interact <u>with</u> them, not isolate ourselves <u>from</u> them.

Even so, a few years after conversion, the average Christian has very few, if any, unbelieving friends. Why is that?

Christians love being together. Can you blame us? We share the same faith and love for Jesus Christ, the same hope of eternal life, the same mission on this earth, and a commitment to the same lifestyle.

Little by little, we've managed to create our own little Christian subculture. If <u>that's</u> all God had in mind for us, He could've taken each of us to Heaven as soon as we trusted Him as Savior.

Instead, God's heart breaks with longing and compassion for people <u>outside</u> the faith. <u>We</u> are His body now. He is counting on us to be His hands, His voice, His eyes.

How will they ever get to know Jesus if we don't open our lives to them, if we cloister ourselves in our little Christian communities where we're most comfortable?

PONDER: Do I have any <u>meaningful</u> relationships with folks who are not yet believers?

PRAYER: Lord, make me sensitive to your longings for people outside my comfort zone and help me move toward them for Your sake with the kindness of Jesus.

May 20
Where's My Focus?

"For the despondent, every day brings trouble; for the happy heart, life is a continual feast." Proverbs 15:15

Despondency is a complicated condition with many possible causes, some even physical. There's no "one-size-fits-all" answer. But God is giving a window into the human heart that might provide helpful insight to those who find themselves struggling to pull out of its grasp. When we are "down," we tend to see everything through a dark lens. We expect the worst, and life seems willing to accommodate us.

I'm reminded of a parable I heard once, of a wise man sitting at the gate of a city, greeting those who approached. One traveler asked, "What kinds of people live in this city?"

The gatekeeper questioned in return, "What kinds of people lived in the place you left behind?"

"They were difficult, self-centered, and mean," he responded.

"I'm afraid you'll find people are like that here also." And the stranger moved on.

Another traveler happened on the wise man at the gate. After exchanging the same questions regarding the town's people, the visitor replied, "Oh, they were wonderful—so loving, giving, and kind! I hated to leave."

"You'll find the same kinds of people here." And the traveler happily entered the city.

PONDER: Where is my focus? Have I counted my blessings lately? Am I expressing gratitude to God and others for them?

PRAYER: Open my eyes to Your blessings, Lord. Help me focus on all that is GOOD in my life.

May 21
Can People Bank On My Word?

"Just say a simple 'Yes, I will,' or 'No, I won't.' Your word is enough. To strengthen your promise with a vow shows that something is wrong." Matthew 5:37

In our culture, words have become simply "tools" used to manipulate and caress our way into, and out of, various situations and relationships, in order to best serve our agendas.

Characters in sitcoms and commercials who shade or evade the truth elicit a good laugh. Politicians and defense lawyers seem more interested in what is expedient than what is true. In that kind of climate, even what's declared under oath becomes suspect.

One who says what he means and means what he says is a rare find in our day. Few people expect it, so when they encounter someone who keeps his word and only speaks truth, that person stands out. *"Let your lives shine brightly before them," (Philippians 2:15b)* says Paul, because a brilliant star against a black sky cannot be hidden. It inspires awe!

Christ-followers embrace truth because God is Truth and always keeps His Word. A simple, "Yes, I will," or "No, I won't," from the mouth of a Christian, should be as good as gold, something people can take to the bank. Anything less dishonors Christ.

PONDER: Is my word trustworthy? Do people know they can count on me to do what I say I'll do, no matter what?

PRAYER: Please, Lord, make me a person of my word. Be honored through what I say and do.

May 22
I'm Just Too Ordinary

"…my work seems so useless! I have spent my strength for nothing and to no purpose. Yet I leave it all in the Lord's hand; I will trust God for my reward." Isaiah 49:3,4

In our minds, the "great" people are those with large followings, those with access to platforms, pulpits, and pavilions. We look at <u>our</u> lives, which, for the most part, seem so ordinary, so mundane. It's difficult to see how the things <u>we</u> do can bring God any glory at all.

If we could only see from God's vantage point, we might feel differently about ourselves and the humble roles we play in the lives of our family members, neighbors, and coworkers. Jesus says, someday, those who <u>appear</u> to be great now will actually be least important, and many of those whom we ignored as irrelevant here will be the most important, the most honored, in Heaven.

No matter what we do, we should do it for <u>Jesus</u>, as <u>His</u> representative *(Colossians 3:17,23,24)*. He knows what honors Him and what doesn't. That is all that matters!

PONDER: Who or what is the true focus of my attention, my energy, in the tedium of everyday life? Do I acknowledge it's really <u>Jesus</u> I'm serving?

PRAYER: No matter how elevated or lowly my work might seem to me, remind me, Lord, that I am actually serving Christ, that my reward will come from <u>Him</u>, not from this world, and that nothing done for <u>Him</u> will ever be done in vain.

May 23

Whose Life Am I Impacting?

"...Hezekiah did not respond appropriately to the kindness shown him, and he became proud..." II Chronicles 32:25

Cured miraculously of a terminal illness in direct answer to prayer, Hezekiah had opportunity to intensify his godly legacy, but something happened in his heart.

We're not told exactly what took place. We know he later humbled himself and repented of his pride *(v. 26)*, but how much damage was done during the years his eyes were on himself rather than God is unknown.

We know <u>one</u> thing for sure: a son named Manasseh was born during the extended 15 years of his life. This little one, so impressionable, was watching his father, absorbing attitudes and a lifestyle which he would someday adopt as his own. And though Hezekiah never worshiped manmade idols, his young son knew instinctively that, in the heart of his father, an altar had been erected to a "god" other than Yahweh.

Manasseh grew up to be one of Judah's most wicked kings. Eventually, he, too, humbled himself and repented. Mercifully, God heard and forgave his sins. No doubt, Manasseh's heart ached with regret and dismay as he looked back over his life, but his influence had already taken its toll.

PONDER: What does my life reveal to those who watch or follow me?

PRAYER: Oh, God, may my heart be so totally yielded to Your lordship, that there will be no doubt about what's most important to me. May those who follow behind me find their way to You!

May 24
Am I An Encourager?

"'…Brothers, if you have any word of encouragement for the people, come and give it.'" Acts 13:15

Paul and Barnabas are in Pamphylia on their first missionary journey. On the Sabbath, they go to the synagogue for services. The man in charge sends them a message asking if they would please bring a word of encouragement for the people.

Easy to do, right, because God had just worked a miracle through them, resulting in the salvation of the governor of Paphos. Anyone could offer a word of encouragement if they'd just experienced something like that!

But look forward one chapter, to *Acts 14:22*. Paul and Barnabas had to flee for their lives to Lystra, where Paul was then stoned and left for dead.

The <u>very next day,</u> they went to Derbe, preached the Gospel, and then journeyed back to Lystra, *"where they strengthened the believers. They encouraged them to continue in the faith, reminding them that they must enter into the kingdom of God through many tribulations."*

Their desire and ability to encourage didn't depend on favorable circumstances. They deliberately chose not to focus on themselves and their problems, but to focus on others' needs.

PONDER: Am I a person of encouragement? Do I offer care for others, despite my own sense of need at the moment?

PRAYER: Lord, I choose to take my eyes off myself. Fix them on You and on the needs of others. Help me receive Your encouragement. Then use me as an encourager of others.

May 25
Who Calls The Shots?

"...Now go out where it is deeper and let down your nets, and you will catch many fish." Luke 5:4

Jesus has been using Peter's boat to speak to crowds on the shore. Afterward, He asks Peter to *"go out where it is deeper..."* Peter insists there are no fish out there. He knows, because he worked hard, all night, and caught nothing!

What Jesus is trying to teach Peter has little to do with catching fish *(vs. 10b,11)*. Someday, Peter will lead Christ's church, but not through his own efforts or abilities. Peter has much to learn, but he seems to be a slow learner.

Remember the Transfiguration? Peter's response was to build three monuments! Instead, God declared it was all about Jesus and allowing Him to call the shots! How about when Peter, in his attempt to walk on water, got boldly out of the boat, but would have drowned had he not beseeched Jesus to save him? By far, though, Peter's worst failure came when, immediately after confidently declaring he would rather die than forsake Christ, he denied even knowing the Lord.

PONDER: Do I ever complain, like Peter, that I've *"worked hard all last night!"* Do I find myself asking Christ to "bless" my own efforts for His Kingdom? What would it look like if every task done in His Name was fully initiated, directed, and empowered by His Spirit alone?

PRAYER: Oh, God, teach me the power of <u>Your</u> Life—lived <u>through</u> me!

May 26
Playing "Hide-And-Seek"

"I could ask the darkness to hide me and the light around me to become night—but even in darkness I cannot hide from you. To you the night shines as bright as day. Darkness and light are both alike to you." Psalm 139:11,12

Have you ever played hide-and-seek with a toddler? Place something over their eyes and pretend you can't find them, and they are giddy with excitement as the hunt begins! They love "hiding" under a blanket, in plain sight, absolutely certain that, because they can't see you, you can't see them either. *"Do it again!"* they beg, over and over. The thrill never seems to diminish.

As these little ones grow older and realize the truth, they often delight in playing that same game with younger siblings. Sometimes the roles are reversed, the older allowing themselves to be the hunted. Always, however, the older sibling <u>knows</u>—it's only a game.

It's amazing, then, that we play that same "game" of hide-and-seek with God, as if He cannot see what we're doing, as if our covert actions, whispered words, and secret thoughts escape His notice.

God warns us: *"…you may be sure that your sin will find you out,"* (Numbers 32:23) and *"…all that is secret will eventually be brought into the open…" Luke 8:17*

PONDER: Am I guilty of trying to hide anything from God, the all-seeing, all-knowing One?

PRAYER: Lord, nothing is hidden from Your sight… even what I conceal from everyone else. I repent and bring everything into Your Light.

May 27

How Desperate Am I?

"...Jacob [was] *all alone in the camp... a man came and wrestled with him until dawn... the man said, 'Let me go, for it is dawn.' But Jacob panted, 'I will not let you go unless you bless me.' Jacob named the place... 'Face of God' for he said, 'I have seen God face-to-face...'" Genesis 32:24-26,30*

Jacob is just hours away from confronting his worst fear. He remembers wronging his brother years earlier and Esau's vow to kill him. He'd begun the journey with confidence, following God's clear instructions to return home.

The closer he gets, however, the more fearful he becomes. Upon hearing of Esau's advancing army, Jacob moves his family to safety and sends servants ahead with gifts.

That's when we find him, alone and vulnerable, in a face-to-face struggle with his Maker.

When God seems about to slip away, Jacob grabs Him, refusing to let go until he receives God's "blessing." When that "blessing" comes, it looks different than Jacob expects, but he is forever changed by the encounter.

PONDER: How desperate am I for the transforming touch of God in my life? Do I hang on tenaciously, as Jacob did, crying out, "I won't let go until You bless me!" Or am I content to go another day, another length of the journey, hoping for a "rematch" along the way?

PRAYER: Lord God, bring me to the end of myself and my resources, so that I will desperately cling to You until You change my life!

May 28
Anonymous Christianity

"The world would love you if you belonged to it, but you don't." John 15:19a

Christ's connotation is obvious: we can't belong to Jesus and be allies with the world at the same time! Our allegiance to Christ automatically sets us up for rejection by the world.

Jesus goes on to say, *"I chose you to come out of the world, and so it hates you… Since they persecuted me, naturally they will persecute you. And if they had listened to me, they would listen to you."* (v. 19b)

Radical obedience to the Lord Jesus will always be met with resistance, even among "lukewarm" believers. The kind of intimacy with Christ that totally transforms a life is welcomed only by those whose hunger for God is also intense.

So, if I'm skating through life without creating a stir of resistance, what is the implication? Could it be that I've not opened my mouth for Jesus lately, or that I'm blending into the world enough to fly under the radar? Perhaps I've cloistered myself with likeminded people and never venture outside my comfort zone.

PONDER: If I was on trial for being a Christian, would there be enough evidence to convict me? Have I been ashamed or fearful of identifying myself as a Christ-follower?

PRAYER: Lord, You said if I want You to plead my case before the Father, I must be willing to stand up for You among people. Fill me with Your Spirit and make me bold for You.

May 29
Straddling Light And Darkness

"For once you were full of darkness, but now you have light from the Lord. So live as people of light!" Ephesians 5:8

Why would anyone who'd been brought out of darkness into God's glorious Light have to be admonished not to return to the shadows? What could possibly cause us to prefer darkness over light?

- **We have something to hide**. If our hearts have been enticed by the things of this world—the lust of the flesh or the pride of life—we may actually prefer darkness. Light may seem a bit harsh and unyielding. Perhaps we find ourselves withdrawing, not even aware we are slipping back into our old ways.
- **We're not ready to change.** We tend to hide what we refuse to surrender. Ultimately, however, in the hiding, we effectively enslave ourselves to whatever we are clinging to and fortify its grip on our lives.
- **Light creates accountability**. It exposes us to the eyes of God and others. We prefer trying to overcome our issues <u>alone</u>, in the dark, so, if we fail, we can still save face. The problem is that whatever we struggle with in secret always seems to get the upper hand.

PONDER: Am I trying to straddle both light and darkness? Are there areas of my life where I prefer to remain in the shadows?

PRAYER: Lord, forgive me for being afraid to bring all of my "stuff" into Your holy Light. Help me to know that's where true freedom resides.

May 30
Using God's Powerful Word

"…he used the Scriptures to reason with the people." Acts 17:2

As we seek to disciple our children and others in the faith, our greatest tool is God's Word. Our goal is to introduce them to what God specifically says in His Word on any given topic.

At times, there will be no clear command. Helping them see what God declares about Himself, about His character and His heart, will enable them to understand how to honor God, even when no specific instruction is laid out for them.

The more of God's Word we introduce them to, the more likely they will be able to live victoriously in the power of God's Spirit.

Sometimes, especially as parents, we refer to God's Word in our conversation, i.e. "The Bible says…," rather than taking time to open the Word of God **with** them, allowing them to **read it for themselves**.

Even more important is helping them find and read the verses in their own Bibles. Then it will no longer be just my voice telling them what God says, or even seeing what is written in my Bible. Reading and acknowledging God's Word, in their own Bibles, is difficult to argue with.

Once they recognize God has spoken directly to them, the impact is powerful and much harder to dismiss or ignore.

PONDER: How often have I simply said, "The Bible says…" rather than helping people view God's Word for themselves?

PRAYER: Thank You, Lord, for the Power of Your Word!

May 31
Call On God In Truth

"The Lord is close to all who call on him, yes, to all who call on him in truth." Psalm 145:18

What does it mean to call upon the Lord "in truth?" How's that different from just calling on Him? It might be important to know, since God very specifically says it's those who call "in truth" that He is close to.

How does one call on God <u>other</u> than "in truth?" Most likely we won't have to look far for the answer to that question, since we're probably all guilty of it to some degree and will see ourselves in the illustrations below (this list is certainly not inclusive):

- Praying for God's will, yet withholding certain options as unacceptable.
- Bargaining with God, saying, "I'll serve you 'if'..."
- Refusing to address the specific sin God is pointing out... focusing instead on peripheral issues that are easier to deal with and make us "look" spiritual.
- Being unwilling to see the truth about ourselves, the selfishness and pride of our hearts, our part in a conflict, etc.
- Being more motivated by the approval of people than by the smile of God.

When we feel God is distant, we might want to check FIRST to see if we've been unwilling to face the truth.

PONDER: God knows the truth. Will I allow Him to make that known to me?

PRAYER: I don't know why it's so difficult for me to live in truth, but I want to. Help me, Lord!

June

June 1

A Severe Mercy

"Notice how God is both kind and severe. He is severe toward those who disobeyed, but kind to you if you continue to trust in his kindness..." Romans 11:22

In our culture, we don't often hear the words "kind" and "severe" used to describe the same person. It's not part of our thinking that those two attributes could coexist in one personality.

This seems especially true when people think about God. People blame God for all the ills of the world, concluding that He cannot possibly be as kind and loving as His Word declares.

Picture with me a parent whose child is bent on kicking and chasing his ball into a busy street. His parents talk to him about the dangers, but he recklessly disregards their counsel. In his mind, they are being too severe. He's sure that, if they really loved him, they'd want him to enjoy his ball without restrictions.

Will they give in and let him play wherever he chooses? Only if they don't really care about him. A truly loving parent will make his obedience in this instance a priority, which may require methods the child will in no way equate with "kindness."

PONDER: Am I like a spoiled child, demanding that God prove He loves me by giving in to my desires? Do I receive His discipline as part of His love and care?

PRAYER: Dear Lord, help me trust that, even in the hard things You allow, I'm being tenderly cared for.

June 2
Nothing God Does Not See Or Know

"Young people, it's wonderful to be young! Enjoy every minute of it. Do everything you want to do; take it all in. But remember that you must give an account to God for everything you do." Ecclesiastes 11:9

Why is it that when we know we're being watched, we are not nearly as apt to do and say things that are wrong as when we think nobody's watching?

- A child quickly pulls his hand out of the cookie jar when Mommy enters the room.
- The boss returns to the office after lunch, and every employee is suddenly seriously engaged in the day's work.
- Upon seeing a patrol car parked near an intersection, dozens of drivers immediately correct their speed.

Being observed by someone bearing authority is highly motivating. That's why we <u>must</u> remember: there is <u>nothing</u> God cannot see, hear, or know!

His intention is not to squelch the fun of those who love life, but to help us avoid the road to heartache and regret.

Over the centuries, many have disregarded His warnings and paid a heavy price for choices made. Forgiveness can be sought and received from our gracious and merciful God, but consequences often last a lifetime.

PONDER: Am I aware of God's gaze upon me at all times, even in the dark? How does it make me feel to know I will stand before Him someday?

PRAYER: Don't let me ever forget, Lord, that I can never hide from the penetrating gaze of Your Spirit.

June 3
Hope So? Or Know So?

"He saved us, not because of the righteous things we had done, but because of his mercy. Because of his grace he declared us righteous and gave us confidence that we will inherit eternal life." Titus 3:5,7

If salvation depends on us and our good works, my friend, then we are destined to live in insecurity. Why? Because we can never be absolutely sure we have performed well enough or worked hard enough. After all, how much is "enough?" What if we stand before God and find out that just one or two more good deeds would've made the difference?

In the quiet, honest moments of the soul, we all know where we fall short of perfection. If we just compare ourselves with other people, we can usually find someone more "sinful" than we. But if **God** is the measuring stick, well… that's a different story!

Thankfully, God wants us to **know** confidently that our eternal destiny is secure! He's not interested in a "hope so" or "maybe" when it comes to our salvation. God says confidence is a gift that comes when we receive His mercy and grace and quit relying on our own efforts toward righteousness.

PONDER: Does the thought of death and what follows bring doubt and fear to my heart or peace and tranquility?

PRAYER: God, I recognize my total inability to make myself worthy of being in relationship with You, and I cast myself now on Your mercy and grace as my only hope!

June 4
A Cosmic Killjoy?

"Keep the commandments and keep your life; despising them leads to death." Proverbs 19:16

How many of us have viewed God's commands as His way of making sure we don't have too much fun as we travel through life? Where did we ever get the idea that God is some kind of cosmic killjoy?

These are lies straight out of the pit of Hell, orchestrated by the enemy of our souls, whose goal, Jesus said, is to *"rob, kill, and destroy"* those whom God loves.

The Lord knows what keeps us from experiencing life's best. His commandments reflect His desire that we live life to the fullest, enjoying all His precious gifts.

Christ is like the "minesweeper" who, having safely navigated the minefield of life, points out the dangers ahead. Yet we are leery. We don't trust His heart.

Satan entices us with the lie he used in the Garden. Once he created suspicion as to God's intentions, he was able to lure Adam and Eve into his trap. We've all fallen prey to that same scheme!

PONDER: How do I see God? Do I believe His desires and plans are for my best, or do I suspect Him of withholding something from me?

PRAYER: Forgive me, Lord, for believing the enemy's lies. I want to know the Truth, which will free me to experience the abundant life You've promised. Your Word is Truth. Intensify my "hunger" for it. Strengthen my desire to know and trust You more!

June 5
Bearers Of Hope

"It seems so tragic that everyone under the sun suffers the same fate. That is why people are not more careful to be good. Instead, they choose their own mad course, for they have no hope. There is nothing ahead but death anyway." Ecclesiastes 9:3

What a difference hope makes! Contemplate with me for a moment those folks King Solomon is discussing. They see nothing worth living for, so they spend their lives in a wild frenzy of pleasure-seeking, hoping somehow to create meaning of their own through lavish self-indulgence. Yet, in the quietest moments of their souls, *"there is nothing ahead but death anyway."*

Know anyone like that? Could it be that we who hope in Jesus are still around because these folks need to hear a word of hope? Has God saved us from despair and destruction so we can huddle together, safe from the corruption of this world, until He takes us home to Heaven?

PONDER: What is my response to people who've ruined their lives and the lives of others in their tragic pursuit of pleasure and meaning in life? Disgust? Anger? Prideful disregard? Or compassion and desperate longing to bring hope to their empty hearts with the Good News of Jesus's love and salvation?

PRAYER: Lord, let me see people as You view them, and then help me do what You would do in response!

June 6
No Need to Worry

"...don't worry about tomorrow, for tomorrow will bring its own worries. Today's trouble is enough for today." Matthew 6:34

Currently, my husband and I walk 1½ miles before dawn each morning on a path designed specifically for such purposes. Over one particularly long section, overhanging branches form a thick canopy, shutting out moon or stars or any nearby manmade light source.

From a distance, that darkness looks so foreboding, but amazingly, when we reach this secluded area, it doesn't seem nearly as dark or fearful as it had earlier appeared.

Anticipation of any event almost always looms larger than life. How much peace, energy, sleep is lost fearfully trying to <u>imagine</u> how dark the darkness will be?

What a waste because God's desire and ability to provide what we need, when we need it, includes more than enough grace and strength to walk through whatever lies ahead! Christ wants our focus on the "now," on His comforting Presence with us.

Living in anxiety about things we fear tomorrow robs us of the ability to fully enjoy today. God invites us to quit worrying and begin trusting Him, but that kind of living cannot be accomplished except as we draw every day, every moment, on <u>His life in us</u>, <u>His abilities through us</u>, and <u>His love for us</u>.

PONDER: Am I a worrier? In what ways do I justify, rather than relinquish, my anxiety?

PRAYER: Lord, teach me to trust Your intimate care and Your constant presence in my life.

June 7
Get Wisdom—Get Life!

"I have written 30 sayings for you, filled with advice and knowledge. In this way, you may know the truth..." Proverbs 22:20,21

Solomon, the wisest man who ever lived, wrote the Book of Proverbs so that we would *"...understand what is right, just, and fair, and... know how to find the right course of action every time." Proverbs 2:9*

He goes on to promise that, if we seek and immerse ourselves in it, *"wisdom will enter your heart, and knowledge will fill you with joy. Wise planning will watch over you; understanding will keep you safe." Proverbs 2:10,11*

There are 30 days in most calendar months. Could it be Solomon intended that these excellent sayings be read again and again, one for each day of the month? Whether it was his intention or not, the Book of Proverbs is divided into 31 chapters, one for every day of the typical month, with an extra for those months containing 31 days.

PONDER: What would my life be like if I would read a chapter of Proverbs every single day? What could God do in and through me, if I took the time to meditate on these wise sayings, asking God how they might be applied to my life, my circumstances, and the current culture of my day?

PRAYER: Lord, give me a hunger and thirst for Your wisdom. Cultivate in my heart the humility to recognize my need for it. Open my understanding to Your eternal perspective through Your Word.

June 8
There's Always Someone Watching

"The local residents… watched them mourning…" Genesis 50:11

There are some moments when we are just too vulnerable to be on our guard. Times of extreme loss—grief, financial reverse, illness, loss of employment, death—these are times we will not have the strength or ability to put on airs, to pretend, or hide what's really inside.

It's in <u>these</u> times that folks in the world watch us most closely, looking to see if the God we serve will come through for us, if being a Christian really <u>does</u> make a difference, if hope can truly carry us when we cannot walk on our own.

And it's in these times that what is <u>really</u> true about us will find its way to the surface.

If we are not in the habit of trusting God in the little things, what makes us think we'll manage to trust when our world is turned upside down? Yet, even then, God can work deeply in our lives, **<u>if</u>** we will but turn **<u>TO</u>** Him, instead of fighting **<u>AGAINST</u>** Him, in our grief and loss.

These times, perhaps more than any others, will give God the greatest opportunity to reveal Himself to a broken and hurting world. In so doing, He gives meaning and purpose to even the most senseless tragedies this life can throw at us.

PONDER: What is my response to the losses in my life?

PRAYER: Lord Jesus, work in me <u>every</u> day, so in the day of trial, I may bring You glory!

June 9

What If The Inconceivable Happens?

"...But others were tortured, refusing to turn from God in order to be set free. They placed their hope in a better life after the resurrection..." Hebrews 11:35

As of this writing, believers in America are still free to follow Jesus and share His love with others. Aside from ridicule by the media, we face very little in the way of persecution.

That's not true in other parts of our world. The day may very well come when, we, too, will find ourselves faced with that inconceivable choice: Jesus or life?

We don't like to think about it, but by avoiding the subject, we set ourselves up for a rude awakening in the event we must ever truly suffer for Christ. A choice like this one must be made <u>ahead</u> of time and reiterated over and over again throughout our lives.

I cannot imagine enduring excruciating pain and loss for my faith. Yet to think of denying Christ for a momentary reprieve from such suffering or death is absolutely <u>unthinkable</u>!

None of us can afford to wait until we're in the moment, with body and emotions screaming for relief, to make that fateful decision.

PONDER: Would I be willing to endure torture, agony, and death, rather than give up my hope in Christ?

PRAYER: Lord, I cannot imagine how, but I know Your grace is sufficient to help me through any trial I could ever face. I choose Jesus… now… ahead of time! I trust You to see me through.

June 10

Jesus, The Wine Maker

"Usually, a host serves the best wine first… but you have kept the best until now!" John 2:10

Jesus is a guest at a wedding feast in which the wine supply runs out. Jesus asks the servants to fill six huge, stone pots with water. As soon as the jars are full, He tells them to take some of it to the Master of Ceremonies.

Imagine the servant's trepidation as he marches to the head table with his "offering." At this stage in the festivities, most of the guests are a bit inebriated, but surely, even drunken partygoers would know something is wrong.

When it comes to wine, the aging process is <u>key</u> to the best taste. "Vintage" equals "premium," right?

However, when the master of the feast tastes this wine, which Jesus has <u>just</u> made, he declares they've saved the BEST for last.

Hmmm…

Could it be that Jesus Christ, the Word made Flesh, the timeless and eternal Son of God, can make something fully aged and mature in the time it takes Him to speak the Word?

PONDER: If God is God, would creating something totally developed, full-grown, and complete be a problem for Him? What hint does this first miracle of Jesus give us about His creative power? Is anything impossible for God?

PRAYER: Lord, I find it difficult to comprehend One so beyond myself. I limit You so often in my mind. Help me acknowledge that, to God, the most impossible tasks are just a "piece of cake."

June 11

How Gracious Am I?

"...The Lord... is gracious in all He does." Psalm 145:13b

A gracious person is one *"...disposed to show grace..."* Webster defines grace as *"unmerited favor or good will, clemency... any kindness, favor, or service freely rendered... something granted in the exercise of favor or discretion and not as of right."*

God is gracious in **all** He does! His kindnesses are given freely and generously, without merit on our part. The Bible makes it very clear that we have all sinned and deserve His wrath and condemnation. *"The soul that sins, it shall die."(Ezekiel 18:4)* Yet God is gracious, *"not treating us as our sins deserve." (Psalm 103:10)*

If we are to be like God, we must allow Him to make **us** gracious people in all **we** do as well. Although offering grace is totally unnatural to the sinful, human nature within, it should be the natural overflow of a life lived in constant, grateful acknowledgement of how undeserving we are of all that God has given and done for us!

PONDER: Would anyone be able to characterize me as "gracious?" Would God? Am I tempted to take God's mercy and grace for granted, as if I have somehow earned it or deserve it? What if God were to treat me as I treat others?

PRAYER: Make me always aware, Lord, that I am alive today, enjoying Your forgiveness and fellowship, only by Your mercy and grace. Make me like You—one who readily offers grace to all whom my life touches.

June 12
So Glad He Knows!

"…God will see it even if no one else does…" Genesis 31:50

These words, spoken by Laban, Jacob's ruthless father-in-law, were intended to instill fear in Jacob lest he mistreat Laban's daughters, who were now his wives.

To Jacob, however, these words brought comfort. He was already very aware of God's ability to see and judge fairly, even in those situations when no one else could possibly know the truth. He said as much to Laban in verse 42: *"…if the God of my father had not been on my side… you would have sent me away empty-handed. But God has seen your abuse and my hard work. That is why he… rebuked you!"*

The all-seeing eyes of God and His ability to know and judge the thoughts and intentions of a person's heart strike terror in some, yet bring unbelievable peace to others. The difference? Relationship.

Personal… intimate… growing relationship with this fearsome God replaces terror with confidence, reverence, love, and gratitude for the tender compassion and care He lavishes on His children.

God demonstrated His unfailing love when He offered His Son as the sacrifice for our sins while we were still His enemies. He loved us <u>first</u> and pursued us with great longing and passion. We needn't fear love like that!

PONDER: Am I <u>comforted</u> by God's ability to see and know everything about me? Why or why not?

PRAYER: Draw me to Yourself, Lord. Help me know and trust You and find comfort in all that You are.

June 13
Even In Politics

"Remind the people to respect the government and be law-abiding, always ready to lend a helping hand. No insults, no fights. God's people should be bighearted and courteous. It wasn't so long ago that we ourselves were stupid and stubborn, dupes of sin…" Titus 3:1-3, The Message

Criticizing and belittling political leaders seems to be a favorite "sport" these days. While there is plenty to complain about, God is asking that those of us who claim His Name evaluate and monitor our words and actions by a higher standard.

There may truly be a need for differing opinions, constructive criticism, or even outright opposition, but our Lord is outlining the **"spirit"** that should accompany the words and actions of all who belong to Him. Sadly, this generous, kind attitude is rarely present in our political discussions and interactions.

Do we think we can somehow mandate righteousness, as if making a law will change men's hearts? **Only** the Spirit of God can change people, and **only** from the inside out! Caustic, angry words, mean-spirited actions, and hateful, judgmental attitudes **never** represent God in a way that draws people to Him.

What we stand for may be totally right, but if we lose the chance to attract people to Jesus, what have we really accomplished?

PONDER: Is it my goal merely to change people's minds and influence their behavior or to win their hearts for Jesus?

PRAYER: Lord, season everything I do and say with the "salt" of Your mercy and love.

June 14

The Omnipresence Of God

"'Am I a God Who is only close at hand?' says the Lord. 'No, I am far away at the same time. Can anyone hide from me in a secret place? Am I not everywhere in all the heavens and earth?' says the Lord." Jeremiah 23:23,24

How incredible is this God Who has revealed Himself to us in His Word and through His Son? He's remarkable beyond our ability to comprehend!

How can He be both near and far away at the same time? If He is everywhere, then it must be true that there is absolutely no place He is not.

That means though I might <u>feel</u> abandoned and alone, I'm really not! When I cry myself to sleep in the lonely hours of the night, He is there. When everyone else in my life jumps ship, God, in His love, remains, whether I sense His presence or not.

Despite my lack of awareness, He has been, is, and always will be "present" through every detail of my life.

PONDER: If I could be truly convinced that I am NEVER out of the range of God's presence, how would that change me? What can I do to keep myself aware of Him in every place and at every moment?

PRAYER: Lord, Thank You for being such an awesome God, so much bigger than my mind can conceive. I worship You as the One and Only True God of the Universe. Receive my praise. Be glorified in my life.

June 15
In Whose Strength?

"...be strong through the grace that God gives you in Christ Jesus." II Timothy 2:1; "Be strong in the Lord and in the power of His might." Ephesians 6:10

What words stand out most often, as you read these passages? I dare say, the words *"be"* and *"strong"* leap off the page with their compelling message. Something within us rises up to accept this noble challenge.

Unfortunately, it's possible to focus on certain words, or portions of Scripture, to the exclusion of others. When we do, we may inadvertently neglect something God wants us to grasp, and miss out on the potential joy, victory, or satisfaction He wants us to experience in Christ Jesus.

Let's look at these passages again, but this time, fixate on, *"...<u>through</u> the <u>grace</u> that <u>God gives</u> you in Christ Jesus..."* and *"...<u>in the Lord</u> and in <u>His mighty power</u>."* How does that change the message?

PONDER: If it's up to <u>me</u> to *"be strong,"* then I've got to muscle my way through the situation, buck up, or try harder. But, if that strength is <u>given</u> me *"<u>in the Lord</u>,"* if it's something I <u>receive</u> through <u>God's grace</u> rather than something I must <u>produce</u>, then my task is simply to make sure I stay connected to Him!

PRAYER: Lord, it's too hard to be strong and "keep it together." Things just keep crashing down around me. Help me to cling instead to Jesus and "rest" in knowing it's all Christ's work, from beginning to end.

June 16
Where Do I Run For Help?

"Because you have put your trust in the king of Aram instead of in the Lord your God, you missed your chance to destroy the army of the king of Aram." II Chronicles 16:7

For 10 years, King Asa of Judah had put his trust <u>completely</u> in the Lord. At one time, when a million-man army from Ethiopia marched against him, King Asa, with fewer than 600,000 ill-equipped men, cried out to the Lord, saying, *"No one but You can help the powerless against the mighty! Help us, O Lord our God, for we trust in You alone." (II Chronicles 14:11)* God soundly defeated their enemy.

Now, however, toward the end of his reign, threatened by the king of Israel, Asa turns immediately to the king of Aram for assistance. Later, when afflicted with a serious foot disease *(II Chronicles 16:12)*, we read, *"...he did not seek the Lord's help, but turned only to his physicians."*

How did Asa move from seeking God first and trusting Him completely to relying on the help of others without acknowledging the Lord?

PONDER: Where do I run when in trouble or distress? Is God my first thought? Even when seeking help from others, am I aware that, ultimately, relief and victory come <u>only</u> from the Hand of God?

PRAYER: Lord, I know that what I do in times of trouble reveals the posture of my heart. May I always be poised to seek You first, for You alone are the Source of all I will ever need.

June 17
The Words Of The Godly

"The words of the godly are a life-giving fountain… like sterling silver… The words of the godly encourage many… The mouth of the godly… gives wise advice… The lips of the godly speak helpful words…" Proverbs 10:11,20,21,31,32

King Solomon lived light years away from the digital age in which we find ourselves. He couldn't have imagined having a "conversation" with someone over email, social media, or text, where words could be "spoken" without any sound except tapping fingertips on keyboard pads.

The wisest man who ever lived would never have dreamed his readers would someday have the ability to engage loved ones, enemies, and even total strangers in serious, real-time conversations from behind a screen, without the benefit of any clarifying body language or human interaction.

How could he have comprehended that, with one, rash touch of a button, our conversations would travel the globe within seconds and be forever recorded in cyberspace?

As Christ-followers, we don't have the "luxury" of spouting our own opinions. Every post, text, or email we send reflects on **Him**. How dare we flippantly, carelessly, or callously respond in the flesh, or with our own understanding, when so much is at stake?

PONDER: Am I willing to let God's Holy Spirit edit every word that comes out of my mouth and off my fingertips, until <u>only</u> what is wise, helpful, encouraging, and life-giving gets past the "send" button?

PRAYER: *"Set a guard over my mouth, Lord, keep watch over the door of my lips…" Psalm 141:3 NIV*

June 18
God's Litmus Test

"...The Lord your God is testing you to see if you truly love him with all your heart and soul. Serve only the Lord your God and fear him alone. Obey his commands, listen to his voice, and cling to him." Deuteronomy 13:3,4

In this passage, the Lord has just warned there will be false prophets who'll dream dreams that come true. They'll promise signs and miracles which will occur. Yet they'll be trying to entice God's people to worship other "gods."

Apparently, God allows the prophecies of these deceivers to come true on occasion to test whether His children will remain steadfast, clinging to that which God has clearly revealed to them in His Word. The ruse is obviously clever, and some will be deceived.

Thankfully, God has given us a <u>test</u> by which we can <u>know</u> what is false and what is true. No matter how convincing the words, deeds, signs, or even wonders, if we are beguiled into loving someone or something instead of, or more than, God, we <u>must</u> turn away.

Sadly, too few believers are familiar enough with God's Word to recognize the subtleties, the intrigue, and the insidiousness of the enemy's enticements. If we allow ourselves to be attracted to what "seems" or "feels" right to <u>us</u>, we may find ourselves led astray.

PONDER: Do I really **<u>KNOW</u>** Scripture enough to use it as a "sword" against the enemy of my soul?

PRAYER: Lord, give me a deep desire to **<u>KNOW</u>** Your Word.

June 19
Don't Bother Me Now!

"Jesus said, 'Let's go off by ourselves to a quiet place and rest awhile...' So they left by boat for a quiet place where they could be alone. But many people... got there ahead of them. ...he had compassion on them... So he began teaching them...." Mark 6:31-34

Jesus had just received news that His cousin, John the Baptist, had been beheaded. Already weary from the stresses of constant travel and ministry, Jesus declared He and His disciples needed to get away by themselves for a while.

They headed across the lake to a quieter spot, only to discover, as they climbed from the boat, that throngs of people had run along the shoreline and were excitedly awaiting their arrival.

His disciples were impatient, wanting to send the crowds away, but, despite His weariness and grief, Jesus was moved with compassion and began teaching them. How did He keep going?

Perhaps the miracle He performed with a young boy's lunch at end of day was a lesson to both the disciples and to us. When we give God what little resources we have left (money, time, possessions, energy), He always gives back <u>more</u> than enough!

PONDER: What's my response when my expectations are hijacked by the needs and demands of others?

PRAYER: Lord, help me be willing to give myself away, knowing my greatest joy and energy will come, not from my carefully laid plans for self-gratification, but in experiencing Your love and power in me as I yield myself to You.

June 20

By Whose Standards?

"We are all infected and impure with sin. When we display our righteous deeds, they are nothing but filthy rags..." Isaiah 64:6

We've all seen the television commercials comparing two socks, one washed with detergent "X," the other with the advertised brand. Everyone suspects the contest has been rigged, but it still sells soap.

I'm reminded of our human tendency to compare ourselves with folks whose lives are "dirtier" or "less desirable" than our own, making our "righteousness" look pretty good.

The problem is that even though I myself, or others, may <u>think</u> I'm "clean," it's not <u>my</u> opinion, or theirs, that will matter on that day when all hearts are open and all desires known.

The only estimation that will truly matter <u>then</u> is the one that unfortunately seems to matter the least now.

Only as we hold our "goodness" up to <u>God's</u> perfect standard can we possibly see how hopelessly lacking we really are. Isaiah had such an experience. *"It's all over!"* he cried when he stood in God's Holy Presence. *"I am doomed, for I am a sinful man!" (Isaiah 6:5)*

Thankfully, however, it's in that humble acknowledgement, coupled with faith in the grace and mercy of Christ on our behalf, that we find ourselves washed in the blood of Jesus that cleanses from <u>all</u> sin.

PONDER: By whose standard do I measure myself?

PRAYER: Lord, You are so holy, I can never deserve Your mercy or earn Your grace, but I thank You for granting them anyway!

June 21
Greed's Many Disguises

"'…Teacher, please tell my brother to divide our father's estate with me.' Jesus replied, 'Friend… Beware! Guard against every kind of greed…'" Luke 12:13-15

This seems like a very reasonable request. The man's brother is obviously acting selfishly. But, instead of castigating the brother, Jesus warns the petitioner about the dangers of greed. Is He being rude and insensitive? Or does Jesus have a valid point?

Greed can be very obvious, like when a brother refuses to share an inheritance with his sibling. It can also be very subtle, cloaking itself as "righteous indignation" or "victimization." Greed's ability to disguise itself makes it especially dangerous to one's spiritual life. Thus, Jesus's warning!

God has promised to care for our every need *(Matthew 6:25-33)* and has asked us to be content with His provision *(Hebrews 13:5)*. Greed is the opposite of contentment. It is the intense desire for something which God, for whatever reason, has not chosen to provide for us.

The petitioning brother was bothered by his sibling's behavior. Though a very natural response to injustice, his question to Jesus revealed his own discontentment with the way God had provided for him to that point.

PONDER: Has greed ever showed up in my heart clothed in less offensive garments like "spiritual concern," "being fair," "standing up for my rights," or a "poor-me" mentality?

PRAYER: Lord, help me recognize greed's many disguises and guard against its insidious grip on my heart. Help me trust **You** for **ALL** I really need.

June 22
Can Daniel's God Deliver Him?

"He [the king] *called out in anguish, 'Daniel, servant of the Living God! Was your God, whom you serve so faithfully, able to rescue you from the lions?'" Daniel 6:20b*

King Darius spent a miserable, sleepless night, wondering if the God of the Hebrews was real and able to deliver. He was in this predicament as a result of a stupid, unalterable law he'd been duped into signing, never dreaming it was a plot against his most trusted advisor, Daniel. Daniel hadn't wavered in His worship and service to God, even though it meant being fed to the lions.

Finally, at first light, Darius rushed to the lion's den, breathless to know whether Daniel's God had indeed rescued him, hoping against hope for a miracle.

God is so ready to prove Himself to anyone who seeks Him. This miracle, though it blessed Daniel greatly, was <u>really</u> for the benefit of the pagan king. Darius embraced Daniel's God, then issued a proclamation of God's praises throughout his kingdom.

PONDER: How many "Dariuses" are there in my life who are hoping that what they see in me is <u>proof</u> that God really does exist? Can I welcome the difficult circumstances of my life as opportunities for God to show Himself?

PRAYER: Lord, give me Your perspective. Help me trust that everything You allow in my life gives You the chance to prove Yourself, not only to me, but also to those who are looking for You, hoping You are really real.

June 23
What A Deal!

"Don't you see how wonderfully kind, tolerant, and patient God is with you? Does this mean nothing to you?" Romans 2:4a

These words were written by the Apostle Paul in the middle of a conversation about judging sinners. In *Romans 1*, he describes people who are *"full of every kind of wickedness, sin, greed, hate, envy, murder, quarreling, deception, malicious behavior, and gossip... backstabbers, haters of God, insolent, proud, and boastful."* These people *"invent new ways of sinning... are heartless and have no mercy." Romans 1:29-31*

"You may think you can condemn such people..." Paul says *(2:1)*, identifying our natural reaction to separate ourselves as far as possible, holding them at arm's length like we would some putrid garbage we can't wait to be rid of. Our judgment and condemnation, however, close the door on God's mercy and only widen the gap between them and the Savior Who came, not to condemn them, but to save them.

PONDER: Have I forgotten that I, too, am a sinner, eternally damned apart from God's kindness to me? Am I any different than those I condemn, except for God's grace at work in my life? In what ways would conscious awareness of how undeserving I am of God's mercy change my response to others?

PRAYER: Forgive me, Lord Jesus, for not offering the same kindness I've received from You to those whose lives are still enslaved by sin and darkness. Teach me how to intentionally build bridges of kindness, love, and mercy to the lost.

June 24
When This Tent Is Dismantled

"For we know that when this earthly tent we live in is taken down [that is, when we die and leave this earthly body], we will have a house in Heaven, an eternal body made for us by God Himself..."
II Corinthians 5:1

Have you ever been tent camping? It's one of my favorite activities. However, dismantling the campsite is always sad for me. The campsite looks so "lonely" once our tents are taken down.

Typically, when it's time to go home, we don't just pick up the tent and carry it. There's a process.

We first remove our belongings and take off the rain cover. We pull up stakes and remove the poles from the loops that secured them. Once that happens, the tent loses its shape and falls to the ground. We must still fold and roll it tightly, stuffing it into its bag. Then we take it home.

When it's our time to die, we might prefer a sudden, unexpected homegoing. However, most of us will be keenly aware of the whole process, as these "tents" are slowly dismantled and our time to die approaches. It's not what we would choose, but God promises His grace will be sufficient. His strength shows up best in our weakness (*II Corinthians 12:9*).

PONDER: Can I trust God to give me His grace through the "dismantling process," as I approach my time to die?

PRAYER: Lord, You will be there with Your grace every step of the way.

June 25

I Wouldn't Have Eaten That Apple!

"The woman was convinced. She saw that the tree was beautiful and its fruit looked delicious, and she wanted the wisdom it would give her. So she took some of the fruit and ate it..." Genesis 3:6

We tend to look upon Eve with a bit of scorn, don't we? After all, she and Adam really messed things up! If only they hadn't eaten the forbidden fruit, we'd never have experienced sickness, sorrow, pain, or death. We'd still be back in paradise, never having lost the innocence and wonder of God's original creation.

We like to think, had <u>we</u> been in that garden, the outcome would've been different. But our track record isn't so great either! How are we at trusting and obeying God? Is there even one of us who hasn't told a lie? Disobeyed a parent? Selfishly schemed to get our own way?

The Bible says, *"There is none righteous. Not even one!" (Romans 3:10)*

God knew when He created mankind that each of us would break His heart and choose our own way. And He also knew what He would do when that happened. He would come to earth as a man, veiled in flesh, to pay for all our sin against Him, so He might buy us back as His beloved children.

PONDER: Why would God even bother with such stubborn, wayward people? How could He love us so?

PRAYER: Amazing love, how can it be, that Thou, my God, should die for me!

June 26
What Will Heaven Be Like?

"Behold, I will create new heavens and a new earth." Isaiah 65:17; "...we are looking forward to a new Heaven and a new earth..." II Peter 3:13; "Then I saw a new Heaven and a new earth, for the old Heaven and the old earth had disappeared..." Revelation 21:1

Someday, Jesus will come and make everything new! God has promised it. He's excited to give it to us and wants us to be dreaming about it. *"...set your sights on the realities of Heaven..." (Colossians 3:1)*

Imagine a new Heaven and earth, completely restored to God's original intent, free from sin, decay, sorrow!

Look around and drink in the magnificence that remains here, in spite of sin's destruction. Appreciate the power of the human mind and body, even though on a collision course with death.

Then, in your mind's eye, remove the potential for death and destruction, eliminate all trace of limitation, all negative emotions, motives, and attitudes, all self-centeredness, greed, and hatred.

Take away all disease and weakness. Remove all thorns and weeds. Imagine a world where goodness permeates everything, because God is good and He reigns supremely, a world where nothing bad, wicked or impure will <u>ever</u> spoil anything again!

PONDER: Do I allow myself to imagine and dream of such a place? Does that make me homesick?

PRAYER: Thank You, Jesus, for showing me that Heaven is my eternal home. Help me anticipate it with great joy and excitement.

June 27
Do Or Die!

"The temptations in your life are no different from what others experience. And God is faithful. He will not allow the temptation to be more than you can stand. When you are tempted, he will show you a way out so that you can endure." I Corinthians 10:13

I can guarantee one thing: What you're going through <u>will</u> "seem" too strong to resist.

That's because the enemy of your soul is a liar. He has no power over the blood-bought child of God except <u>deceit</u>, so he does all he can to make us **"feel"** alone, helpless, defeated, obligated to give in to the stampeding urges demanding satisfaction.

If God's Word is <u>true</u> (and it is!), then it all comes down to one thing: how badly do I <u>want</u> to win this battle with sin and self, the flesh and the devil? Jesus **DEFEATED** Satan at the cross. He lives **IN** me. Therefore, *"I CAN do everything through HIM who gives me strength." (Philippians 4:13)*

If I believe God and am determined to overcome, then, through the power of God's Spirit, I will **look for**, and **take**, the way out God has promised.

That kind of resolve would rather die than yield. When those are my only choices, it's amazing how readily my heart detects the escape route!

PONDER: Have I come to that place where I would rather die than yield to temptation?

PRAYER: No matter what You have to do, Lord, get my heart to that place!

June 28
When God Goes Before Us

"…I will make people throughout the earth terrified because of you. When they hear reports about you, they will tremble with dread and fear." Deuteronomy 2:25

After wandering in the wilderness for 40 years, the people of Israel are finally preparing to cross Jordan and take possession of the Promised Land. Incredibly, the Canaanites, whom Israel has feared all these years, are now trembling with dread at the mere mention of their name, because the Lord has struck terror in their hearts.

Apparently, impacting people's thoughts and responses is not a difficult task for Almighty God. If we could only comprehend and trust the power of the God we serve!

Proverbs 21:1 declares, *"The king's heart is like a stream of water directed by the Lord; he turns it wherever he pleases."*

Again, *Proverbs 16:7* says, *"When the ways of people please the Lord, he makes even their enemies live at peace with them."*

This doesn't negate all effort on our part, but so much of the time and energy we expend creating our desired impression could be more productively channeled into staying intimately connected to the One Person in the Universe who knows what, when, where, why, how, and with whom everything will best be accomplished.

PONDER: Can I trust God to go before me in every situation, to prepare people's hearts for the outcome He sees is best?

PRAYER: Forgive me for striving so hard to accomplish what, though impossible for me, is so simple for You.

June 29

Am I As Alive As I Appear To Be?

"I know all the things you do, and that you have a reputation for being alive—but you are dead." Revelation 3:1b

Jesus is dictating a letter to Christians here—members of the church at Sardis. Obviously grieved by what has taken place in their lives, He calls them in verse 3 to *"Repent and turn to me again,"* because *(v. 2) "your actions do not meet the requirements of my God."*

Surely they are doing something right, wouldn't you think? These are people with a reputation for spiritual vitality. Unfortunately for them, the Lord isn't impressed.

Apparently, these believers have allowed themselves to be lulled to sleep, totally unaware how far they have drifted from vital relationship with the Living God. Had Satan been more blatant, they would surely have recognized His schemes. But He works insidiously, subtly enticing our hearts away from our first love. Jesus calls us *(v. 2)* as He did those early believers, to *"Wake up!"*

PONDER: Where does my passion lie? …in doing things FOR Jesus, or in coming to know and love Him with my whole heart? Have I allowed good works, deeds of righteousness, or spiritual activity to preempt my desire for Christ Himself?

PRAYER: Lord, forgive me for focusing on the "doing" while my <u>love</u> for You slowly cools. Wake me to the subtle danger of losing my passion for You. May the good things I do flow out of a heart deeply and profoundly in love with the Savior.

June 30
Fulfilling My Heart's Desires

"He [Christ] died for everyone so that those who receive his new life will no longer live for themselves..." II Corinthians 5:15

This verse makes us a bit uncomfortable, really, because we rather <u>like</u> living for ourselves. We're not too happy when anyone, even God, suggests we do otherwise.

In our minds, things fit together quite nicely. The place where I live is MY house, the things I possess are MY things, the hours in my day are MY time. Don't get me wrong, I'm happy to share them... AFTER I've figured out what I want and when!

Sadly, the more I grasp and manipulate things to my advantage, the less they turn out like I hoped they would. I usually end up quite empty, lacking the real satisfaction I thought "getting my own way" would bring.

According to Jesus, we must:

- Lose our life to find it *(Matthew 16:25)*
- Seek His kingdom <u>first</u> so He can give us all the other stuff we need *(Matthew 6:33)*, and
- Delight ourselves in Him so He can safely give us the desires of our hearts *(Psalm 37:4)*.

The real problem is, we're just not sure we can trust Him on this one.

PONDER: Does my life center around Christ and others? If my answer is "Yes," is there any proof of it in the way I live and talk and spend my time?

PRAYER: Lord, help me trust that You know best how to fulfill my heart's deepest longings.

July

July 1
Somebody, Please Turn On The Light

"You are the light of the world... No one lights a lamp and then puts it under a basket. Instead, a lamp is placed on a stand where it gives light to everyone in the house." Matthew 5:14a,15

Satan is clever. Deception is his game. We don't recognize the "basket" we're "under" and just how little light actually makes its way out into the darkness.

I, like you, prefer the company of other believers—and we do need each other—but we'll have all eternity to enjoy our believing friends. In the "here and now," a whole world that Jesus loves and died for is wandering in the dark. Our light is too often hidden inside the four walls of our churches and our homes, rather than set on a lampstand, out in our neighborhoods and workplaces.

We're all acquainted with unbelievers. We can't help crossing paths occasionally. But where do we spend our time and attention?

Being "light" means **deliberately choosing** to invite lost people into our sphere, to "do life" with us, to see the difference Jesus makes in our relationships, in the trials and heartaches of life, and to build trust and be available when they find themselves at life's crossroads.

PONDER: Am I deliberately choosing to initiate relationships outside the Family of God? If not, why not?

PRAYER: Lord, open my eyes to the lostness of people around me. Give me a glimpse of their final destiny. Break my heart with Your love for them.

July 2
Can God Use That?

"And we know that God causes everything to work together for the good of those who love God and are called according to <u>His</u> purpose for them." Romans 8:28 (emphasis mine)

God is not promising here to make every bad thing good. He **does** promise, however, that, to those who love Him and seek **His** purpose for their lives, He will cause **everything** to work together for **their** good. In the very next verse, God reveals what His purpose is: to make us like His Son, Jesus Christ.

God is declaring that anyone committed to His will can rest assured that God will use any trial—any person or situation, whether good or evil, just or unjust—to reshape our attitudes, motives, thoughts, words, and actions to look more and more like those of Jesus.

For anyone with a heart for God, that should be wonderful news! Could such an awareness change my response to what I'm facing right now? Might this assurance enable me to walk through my most difficult circumstances, including the most trying of people, with my heart on "full alert," actively seeking to discern what God intends to accomplish in **me**?

PONDER: What is my response to difficult people and circumstances? Does it ever occur to me that God might be doing His **best** work in my life through **them**?

PRAYER: Lord, Your likeness is my longing. Forgive me for fighting against the very tools You would use to make me more like You.

July 3
Too Bland, Too Salty, or "More, Please!"

"You are the salt of the earth. But what good is salt if it has lost its flavor?" Matthew 5:13a

Most of us would rather go hungry than eat bland, flavorless food. Salt is the one ingredient that can impact our enjoyment of almost any dish. Though there are many uses for salt, Jesus focuses here on its ability to create mouthwatering delight.

We, in whom Christ lives, are to be "salt" in a world where life has lost its flavor. Sadly, many who "claim" Christ's name have little or nothing to offer except hypocrisy and self-righteous judgment.

Additionally, salt must get out of the shaker if it's to improve the taste of anything. We cannot retreat into our little Christian "bubble."

Unfortunately, some, in a misguided effort to make a difference, take the lid off the shaker and dump, rather than sprinkle, salt into the stew.

"Too salty" is perhaps even worse than not salty enough, for if something is tasteless, we can at least add salt to improve its flavor. Once too much salt has been poured into our recipe, however, it's impossible to rectify. The whole meal is ruined and must be thrown out.

PONDER: Am I hiding in the "shaker?" Do I tend to dump on people? Or does my life make their mouths water to know God?

PRAYER: Lord, please sprinkle Your rich flavor, moment by moment, through my life into the hearts of those who are hungry for what only You can give.

July 4
Do My Eyes Give Me Away?

"... things the Lord hates... haughty eyes..." Proverbs 6:16,17

At the top of God's <u>Most Hated List</u> is "haughty eyes," eyes that look down on another human being.

As broken beings ourselves, we're often comforted to find we are not alone in our brokenness. Unfortunately, we also seem to get some strange satisfaction in discovering we are actually "better" than others, at least to some degree. Perhaps it's the only way we can continue feeling "good" about ourselves.

For those folks who can't seem to get their act together, who are sloppy in dress and manners, who've squandered their money, who've obviously indulged their appetites for food or harmful substances, who've been caught doing something we'd never dream of doing, our hearts are quick to make the comparison, and our eyes give us away.

To Jesus, each person is precious! Those we disdain are wounded, hurting people, trying in vain to dull life's pain, to fill the emptiness inside.

Ironically, even <u>our</u> haughtiness is a vain attempt to satisfy a need—the need for significance. It's such a deadly attitude, however, because it makes us <u>think</u> we are actually okay when we're not!

PONDER: What do I find particularly offensive in others? Have my "haughty eyes" offended God?

PRAYER: Give me your insight into the hearts of others. Help me see them as You do—wounded people, seeking healing and wholeness in all the wrong things. Fill my heart with Your compassion, and let it shine out through my eyes.

July 5
In Eternity, Will It Even Matter?

"Do not waste time arguing over godless ideas and old wives' tales. Instead, train yourself to be godly." I Timothy 4:7

How easy it is to get sidetracked with peripheral issues. How much energy and time do we spend researching and defending positions that, even if we're right, have little to do with producing godly character in us or helping others find their way into God's forever family?

Think about it! If it was <u>your</u> job to keep people from hearing and responding to the Gospel, what would you do? Satan is no fool! If he can get us arguing about **ANY** thing, he can get our eyes off the **MAIN** thing.

And we are not the only ones impacted by such a distraction. Unbelievers watching our lives are not observing what God <u>intended</u> from His people.

What is the main thing? To know Christ and make Him known… to allow His Spirit to make us like **Him**—to live in such a winsome way that those seeking Truth will be attracted to the Jesus they <u>see</u> in <u>us</u> and be drawn into relationship with **Him**.

PONDER: In what ways have I played into the devil's hands, fulfilling <u>his</u> game plan instead of Christ's? In light of eternity, will the issues I'm so preoccupied with even matter?

PRAYER: Lord, guard my heart and mind from the allure of winning an argument or defending a doctrine at the expense of seeking to become a **Christlike ambassador** of the Living God.

July 6
Putting Things In Perspective

"And I am praying that you will put into action the generosity that comes from your faith as you understand and experience all the good things we have in Christ." Philemon 1:6

The more we understand and experience what we've been given in Christ, the kinder and more merciful we become toward others. Those of us who are harsh, judgmental, legalistic, or unforgiving need to come face-to-face with our own desperate need of the mercies of God. We know in our heads we "need" a Savior, but are not convinced in our hearts. We've done a pretty good job, after all, of putting our lives together—pulling ourselves up by the bootstraps, fixing what needed to be fixed—and we feel God is now somewhat obligated to us.

Because we've managed to create a rather good-looking "righteousness," we expect others to do the same. We have little patience with folks who can't seem to "get it together."

One good glimpse of the motives of our hearts in God's Holy Presence would forever shake us to the core of our being. We would cry with Isaiah, *"Woe is me! I'm doomed!"* From that moment, we would cling desperately to the mercy of God, knowing that without it, we are utterly and hopelessly lost!

PONDER: What does my response to others reveal about my understanding of, and experience with, the mercy and grace of God?

PRAYER: Lord, let me see my heart's true motives and have mercy on my soul!

July 7
My Way Or The Highway!

"Fools have no interest in understanding; they only want to air their own opinions." Proverbs 18:2

This passage hit me pretty hard. I tend to be one of those persons who forms opinions and then tries to "sell" them with great enthusiasm. After all, I know I'm right! And, in many cases, I am.

But good, honest, sincere, intelligent people can come down on different sides of certain issues, especially those for which God's Word is not absolutely clear. And make no mistake: there **are** issues over which God has left some ambiguity. These tend to divide God's people. Scripture is very clear about the divinity of Jesus, His virgin birth, death, and resurrection, salvation by grace through faith—these things unite us. However, there are a variety of opinions regarding spiritual gifts, free will, Christ's Second Coming, etc., that can be supported by some scriptures and questioned by others.

Perhaps God wanted it that way, so we could learn the wisdom of seeking understanding, rather than slinging opinions. Maybe He is more interested in our finding and embracing what unites us than in building walls over what divides us.

By seeking understanding, we **value** each other and thus open our hearts to relationships which otherwise might never occur.

PONDER: Am I more interested in proving I'm right than in understanding and building relationship with the other person?

PRAYER: Help me value understanding more than my own opinions, Lord, so I can build relationships through which You can work.

July 8
Are My Good Deeds To Be Seen Or Not?

"…let your good deeds shine out for all to see, so that everyone will praise your heavenly Father." Matthew 5:16; "Watch out! Don't do your good deeds publicly, to be admired by others…" Matthew 6:1

Wait a minute! Isn't this double-talk? How can I do my good deeds for all to see, if I don't do them publicly? Hmmmmm…

As is so often the case, Jesus is talking here about motive! The very same deed, done in the very same way and in the very same venue, can glorify God or glorify self. The difference is something only God can see, because He is the only One who can look into my heart.

When we do our good deeds for the glory of God, it won't matter whether anyone sees or not. We do and say what Jesus asks of us, that **He** might be honored and lifted up. If someone sees and acknowledges us, we give God glory. If not, that's okay, because we did it for **Him**, not ourselves.

PONDER: How motivated am I to give and serve when I <u>know</u> no one but God will ever see? When I <u>do</u> serve others (my spouse, kids, church, pastor, coworkers…), how do I feel when no acknowledgement comes?

PRAYER: Lord, You alone can see into my heart and reveal the motives behind what I do. Help me know when it's <u>my</u> "glory" I'm seeking. Purify me, so that You will be glorified in all I do and say.

July 9
God Looks At My Heart

"Oh, that my actions would consistently reflect your decrees! Then I will not be ashamed when I compare my life with your commands."
Psalm 119:5,6

This is the cry of one whom God declares, *"a man after my own heart."* (Acts 13:22) Yet David's life didn't always reflect God's commands. Sadly, there were times when he succumbed to the selfish, carnal nature within.

David was not perfect, but God didn't declare him "perfect." God loved David's heart.

It's obvious, isn't it? Our "performance" is not what God is measuring. He knows our weakness, that we are made of dust. *(Psalm 103:14)* There was only one perfect Man, the Lord Jesus Christ.

So then, does God not care when we sin? Of course He does! Sin robs us of the abundant life God paid such a high price to give us. But *Romans 5* makes it clear that *"where sin abounds, grace abounds even more."*

It's the <u>heart</u> that God listens to most intently.

The Lord is merciful to those who acknowledge, confess, and forsake their sin. God's gracious response to my sin only deepens my devotion to Him. But a heart without a desire to please God is immune to the Holy Spirit's pleadings and hardens itself against God's voice.

PONDER: What's my attitude to God's Word? Take it or leave it? Pick and choose? How would God describe the condition of my heart?

PRAYER: Look deep inside me, Lord. May what You find there bring You much joy.

July 10
The Fragrance Of My Life

"…he [God] uses us to spread the knowledge of Christ everywhere like a sweet perfume." II Corinthians 2:14b

Have you ever caught a whiff of fragrance that made you want to lean in for more? Have you ever asked someone what perfume they were wearing because the scent was so alluring you just had to know what it was, so you could get some, too?

The Lord wants to permeate our lives, our countenances, our attitudes and actions, so that those who encounter us will be drawn in that same way and want to know what makes us so appealing.

Some people wear so much cologne their fragrance is overpowering, almost nauseating! Others use perfume to cover poor personal hygiene. Cologne is not a substitute for cleanliness. The combination of body odor and perfume can be terribly offensive.

The parallel is obvious, isn't it?

The delightful essence God desires we wear is <u>not</u> something we ourselves can produce or apply to our own lives. It results from a heart that's been forgiven and scrubbed of its sin, that is fully yielded to the Lordship of Jesus Christ, and lived for His glory.

PONDER: What kind of aroma does my life emit? Is it sweet? Does it draw people to Jesus?

PRAYER: Lord, make my life a sweet, beautiful fragrance that attracts people to You.

July 11
Sin Changes Everything

"And you will desire to control your husband, but he will rule over you." Genesis 3:16

Before the fall, Adam and Eve lived without shame, clinging to each other with the knowledge that they were perfect for each other. Adam recognized the gift God had made, especially for him, from his very own body.

Their feelings of mutual appreciation and dependence created a peaceful, supportive, loving environment. Adam was well aware he was incomplete without Eve. Eve recognized that without Adam, she would never have existed.

Now, something has changed. No longer transparent in each other's presence, they make garments to hide their nakedness. Rather than celebrate each other, they play the blame game. The peace, tranquility, freedom, and joy they had once experienced has been replaced with fear, suspicion, manipulation, and desire for control.

From that day to this, even the deepest affiliations have suffered from these same inclinations. Only the unconditional, selfless love of God poured out in our hearts is sufficient to overrule the sinful tendencies inherited from our first parents in the Garden of Eden.

PONDER: Am I ever manipulative, controlling, or self-centered in my associations with others? How is **that** working for me?

PRAYER: Building an intimate connection with another person can be like trying to fill holes in a leaky boat. I just get one hole plugged, and another leak springs up. Please help me, Jesus! I recognize that only by denying my selfish tendencies and yielding to Your control will I ever experience the relationships my heart longs for.

July 12
Getting Quiet Enough To Hear

"May He give you the power to accomplish all the good things your faith prompts you to do. Then the name of our Lord Jesus will be honored because of the way you live..." II Thessalonians 1:11b,12a

What good things does my faith prompt me to do? Am I doing them or putting them off, allowing my busy schedule, favorite TV programs, or personal desires to dictate when, or even if, I respond?

Perhaps I seldom sense the prompting of the Holy Spirit to do good things. Why is that, I wonder? Could it be that I have drowned out His voice with all the noise and clutter I've allowed in my life?

Elijah discovered that God doesn't speak in the earthquake, wind, and fire. Rather, His voice is "still" and "small," and we must take time to listen, get quiet, and rest in His presence if His promptings are to be discerned.

What a shame that, in a world so desperately in need of Jesus, my inability to sense His promptings, or my failure to accomplish the good things He inspires might hide Him from those who are in such need of His love.

PONDER: How sensitive is <u>my</u> heart to the voice of God? What is it that, too often, drowns out His promptings?

PRAYER: Lord, forgive me for getting caught up in a lifestyle that minimizes Your impact on this world through my life. Draw me to that place where honoring You is my deepest desire.

July 13
Frantic Or Restful?

"Unless the Lord builds a house, the work of the builders is wasted. Unless the Lord protects a city, guarding it with sentries will do no good." Psalm 127:1

When will we finally comprehend that all human effort is futile unless directed and fueled by God's Spirit? We work so frantically, plan so carefully, build so elaborately. At times little or nothing is accomplished. Even when success <u>is</u> achieved, we dare not let up, even for a moment.

The very next verse says, *"It is useless for you to work so hard from early morning until late at night, anxiously working for food to eat, for God gives rest to his loved ones."*

Would God prefer I do nothing? Of course not! He's not suggesting we don't plan well and work hard, but too many of us approach our lives as if everything depends on <u>us</u>. That creates a frantic "weight" God never intended us to carry.

The quiet "center" that comes from acknowledging that God loves us, provides for us, has our best interest at heart, and can be absolutely trusted to do what's right concerning us enables us to "rest" even as we work, knowing that everything ultimately depends on <u>Him</u>, not on us.

PONDER: In my deepest heart of hearts, who or what am I really trusting in?

PRAYER: Lord, I want You in the driver's seat of my life. Make obvious to me the difference between how I "do life" and how You designed it to be lived.

July 14
Will I Be Ready?

"Watch out! Don't let your hearts be dulled by carousing and drunkenness and by the worries of this life. Don't let that day catch you unaware, like a trap." Luke 21:34

Do we have any idea the dulling affect this world has on our hearts? In this chapter, Jesus envisions the events surrounding His Second Coming, describing disasters and turmoil that will terrify all mankind. Christians will be greatly persecuted, even killed, for their beliefs.

Being faithful throughout such suffering will be crucial because Scripture makes it clear that *"those who endure to the end will be saved." (Matthew 24:13)* That's why Jesus warns us to stay alert, not allowing ourselves to be "lulled to sleep" by this world.

Most of us don't really think Christ's return will happen within our lifetime. After all, people have been warning of it for centuries. It hasn't happened yet!

I have news for us all. Every person <u>will</u> experience Christ's return within his/her lifetime. Whether when He splits the skies at His Second Coming, removes us quietly from a hospital bed, or snatches us quickly in a fiery car crash, He <u>will</u> come for each of us.

Dulled hearts will be suddenly terrified and ashamed as they stand in His Holy Presence to give an account of the way they have lived.

PONDER: Suppose today is <u>my</u> day to stand before God? Does that thought fill me with peace? Fear? Shame?

PRAYER: O, God, have mercy! Make me ready for Your coming!

July 15
On Death And Dying

"A wise person thinks a lot about death…" Ecclesiastes 7:4a

In our culture, the subject of death and dying is almost "taboo."

Not only are we reluctant to discuss it, we avoid viewing the body of deceased friends and loved ones, shield our children as much as possible from the dying process, and want memorial services to be short, or even nonexistent, so we can get back to "normal" as quickly as possible. But think about this: Death is the **one** thing in life that is absolutely **guaranteed**! It's no respecter of persons, old or young, and it often comes without warning.

To avoid dealing with death's inevitability is to cheat family members and friends of the chance to say and do those things which can never be communicated once the loved one has died. Even worse, it robs each individual of the opportunity to get prepared for the "hereafter."

Jesus Christ offers eternal life for **anyone** who will call on Him in faith, but those who refuse to entertain their own mortality find it easier to ignore their need of a Savior, and someday, it will be too late!

PONDER: How "comfortable" am I with thoughts of my own demise or the death of someone I love? Am I an avoider? Or will I take time to contemplate and prepare for what I cannot prevent?

PRAYER: Lord, You conquered death when You rose triumphantly from the grave, forever removing its fear and sting. I will trust Your gracious provision!

July 16
Take Your Medicine

"A cheerful heart is good medicine, but a broken spirit saps a person's strength." Proverbs 17:22

The Doctor has prescribed some medicine, but He cannot make me take it. I have to choose to follow his orders. If I don't, I cannot hope to feel better.

But how can I apply a cheerful heart, when I don't feel the least bit cheerful? Good question! Here are a few applicators that might help:

1. **Fix (fasten, secure) my thoughts on Christ** *(Isaiah 26:3; Hebrews 3:1)*. I am only capable of one emotional "focus" at a time.
2. **Trust in the Lord** *(Proverbs 3:5,6; Philippians 4:6,7)*. I cannot trust and fret at the same time.
3. **Take charge of my thoughts** *(II Corinthians 10:5)*. Refuse to allow myself to dwell on things that don't honor Christ.
4. **Choose to think only on what is good and right and pure, etc.** *(Philippians 4:8)*.
5. **Recall and count my blessings, both physical and spiritual** *(Psalm 103:2)*. I may have lost sight of them, but they are there.
6. **Express praise and thankfulness** *(I Thessalonians 5:18)*. Speak my gratitude aloud to God and others. Write notes of appreciation or call, if necessary, but I must find a way to give expression to my gratitude.
7. **Find someone with a need and be the one to meet it** *(Luke 6:38)*.

PONDER: Am I following Doctor's orders? Or am I content to wallow in self-pity and despondency?

PRAYER: Lord, help me get up, right now, and take my medicine!

July 17

Am I Listening?

"So pay attention to how you hear. To those who listen to my teaching, more understanding will be given. But for those who are not listening, even what they think they understand will be taken away from them." Luke 8:18

Jesus is warning here against a careless attitude toward God's Word. We cannot afford to just "read" the Bible like we would read any other book.

Notice that Jesus did not say to be careful how we "read." Nor did He promise more understanding for those who "read" His teachings. No. He spoke of "hearing" and "listening" and warned us to pay attention to "<u>how</u>" we do it.

Do we merely "read" our Bibles? Do we approach God's Word like a "smorgasbord," picking and choosing what interests and inspires us, ignoring what we feel we can safely disregard or postpone?

Or do we come to our Bibles with a desire to <u>hear</u> God's voice, to know what He is <u>saying</u> to us—today, specifically—about our lives, our attitudes, our habits, our motives? Are we listening to discern God's purposes and how He plans to fulfill them in and through us?

PONDER: What's my approach to God's Word? Do I <u>expect</u> God to speak to me? Am I listening?

PRAYER: Each time I open Your Word, O God, help me not just see words on a page, but may I tune my "ears" for Your Spirit's voice. Speak directly to my heart, Lord, because, from now on, I'll be "listening."

July 18
The Same Ole Lie

"In the middle of the garden, He placed the tree of… the knowledge of good and evil. …God warned… 'If you eat its fruit, you are sure to die.'" Genesis 2:9b,17

For centuries, folks have speculated on the species of the forbidden tree as if the answer to that question were somehow significant. In actuality, the real drama centers on the relationship of the two newly formed humans with their God.

The forbidden tree simply represented a <u>choice</u> to be made—the <u>only</u> choice required of them since they were given free and abundant access to <u>everything</u> else on earth.

Would they trust God, this One who had just created an incredible world for their enjoyment, who had breathed His life into them… this Friend with whom they walked each evening, basking in the security of His love and the glory of His creation? **<u>All He asked was their trust and obedience</u>**.

But Satan, the father of lies and archenemy of God, reasoned that if he could just raise questions as to God's trustworthiness, he could lure humankind to its damnation. He succeeded in the Garden, and, tragically, his success continues to this day.

PONDER: How about me? Do I fully trust God? How would my life be different if I wholeheartedly believed and obeyed <u>everything</u> God has revealed in His Word about Himself, about Creation, about life and salvation, about the destructiveness of sin?

PRAYER: Lord Jesus, forgive my unbelief and rebellious pride. Help me recognize and renounce the enemy's lies.

July 19
Never, Lord!

"...If God says something is acceptable, don't say it isn't... Three men have come looking for you... go with them without hesitation... for I have sent them." Acts 10:15,20

The Holy Spirit is speaking here to Peter, requesting he do something that, all his life, he had considered forbidden and revolting. A good Jew would <u>never</u> eat animals God had labeled "unclean." Why was the Lord even asking such a thing?

We don't know what kind of animals were in that sheet, but we can guess by Peter's response, "Never, Lord!" Peter was aghast, repulsed by the very thought.

The lesson to be learned here is not as much about food as about God's love for the unlovely and His ability to transform even the worst of sinners.

To God, those whose words, deeds, and appearance repulse us are eternal souls, created in His image, blinded by the god of this world, and in need of <u>someone</u> to show them the way back to their loving Heavenly Father.

PONDER: Are there some folks whose lifestyles and philosophies nauseate and disgust me? If God wanted to use **me** to show them His love and mercy, would I, like Peter, cry, "Never, Lord!"?

PRAYER: Jesus, you'll have to be the One to convince and enable me, like you did Peter, to look at people the way You do. Help me not miss out on the miracles of Your transforming power, simply because I am too prejudiced to let you love the "unclean" through me.

July 20
The Difference Between "Then" And "Now"

"He [Abraham] responded, 'The LORD, in whose presence I have lived, will send his angel with you and will make your mission successful.'" Genesis 24:40

Abraham lived in the days before the Holy Spirit was poured out into the hearts of all believers. God's salvation and the constant indwelling of His Spirit were still promises for the future.

God did speak to Abraham, and even appeared to him, on more than one occasion, but there were often many years between each instance. So how could he say he had <u>lived in the Lord's presence</u>?

Somehow, Abraham managed to embrace each day with a conscious awareness of God, even when God wasn't speaking or revealing Himself. For Abraham, there was apparently an ever-present expectation that God could "show up" at any moment. And <u>that</u> changed his life!

As a believer, I have an <u>advantage</u> over Abraham in that my <u>body</u> is the "dwelling place" of God. Christ lives <u>in</u> me! *(Col. 1:27)*

PONDER: Do I spend my life in the constant awareness of His presence? Do my words, choices, reactions reflect that consciousness?

PRAYER: Lord Jesus, make me aware of the <u>reality</u> that You actually live <u>inside</u> of me. You are <u>closer</u> to me than any human being could ever be. Wherever <u>I</u> go, <u>You</u> go. When <u>I</u> walk into a room, the <u>Holy Spirit</u> enters as well. May that truth change the way I think… and what I do… and how I respond, today—and the rest of my life!

July 21
Does God See Or Not?

"'The Lord isn't looking,' they say, 'and besides, the God of Israel doesn't care.'" Psalm 94:7;

"The Lord sees clearly what a man does, examining every path he takes." Proverbs 5:21

Does He see us or not? In the Psalm above, people who <u>think</u> they know more than God, discount what He says about Himself and His ability to know what's going on. Their conclusions are drawn from their own limited experiences, yet they live their whole lives as if their assumptions are correct.

But what if they're wrong? What if they come to the end of life and find that God **has** been watching after all?

PONDER: Assuming there really is a God, isn't it rather arrogant to think that any mortal could ever hope to figure Him out? In those times when it doesn't "feel" to <u>me</u> like He cares, should I trust my own conclusions? Wouldn't I need to know as much as God knows to fully understand Him and His ways?

PRAYER: Lord, help me recognize the source of the voices that arrogantly defy Your Word, both within my own heart and out of the mouths of others. Help me choose to believe what You have said over and over in the Bible… that I am seen and known intimately by God. May that thought motivate me to seek to <u>know</u> You—<u>really</u> know You—and to live in such a way that I won't be afraid or ashamed when death finally ushers me into Your presence.

July 22
God, Do You Have To Do It That Way?

"Then, spitting onto his own fingers, he [Jesus] touched the man's tongue with the spittle... and commanded, 'Be opened!' Instantly the man could... speak plainly!" Mark 7:33b-35

This man was a deaf-mute, but he could <u>see</u> what Jesus was doing. Was he repulsed, as I am, at the thought of someone spitting on their fingers and putting the spittle on <u>my</u> tongue? Was he tempted to push away at that moment, gesturing that he would find another solution to his dilemma?

Why does Jesus choose such a method for this man's healing? Surely, He could just say the words and make it happen.

And what about the blind man in *John 9*? Jesus spat on the ground, made mud with His saliva, and smoothed the mud over the man's eyes before telling him to go wash in the pool of Siloam. At least the blind man couldn't see what Jesus was doing! He surely <u>heard</u> Him spit, however, and <u>felt</u> the resulting wet, gooey substance on his eyes.

So often, the ways of God escape our understanding. Many times they **offend** us. But can you recognize that Jesus is inviting **trust** here? Had the man refused to allow Jesus's spit to touch his tongue, he'd have gone to his grave unable to speak!

PONDER: How many of God's "healings" have I refused because they came packaged in ways that didn't resemble my idea of a miracle?

PRAYER: Forgive me, Lord for questioning Your ways. Deal with me as You see fit.

July 23
Which Is The Real Me?

"...I will lead a life of integrity in my own home." Psalm 101:2b; "...David returned home to bless his own family..." II Samuel 6:20a

Why is it so much more motivating to live out a life of sacrifice and service at work than at home? Why do we find it easier to spread compliments, extend praise, and do our best listening with those outside our family circle?

After keeping a tight rein on our appetites, attitudes, and words throughout the day, how many of us "let it all hang out" upon our arrival at home?

So often, our spouses and kids face the brunt of all the tensions that have built up inside throughout our day. By the time we get home, after expending ourselves in pursuit of whatever filled our agendas that day, we have very little left to give those we love the most.

In both of our passages today, we find David very concerned about what happened in his own home. A big part of being a person of integrity is to actually **"BE"** what I **"APPEAR"** to be, to make sure that my life is the same in private as in public.

PONDER: Would my family members call what happens when I get home a "blessing?" Would they recognize the "me" that others see, as the same "me" they encounter at the end of the day?

PRAYER: Lord, transform me into a person whose integrity will bless those most intimately touched by my life.

July 24
Who Touched Me?

"'Who touched me?' Jesus asked. Everyone denied it, and Peter said, 'Master, this whole crowd is pressing up against you.' But Jesus said, 'Someone deliberately touched me, for I felt healing power go out from me.'" Luke 8:45,46

The Lord apparently knows the difference between a deliberate, faith-inspired touch that longs for and expects results and the casual stuff we usually call "touching."

This crowd is intense, jostling each other on the road. One timid, disease-ridden woman, who'd spent her life savings on doctors without success, barely gets her fingers on the hem of Jesus's garment, and all of Heaven stops to grant her request.

It was her deliberate, desperate, faith-filled touch that caused healing to flow from Him. Jesus only confirmed her healing, after the fact.

God is attracted to our humble acknowledgement of need. A broken, contrite heart that looks to Him expectantly will not be turned away.

When we, too, pull our eyes away from human resources, recognizing our only hope lies in getting close enough to the Savior to "touch" the hem of His garment, we will find ourselves the grateful recipients of a miracle.

PONDER: Is my approach to God casual? Take it or leave it? Am I content with the world's "doctors?" Or is God my deliberate and desperate choice?

PRAYER: Trembling, I come. Desperate, I reach for You and You alone. My faith is small, Lord, but You are big and the only answer to my need.

July 25
Is God Big Enough To Do This?

"...the Lord your God is the one who will cross over ahead of you like a devouring fire... He will subdue them so that you will quickly conquer them and drive them out, just as the Lord has promised."
Deuteronomy 9:3

This scene takes place just before the Israelites cross the Jordan River to take the city of Jericho and all the land of Canaan.

To the human eye, it will "look for all the world" like the children of Israel are fighting the battle. In reality, though, the enemy will have <u>already</u> been conquered, served up on a silver platter by the God of the Universe.

The Lord Himself will go ahead of them. He (the Lord God of Heaven) will handcuff their enemies, so that His people can easily conquer them.

That's what He'd said He'd do 40 years earlier. The promise had been just as trustworthy <u>then</u> as on this day, but their ancestors had succumbed to fear, refused to follow God into the conquest, and died while wandering 40 years in the wilderness.

Not much has changed since then. Canaan is still filled with fortified cities and giants. But this time, Israel will enjoy the fruits of victory because they will follow the Lord of Heaven's Armies into the impossible.

PONDER: What looms large in my life right now? Will I trust God or give way to fear?

PRAYER: Lord, don't let me allow fear and unbelief to rob me of the provision You want to give me.

July 26
How Will They Ever Know?

"When they heard that the Lord was concerned about them and had seen their misery, they bowed down and worshiped." Exodus 4:31b

That's the word we need to get out to people <u>everywhere</u>. God is concerned about them and sees their misery! He cares. He has made provision through Jesus Christ to lift their burdens, heal their brokenness, and change their lives.

That's such good news!

It's not like people haven't heard about Jesus. Most people have at least a vague understanding of God, but there is a definite disconnect between their understanding and their experience.

Could it be they believe God values them the way His people do? If they perceive the church as an exclusive club into which only those willing to abide by the "rules" are invited, then those whose lives are still a mess <u>may</u> assume they are unwelcome to God Himself.

We are Christ's body, through which He wants to touch and speak and love those who are lost and hurting. We must shed our "fear of contamination," go where broken people hang out, and "get down in the trenches" to show them how deeply God cares about them! Perhaps then they will finally believe they are **treasured** by the God we represent.

PONDER: What keeps me from spending time with folks caught in sin's trap? Pride? Fear? Busyness? Do I even know any?

PRAYER: Jesus, be Lord of my life! Give me YOUR heart for people damaged by sin. Show <u>them</u> how much You love them... through me.

July 27
Use What You Have

"...to those who use well what they are given, even more will be given. But from those who do nothing, even what little they have will be taken away." Luke 19:26

Ever know people who complain because they have so few talents or abilities? They are like the man in this story. Because of fear, envy, and lack of trust in his master, he hid what was given. He incurred his master's wrath and forfeited what little he had.

God is not worried about how much or little we have. His concern is whether we <u>acknowledge</u>, <u>use</u>, <u>develop</u>, and <u>expand</u> what He's entrusted to our care. Those who use well what they've received will be given even more.

PONDER: Have I been comparing myself to others, consumed with how little I have in contrast? Have I been feeling cheated, mistrustful of the God Who decided to give me "so little?"

Will I risk taking an honest look at my life and identify, with His help, those interests and abilities He <u>has</u> placed there? Even if, at this moment, they seem miniscule, am I willing to "dust them off" and begin using them for His glory?

PRAYER: Help me, Lord, to trust Your love and wisdom for me. Help me to thank You for whatever purpose You had in mind when You made me <u>just</u> the way You did. From now on, I determine to use what You <u>have</u> given me with a heart of gratitude and for Your Glory.

July 28
Is Bitterness Ever Worth It?

"…God… devises ways to bring us back when we have been separated from Him." II Samuel 14:14b

These words were spoken by an old woman, trying to help King David see the importance of reconciling with his estranged son Absalom. Though the king followed her advice by allowing Absalom to return to Jerusalem, he still refused to see his son for two more years.

By the time David was finally persuaded to allow his son back into his presence, hurt and bitterness had already sparked a plot in Absalom's heart to steal the kingdom from his father. David had to flee for his life. In the ensuing battles, his son died. No doubt, the king's prolonged, agonizing grief was exacerbated by his deep regret.

Even though David was known as a "man after God's own heart," in this matter (and several others, too), he missed the heart of God completely and paid a high price for it.

PONDER: What about the broken relationships in my life? Am I devising ways to bring about reconciliation? Am I willing to follow the example of Jesus Christ, who went all the way to the cross to bring me back into relationship with Himself?

PRAYER: Lord Jesus, I want to be like You. I want the heart of God. Open my heart to those I struggle with right now. Fill my mind with creative ways to restore our relationship and give me grace to live in forgiveness and reconciliation.

July 29
I Can Never Outgive God!

"...a farmer who plants only a few seeds will get a small crop... the one who plants generously... a generous crop. ...God loves a person who gives cheerfully. And God will generously provide all you need..." II Corinthians 9:6-8a

Are we bothered by verses like these that seem to indicate that we should <u>expect</u> God to give generously in return for gifts given in His Name? Somehow, we're not sure giving should be tied to any thought of receiving something in return, so we tend to "play down" those Scriptures that promise reward for good works done.

Obviously, God is not interested in blessing selfishness in any form. But think with me a moment: **Being generous with my time, energy, or resources means I will have less left over, perhaps not even enough to meet all my own needs/desires.** That's not typically something a selfish heart would be inclined to pursue.

In the moment of decision, my desire to be generous comes into direct conflict with my innate compulsion to make sure I/mine have "enough." Only trusting God, as the **Provider** of all I need and the **Replenisher** of all I give away, will enable me to give beyond my "comfort zone."

PONDER: Is it possible to "give" without being "generous?" What determines whether what I give is generous or not?

PRAYER: Dear Lord, You will never be in anyone's debt. You will always outgive even the most generous person. Help me to trust Your Word and live my life accordingly.

July 30
Gaining Perspective

"...I grieve over my loss. Yet I still dare to hope when I remember this: The faithful love of the Lord never ends! His mercies never cease. Great is his faithfulness; his mercies begin afresh each morning." Lamentations 3:21b-23

In this chapter, Jeremiah recounts his own immense suffering. In earlier verses, we can almost feel the anguish and bitterness he expresses. Yet, even while enduring such intense distress, he remembers God's love and faithfulness, and he is comforted.

Bringing God into the midst of our pain gives perspective that would otherwise elude us. You see, life is not always fair! Bad "stuff" happens to good people. When it does, we have only two choices.

Some will rail against God in agony, stiff-arming Him with anger and bitterness. Others will turn toward Him for strength, shelter, peace, and purpose even as they endure their turmoil.

Choose the first and go it alone, angry, and miserable. Open your heart to the comforting presence of God, whose love never ends, whose mercies never cease, and find hope beyond this present moment!

PONDER: When life treats me unfairly, what is my response? Do I see God as the enemy or as the only One who can bring meaning to my present suffering, strength to endure my afflictions, and hope beyond this life?

PRAYER: Lord, I need You too much to shut You out of my life. I turn to You, now. I choose to trust You and cling to Your love and mercy.

July 31

Is It Mere Imitation?

"...you should imitate me, just as I imitate Christ." I Corinthians 11:1

Although Paul made it clear in *Galatians 2:20* that the Christian life is about trusting Christ to live His life in us, he talks here about imitating Christ, because each of us still has choices to make. In every specific life situation, we are bombarded with opposing motivations and conflicting voices. Whose life will actually be lived out in my body?

By choosing what I know Christ would choose, I am "imitating" Him. However, I must recognize that I don't have the power to pull it off, even after making the decision. It's Christ's life <u>in</u> me that gives me confidence that, as I choose to do what I know He would do, He will provide the love, the joy, and everything else necessary, to follow through.

By faith, I recognize that, because Christ lives in me, there is plenty of joy within me, even in the midst of adversity, to make my song <u>real</u>, if I will but <u>choose</u> to sing it.

The <u>choosing</u> is the imitating. The song itself can <u>only</u> be sung by <u>Jesus</u>. It should thrill and amaze us that He desires to sing His song using our voices, our tongues, our hearts.

PONDER: Whose life most often gets lived in my body, Christ's or mine? What does it mean for Christ to live <u>His</u> life <u>through</u> me? What hinders that in my life?

PRAYER: Lord, help me experience Your life in me!

August

August 1

Enthusiastic, But Wrong!

"David and all Israel were celebrating before God with all their might, singing songs and playing all kinds of musical instruments... the Lord's anger was aroused... Uzzah died there in the presence of God." I Chronicles 13:8,10

David had just been declared king of Israel. In his exuberance, he invited all the priests and Levites to join him in returning the Ark of God to its rightful place in the Tabernacle of God.

Earlier, the Philistines had captured the Ark in battle, but suffered so greatly while in possession of it, they'd returned it on a cart drawn by two oxen. David and the Israelites celebrated with all their might as they began this trek. But there was one problem: they'd neglected the specific instructions given by God as to how to safely transport it.

When the oxen stumbled, Uzzah reached out to steady the Ark of God, and all Israel was suddenly gripped with the fear of the Lord. This was no ordinary box. No amount of spiritual fervor could make up for <u>disobedience</u> to the <u>known</u> will of God, whose instructions had been given to <u>protect</u> His people from this <u>very</u> thing.

Later, the Ark was transported safely, this time hanging on poles through loops specifically designed by God Himself for that purpose.

PONDER: Are there any clear teachings of Scripture I have compromised or ignored? Am I enthusiastically "serving God" in ways He cannot bless?

PRAYER: Lord God, forgive me for presuming I can follow You on <u>my</u> terms.

August 2
A True "Con Artist"

"You may think you can condemn such people, but you are just as bad…! When you say they are wicked and should be punished, you are condemning yourself, for you who judge others do the very same things." Romans 2:1-4

It's so easy for us to assign questionable, even wrong, motives to others as we observe their behavior and hear their words. We are quick to assume we know what they are thinking and what their underlying motivations are.

Once that judgment is made, we will find everything they do and say colored by our assumptions. Unfortunately, and all too often, our conclusions about those folks find their way into our conversations with friends and family. These dear folks may never have thought about it on their own, but, now, after talking with us, they can more easily see the "truth" as we do.

Conversely, however, when it comes to our **own** motives, we are tremendously skilled at rationalizing and justifying them. In our minds, we manage to package our arrogance as "teaching" or "guiding." We manipulate people in the name of "concern." Our need to control is disguised as "protection." We exploit people while telling ourselves we are really "helping" them or giving them an "opportunity."

PONDER: Sound familiar? If we're honest, it does. But there is One from whom we cannot hide our true motives.

PRAYER: Oh, God, deliver me from the temptation to malign the motives of others while, at the same time, justifying my own.

August 3

God Lives In Me!

"...For we are the temple of the Living God. As God said, 'I will live in them and walk among them...'" II Corinthians 6:16

God Himself, in all His fullness, lives in every person who has received Christ as Savior and Lord.

That means, as born-again believers in Jesus Christ, we already have **ALL** of God living within us right now. There's nothing we can do to receive more of God than we've already been given.

Think of it! Every attribute, power, and quality of God is at our disposal because He resides within our bodies at this very moment!

So why don't our lives reflect this truth?

Good question! It's possible we don't even realize or comprehend what we've been given. Or perhaps we stay so preoccupied with the cares of this life that we simply fail to live in the <u>awareness</u> of His presence within.

Sadly, I'm afraid, for far too many of us, it's because, although we have all of God, He does **not** have **all** of us.

PONDER: How would my life be different if I could truly believe and live in the awareness and power of Christ's life **in** me? How would that affect my attitudes, my words, my reactions and responses to the people and circumstances I encounter every day?

PRAYER: Lord Jesus, help me recognize that You have taken up residence in my body. Show me what that means. Help me live in the joyful confidence that You have made Yourself at home within me.

August 4

How Much Does God Know About Me?

"But I know you well—where you stay and when you come and go." II Kings 19:27

God is speaking to the king of Assyria, who's been threatening King Hezekiah and the people of Judah, haughtily defying their God. The Lord replies in verse 22, *"Whom have you been defying and ridiculing? Against whom did you raise your voice? At whom did you look with such haughty eyes? It was the Holy One of Israel!"*

King Sennacherib had no idea who he was dealing with! But Almighty God knew <u>him</u>, through and through. The Lord of the Universe saw everything he did… heard everything he said. Someday, Sennacherib will stand before God at the Judgment. This pompous king will know then Who he so arrogantly defied. But it will be too late.

Each of us must someday give account to God as well. Perhaps we're not guilty of actually defying the God of Heaven. Our temptation may simply be carelessness or apathy.

Some of us tend to fit God neatly into a spiritual "compartment." You know, church on Sunday, personal devotions each morning. But after that, it's "business as usual." We may look spiritual enough to others, but is God convinced?

PONDER: What would change in my life if I really believed God observes and evaluates every detail of it?

PRAYER: Lord, You are always near, watching, knowing everything I do and say. Make me aware of Your presence, and may that awareness change my life.

August 5

Free Indeed!

"For you are a slave to whatever controls you." II Peter 2:19b

We know that! Don't we? But we think in terms of <u>big</u>, <u>bad</u> things like substance abuse or other enslaving addictions. Peter doesn't put any qualifiers on this statement. Nothing is exempt from scrutiny here, and that's what makes me squirm.

Perhaps what I can't get enough of is the praise or appreciation from people. Or could it be that I am constrained by a need to prove my worth to someone?

How about the bitterness that springs from an unforgiving heart? Or the need to "fix" everything and everyone whose brokenness intersects with my life? Is it possible that even that which "appears" outwardly good might be motivated by unhealthy inner compulsions I can't break free of?

In all these and myriad other "addictions," we find ourselves crying out like Paul, *"O wretched man that I am! Who will rescue me from this body of death?" (Romans 7:24,25)* But, *"thanks be to God,"* the answer is still the same: **_Jesus Christ!_** He is our Rescuer, our Redeemer, our Sanctifier! Through Him, we <u>can</u> find release and freedom!

PONDER: Is there anything driving, compelling me that, if I'm honest, I really can't just turn off and ignore?

PRAYER: Lord, search my heart. Point out any compulsion that arises from something other than the love and mercy of God at work in my life. Give me the courage to bring it into the Light of Your Truth. Then set me free.

August 6
How Can I Know For Sure?

"But seek ye first the kingdom of God and His righteousness, and all these things will be added unto you." Matthew 6:33 KJV; "And he will give you all you need from day to day if you live for him and make the Kingdom of God your primary concern." Matthew 6:33 NLT

Is there some kind of litmus test that would help me know if I've put God, His Kingdom, and His righteousness first on my list of priorities? Most of us would declare outright that God is at the top of our list, family second, etc., etc. If that is <u>true</u> in my life, then the choices I make every single day will reflect it.

PONDER: When I look at my checkbook register or my credit card statement, does my love for God show up anywhere?

In my use of time, how much does God get in a typical day, week, etc.?

When I'm not obligated to think about anything pertaining to responsibilities at work or at home, what do I find myself thinking about?

What captures my attention when I first rise in the morning?

PRAYER: Lord Jesus, I'm afraid I very often seek after "all these things" first and give you the "leftovers." Right now, I deliberately choose to begin rearranging my life to make room for You. Stir up a hunger and thirst in my heart, that I might not be satisfied until You, Your kingdom, and Your righteousness are truly my top priority.

August 7

Trusting—No Matter What

"Can we find anyone else like this man, so obviously filled with the spirit of God?" Genesis 41:38b

These words were spoken by Pharaoh about Joseph, after God used him to interpret the king's troubling dreams. Pharaoh was not a believer in the one, true God. Yet He recognized God's Spirit at work in the man who stood before him. As a result, this powerful ruler immediately gave Joseph control over all the affairs of his kingdom.

What had prepared Joseph for this moment? He'd kept his heart centered on God and refused to succumb to bitterness.

Though sold as a slave by jealous brothers, lied about by Potiphar's devious wife, imprisoned for years, and forgotten by one who'd promised a good word on his behalf, Joseph had honored God, worked hard to serve others, and trusted his Lord, even when everything looked and felt hopeless.

His heart was tuned to God, so when the moment came for God to move on his behalf, Joseph knew what to do. This godless ruler recognized the hand of Almighty God and gave unprecedented authority to this unknown foreigner who, just a short time earlier, had been rotting in the palace prison.

PONDER: Is my heart centered on God, tuned-in and trusting, like Joseph's, even in the midst of circumstances I don't like or understand? Or has bitterness, resentment, and mistrust consumed my energies and dulled my senses to God's voice and His movements?

PRAYER: Oh, God, bind my wandering heart to Thee!

August 8

Why Didn't They Leave? (Part 1)

"...the Israelites had many children and grandchildren. In fact, they multiplied so greatly that they became extremely powerful and filled the land." Exodus 1:7

The descendants of Jacob had moved to Egypt to survive a serious famine. After the famine, they surely could have departed. They chose to stay put. Their children, born in Egypt, had never known life anywhere else.

Egypt was home—its food, customs, and lifestyle familiar and comfortable. Surely, they'd heard of the land promised them by God. They must've been aware of Joseph's instructions to carry his bones to Canaan when they left. Why were they content to stay in Egypt?
The Old Testament stories are recorded to warn and teach us. Will we learn their lessons?

The Apostle John cautions in *I John 2:15, "Stop loving this evil world and all that it offers you, for when you love the world, you... do not have the love of the Father in you."*

Unfortunately, we <u>do</u> love this world, its pleasures, riches, and fame. Though Jesus calls us "out of Egypt," we choose to stay. Why? Perhaps we feel more "at home" there than in the Promised Land.

PONDER: What's <u>my</u> relationship with this world, its values and lifestyle? Am I trying to straddle the fence, seeking to accommodate both the Lord <u>and</u> worldly pursuits?

PRAYER: Open my eyes, Lord, to see the insidious nature of this world's philosophy. Give me Your Heavenly perspective. Help me see the eternal consequences of clinging to worldly pleasures.

August 9

Why Didn't They Leave? (Part 2)

"...the Israelites had many children and grandchildren. In fact, they multiplied so greatly that they became extremely powerful and filled the land." Exodus 1:7

Why didn't they leave Egypt while they had the chance? They went there a free people. At some point, when they realized they'd lost favor with the pharaoh, they were still strong enough to leave. So why stay?

Sadly, even before cruel slave masters cracked whips over their backs, their hearts had become enslaved to Egyptian pleasures and privileges they were <u>not</u> willing to relinquish.

They loved Egypt more than Canaan, more than God. Although they <u>knew</u> God had promised them a land of their own, they were in no hurry to say "goodbye" to the life they loved.

By the time they actually "felt" the pain of Egyptian cruelty, it was too late. They'd become slaves to a tyrant over whom they had no power.

How like them we are at times. We are so easily seduced by the allure of sin. We fail to comprehend that its tentacles are wrapping themselves around our hearts and lives.

At some point, we, too, will "wake up" to realize we have become enslaved by the very things we <u>thought</u> would set us free.

PONDER: Do the pleasures of sin so allure me that I cannot see their potential to enslave?

PRAYER: Lord, open my eyes that I might reject the promises of "Egypt" to experience the "land flowing with milk and honey" that Jesus offers.

August 10

Would I Die For Christ?

"I will rejoice even if I lose my life, pouring it out like a liquid offering to God..." Philippians 2:17

Paul writes from prison, not knowing how much longer he will live, but anxious that believers everywhere hold true to their faith, with joy, no matter what they are called on to endure for the sake of Christ.

We find it difficult to imagine rejoicing at the thought of losing our lives. Yet here is Paul, very aware that his death could be imminent, still somehow filled with joy at the thought of dying for Jesus, of pouring out his life as an offering to the God he loves.

We have been so free of persecution in our culture that it's difficult for us to relate to such sacrifice. In many parts of the world, however, Christian brothers and sisters are being given the ultimatum, "Deny Christ or suffer! Deny Jesus or die!"

What would we do? Of course we can hope and pray such suffering never comes our way, but, whether or not we're ever faced with such persecution, shouldn't the question it raises already be settled in our hearts? Shouldn't its answer be lived out daily in our lives?

PONDER: Do I choose Jesus <u>NOW</u>, in the everyday opportunities I have to "die" to myself and give my life away?

PRAYER: Lord, I <u>do</u> choose You! Give me the grace I need to pour out my life as a living sacrifice <u>every</u> day and in <u>every</u> way!

August 11

Because God Said So!

"So take courage! For I believe God. It will be just as he said." Acts 27:25

The Apostle Paul is aboard a ship bound for Rome to stand trial before the emperor. They've hit terrible weather, and their hopes of riding out the storm have dwindled.

In the night, an angel reports to Paul that he will indeed get to Rome and that all on board will be saved, even though the ship will eventually break apart in the storm. That is good news, although there are terrifying hours ahead.

As the sea continues to rage against them, Paul chooses to "rest" in the promise of God rather than give way to the terror of the wind and waves threatening their lives.

His choice not only brings peace to his own heart, but gives him opportunity to witness to the power of God and encourage others on board the ship (*Acts 27:36,37*).

PONDER: When difficulties threaten my life, what/who gets my attention? Do I focus on the winds and waves looming overhead or the God Who promised to work all things out for my good? Do I choose to rest in God's Word and allow my heart and mind to be comforted by it? Do I believe God, even when everything is falling apart around me?

PRAYER: Help me <u>love</u> Your word, Lord, and <u>know</u> it so well that in the storms of life, I can say with Paul, *"I believe God. It will be just as He said."*

August 12

Take Time To Smell The Roses

"How amazing are the deeds of the Lord! All who delight in him should ponder them. Everything he does reveals his glory and majesty…" Psalm 111:2,3

For anyone willing to look carefully, God has described Himself thoroughly in everything He has done. God further identifies Himself in countless ways every day through His protection and abundant provision.

This passage presents a challenge to those of us who claim to delight in the Lord: **ponder His deeds… think deeply about everything He does**. To accept that challenge, we must <u>slow</u> <u>down</u> enough to notice.

We can't be satisfied with a casual glance at the sunset or beautiful butterfly. Nor should we be content with fleeting thoughts about God's care in a near-miss accident or the "coincidence" of finding that missing item right after asking the Lord to show us where it was.

God is actively at work around us! Do we really notice? He desires to reveal His glory and majesty. He loves to delight us. Are we amazed?

Is God able to thrill us with His mighty deeds, or do we rush on by, too busy to notice? Or, worse yet, yawn in complacency?

PONDER: When is the last time I slowed down enough to study the beauty of a tiny wildflower? How long since my heart stopped at the sight of a snow-covered peak?

PRAYER: God, does my lack of appreciation grieve Your heart? Open my eyes. Amaze me as I look at Your works, O Lord!

August 13

Let God Decide That!

"He [God] *said to me, 'You are my servant... and you will bring me glory.' I replied, 'But my work seems so useless! I have spent my strength for nothing and to no purpose. Yet I leave it all in the Lord's hand; I will trust God for my reward.'" Isaiah 49:3,4*

Sometimes, we may find ourselves, like Isaiah, questioning whether or not we've made much difference in this world for God.

From our finite perspective, it can look, and feel, like we've fallen woefully short of our goal.

The enemy of our souls loves it when we evaluate our lives by what we can see, hear, or measure with statistics. Though not his only strategy, Satan seeks to discourage us with the lack of "evidence" so we will feel useless and lose heart along the way.

Isaiah spent his strength in the service of the Lord, but didn't seem to have much to "show" for it, at least from his perspective.

Rather than try to measure his success by what "seemed" true to his limited understanding, however, he believed God, who said, *"You will bring me glory,"* and left *"it all in the Lord's hand."*

PONDER: Have I believed the enemy's lies that what I have done for Jesus is wasted or insignificant? Have I allowed Satan to label me a "failure" or "worthless?"

PRAYER: Lord, as I love and serve You, I will trust that little is much when offered to You with a sincere heart.

August 14

God Gets The Blame For Our Mistakes

"The people refused to enter the pleasant land, for they wouldn't believe His [God's] *promise to care for them. Instead, they grumbled in their tents and refused to obey the Lord." Psalm 106:24,25*

The Israelites could have enjoyed the Promised Land 40 years earlier had they just believed God's Word. He had promised to lead them to a land *"flowing with milk and honey." Exodus 3:8*

Hadn't He already proved His power over the Egyptians, made a road through the Red Sea, and promised to subdue all the nations occupying the land of Canaan? They just simply didn't believe Him!

Isn't it typical of us humans to blame God for our self-made predicaments and then throw a "tantrum?" The Israelites had made the bed they must now lie in, yet they grumbled against God as if it was <u>His</u> fault, and refused to obey and honor Him.

PONDER: How many of the difficult circumstances in <u>my</u> life are the result of my own failure to trust and obey God? How often have I wallowed in self-pity, choosing to blame God rather than accept the consequences of my own choices and humbly seek His grace and restoration? Why is it so much easier to grumble and rebel against God than to "backtrack" and seek His forgiveness?

PRAYER: Oh, God, forgive and cleanse the rebellion of my heart. Help me humbly seek You instead of trying to "go it alone." I want to <u>know</u> You better so I can <u>trust</u> You more.

August 15
Walk The Talk!

"Son of man, let all my words sink deep into your own heart first. Listen to them carefully for yourself. Then go to your people..."
Ezekiel 3:10,11

How much easier it is to identify what my neighbor, my spouse, or my coworker needs to hear than to allow the spotlight of God's Word to shine into my <u>own</u> heart, revealing <u>my</u> motives and attitudes, pointing out areas of disobedience or unbelief in <u>my</u> life!

This may be especially true for those responsible for communicating spiritual truths: pastors, evangelists, teachers, parents, and youth leaders. It's much easier to approach God's Word in search of a lesson to be shared than to absorb it as a message to be lived.

Thankfully, even when our study is for the benefit of others, the Holy Spirit can use the truth of Scripture to penetrate and transform our own hearts.

The temptation, however, is to teach and preach truths from God's Word that we've <u>never</u> bothered to live. We figure we'll get around to applying them eventually. The problem is, once we've "preached" that message, there's another to prepare, and another. Oh, well...

Meanwhile, the discrepancy between our words and our actions grows so large our listeners can't "hear" what we say.

PONDER: Am I guilty of applying Scripture to others without first allowing God to build it into my life?

PRAYER: Lord, make me aware of those areas where my "walk" doesn't match my "talk" and do a deep work of transformation in my life.

August 16

What's Behind The Façade?

"...the sins of some people are obvious... But there are others whose sins will not be revealed until later. In the same way, the good deeds of some people are obvious. And the good deeds done in secret will someday come to light." I Timothy 5:24,25

What we "see" when we look at others may or may not be the truth. What they see when they look at us may not be true either. We humans are masters at manipulation and façade, carefully projecting only the images that cast us in the best light.

Our good deeds are far too often designed to draw attention to ourselves, make us look good in the eyes of others. Bad habits and attitudes, secret sins and thoughts, are stealthily hidden, so as not to impact the reputation we've striven so hard to create.

How is it we've forgotten that God Himself sees and knows <u>everything</u>? He knows our thoughts, before we think them. He sees the <u>motives</u> of our hearts and recognizes the <u>attitudes</u> beneath our "kind" words and "good" deeds. And He promises to expose them someday for everyone to see, if not in this life, at the Judgment.

<u>Only</u> those covered by the cleansing blood of Christ, clothed in His righteousness alone, will stand in confidence on <u>that</u> day.

PONDER: What am I shielding from the view of others? Myself? God?

PRAYER: Lord, I'm tired of hiding the real me! Help me bring everything into the light of Your Holy Presence.

August 17
God Must Need My Help

"The son of the slave wife was born in a human attempt to bring about the fulfillment of God's promise. But the son of the freeborn wife was born as God's own fulfillment of his promise." Galatians 4:23

God made a promise to Abraham that he would have a son. Many years came and went. Still, no baby. Since God was obviously "unable" to make good on His promise, Sarah and Abraham decided to "help" God. The resulting grief is well documented in Scripture and plays itself out in modern-day conflicts in the Middle East.

In this passage, Paul is illustrating the human tendency to attempt, in our own strength, what only God can do. God declares that He has made us who know Christ to become *"the righteousness of God in him* [Christ Jesus].*"* (II Corinthians 5:21 NIV)

Sadly, however, we find it difficult to trust what God says about us. Instead of <u>resting</u> in His provision through Christ, we <u>strive</u> to create a righteousness of our own.

PONDER: Why is it so difficult for me to admit I cannot just "do it myself?" Why do I find it so difficult to "trust" what God says about me? Do I even **<u>know</u>** what God says about me? Am I willing to search the Scriptures to find out?

PRAYER: Oh, God, I acknowledge that my attempts at righteousness will never gain the relationship with You I long for. I choose now to exchange all my striving for the "**<u>rest</u>**" that comes in <u>trusting</u> You.

August 18

Peace Is Found Only One Place!

"I am leaving you with a gift—peace of mind and heart. And the peace I give is a gift the world cannot give." John 14:27

It's what we're all searching for—peace of mind and heart—but it seems the more we pursue it, the more elusive it becomes. When we finally obtain whatever we thought would produce this peace, we discover we must continue looking elsewhere.

That's because the peace Jesus speaks of is <u>only</u> found in right relationship with God. Jesus said there's only <u>one</u> way into that relationship. The Apostle Peter agrees in *Acts 4:12: "There is salvation in no one else! God has given no other name under Heaven by which we must be saved."*

If there'd been another way, God would have used it. To take on human flesh with all its limitations, to be condemned for sins He'd never committed (your sins and mine), to suffer and die a cruel death in our place so we might be forgiven—this would obviously not have been God's <u>first</u> plan of attack had there been **<u>ANY OTHER WAY</u>**!

Only when we finally humble ourselves enough to accept the fact that Christ is the only one who can meet the deepest longings of our hearts will we experience the PEACE for which we seek.

PONDER: What things have I been pursuing in my effort to find peace? What keeps me from simply trusting the loving heart of God?

PRAYER: I'm tired, Lord! My way hasn't worked. You alone can give me the peace I seek!

August 19
Is Jesus Really God?

"Jesus... said to Thomas... 'Don't be faithless any longer. Believe!' 'My Lord and my God!' Thomas exclaimed. Then Jesus told him, 'You believe because you have seen me. Blessed are those who believe without seeing me.'" John 20:28,29

Believing didn't come easy for Thomas. In this passage, Jesus first encourages Thomas to <u>choose</u> to believe, in spite of his doubts. Then moments later, Jesus praises Thomas for his belief. So what changed?

Between Christ's two statements, Thomas acknowledges Christ's Resurrection by declaring Jesus to be, *"My Lord and My God!"* Amazingly, Jesus not only **<u>allows</u>** Thomas to declare Him God, but actually **<u>blesses</u>** him for it.

Jesus is well aware that Scripture forbids the worship of anyone or anything but God. When tempted by Satan in *Matthew 4:10*, Jesus stated unequivocally, *"You must worship the Lord your God and serve only him."*

Knowing what Scripture demands, why would Jesus allow Thomas to worship Him as God? **Because He <u>is</u> God!** Jesus had encouraged Thomas to believe it, and now, Jesus praises him for drawing that conclusion.

You and I are those Jesus referred to, who must <u>choose</u> to believe without seeing what Thomas saw. That requires faith. But even faith is a gift of God *(Ephesians 2:8)*.

PONDER: Am I, like Thomas, stumbling over what I cannot fully comprehend with my finite mind? Will I choose to trust Jesus's words rather than my own understanding?

PRAYER: Lord Jesus, I acknowledge You, by faith, as my Lord and my God!

August 20
Looking Back To Move Forward

"Those who are wise will take all this to heart; they will see in our history the faithful love of the Lord." Psalm 107:43

The Psalmist has just recounted four stories of different people, each having found himself in a desperate, life-and-death situation, crying out to the Lord for His mercy and deliverance. Whether the calamity is self-inflicted by rebellion or foolishness, or caused by factors completely outside their control, God dramatically intervenes and, in all four illustrations, brings peace, health, and freedom!

In our lives, when God miraculously comes through for us, we feel certain the memory is forever etched in our minds. Yet, amazingly, the very next time we're in a tight place, we find ourselves, once again, anxious and fearful, grasping for some means of regaining control.

It's not that we've forgotten God's miracles of the past, but present circumstances have a way of filling our vision and commandeering our thoughts. We need the Psalmist's reminder that it's a wise person who <u>deliberately</u> chooses to look back and see in his/her history the faithfulness of God, focusing on all the ways His love and care and power have been demonstrated over and over in our lives.

PONDER: What are the specific times and ways God has protected and helped me in my history? Am I allowing His past faithfulness to inform my response to these present circumstances?

PRAYER: Forgive me, Lord, for not taking the time to remember, so I can trust You more.

August 21

You Can't Afford To Get This Wrong!

"God Himself will be with them. He will remove all their sorrows, and there will be no more death or sorrow or crying or pain. For the old world and its evils are gone forever." Revelation 21:3b,4

God is giving us a peek at Heaven. Sound good? It does to me, especially after saying "goodbye" to a dear friend, watching her slip into eternity.

Scripture answers questions that plague our hearts in those moments. Where is she? Will I ever see her again? Is "dead" just dead, or is she still alive somewhere?

For the one who has been redeemed by Christ's atoning sacrifice on Calvary, God's words offer unbelievable assurance and confidence. For those who don't know Him, <u>no</u> such comfort arises in their hearts.

The Bible is clear: *"only those whose names are written in the Lamb's Book of Life" (v. 27)* may enter this heavenly home. Everyone else is cast into the lake of fire forever and ever *(Rev. 20:15)*, not because God wills it, but because they've rejected the **<u>only</u>** way to escape it, which He Himself provided at immense cost.

Romans 3:23; 6:23; John 3:16; 14:6; 1:12; I John 5:11,12.

PONDER: Am I ready to die? Does that thought comfort or terrify me? What keeps me from trusting God's provision for my rescue from the lake of fire?

PRAYER: God, You know me completely. You know the truth about my relationship with You. Someday my heart will be exposed. Help me get right with You **<u>now</u>**!

August 22

The Waiting Game

"Until the time came to fulfill his dreams, the Lord tested Joseph's character. Then Pharaoh sent for him and set him free." Psalm 105:19,20

God had given Joseph a couple of dreams as a young man, which he understood to mean that he would be a great ruler someday and that even his own family would recognize and submit to his authority. Yet the road to the fulfillment of those dreams was fraught with misunderstanding, abandonment, isolation, betrayal, false accusations, slavery, and even imprisonment.

It's obvious to us in Scripture that God had a plan, and Joseph was right smack in the middle of it. But Joseph had no such perspective, though he remained loyal to his God through it all, serving Him faithfully during his years as Potiphar's slave and, later, in an Egyptian prison.

He could not have known his character was being tested, that a grand "prize" awaited him. What if Joseph had chosen bitterness and retaliation? How might that have affected the future of God's chosen people, through whom the promised Messiah was to come?

PONDER: When faced with circumstances similar to Joseph's, what is my response? Do I wait quietly and trust confidently in God, Who promises to work all things out for my good and His glory? Or do bitter, anxious thoughts steal my peace and dictate my choices?

PRAYER: Oh, God, help me quiet my heart and trust Your purposes, even when I can't see evidence of them in my present circumstances.

August 23

I Have A Right To Be Happy, Don't I?

"...We must not just please ourselves...Christ didn't live to please himself." Romans 15:1,3

We live in a "me" culture. From the time we are born, everything revolves around our personal pleasure, comfort, longings, and desires. We don't need any encouragement to be self-absorbed. It comes naturally and shows itself at a very young age.

Unfortunately, even well-intentioned parents can inadvertently contribute to this attitude by centering their family life around their children rather than training children to consider the needs of the family and others. That lifestyle reinforces the notion that it's "all about me."

Media blasts also play a defining role: *"You need this! You want this! You deserve this! You should have this! You won't be happy without this!"*

We can even find it in religion. God's love is often misconstrued to imply that His ultimate goal for me is that I "be happy," that He would never ask me to give up something I really want or do anything that would make me uncomfortable.

However, to be a Christ-follower, Jesus declared I must deny myself and take up my cross. Denying self means saying "no" to the selfish part of me! The cross, for Jesus, held only one meaning: DEATH... to self-centeredness, self-absorption, self-serving attitudes, words and actions.

PONDER: Who is the center of my "world?"

PRAYER: Lord, help me escape the enemy's trap. Help me see that only in "crucifying" the selfish part of me can I ever be truly "free." Help me die to self.

August 24

Impulsive Choices Can Devastate A Life

"Watch out for the Esau syndrome; trading away God's lifelong gift in order to satisfy a short-term appetite. You well know how Esau later regretted that impulsive act..." Hebrews 12:16,17, The Message

One impulsive act, one fleeting moment in time that may seem like the most important of all moments, and we can unalterably turn the course of our lives in ways we will forever regret.

Yielding to the urgent impulses of our bodies and/or emotions will lead us down that trail of tears. Learning to view what I'm experiencing with perspective—God's eternal perspective—will protect me from such tragic foolishness.

Sadness, heartache, pain, disappointment, feelings of inadequacy, loneliness... these are all part of the human condition and impact each of us. For some, these feelings are more fleeting than for others, but in the moment, they can consume us to the point that we are tempted to yield to their demands to give up and give in.

God has promised that though *"weeping may last through the night... joy comes with the morning." (Psalm 30:5)* For some, "morning" may not happen until Jesus takes us home to be with Him, but it will come, and nothing in this world is worth trading for that glorious hope!

PONDER: Have I lost God's perspective? Am I really willing to trade the assurances of my God for the possibility of temporary relief?

PRAYER: Lord God, open my eyes. Help me see what You perceive and choose what You know is best.

August 25

If It Doesn't Fit...!

"'...I can't go in these...' he protested... 'I'm not used to them.' So David took them off again. He picked up five smooth stones from a stream and... started across the valley to fight the Philistine." I Samuel 17:39,40

Saul talks David into wearing the king's armor. It doesn't fit, and David's not used to it. How differently would this story have ended, had David headed into battle in someone else's gear?

Each of us thinks, *"If I could just be like 'so and so,'* then *I could serve God."* But no matter how effectively God has equipped someone else for <u>their</u> encounters, His plan for **YOU** requires that you be **exactly** the way He made <u>you</u>.

The Lord specifically designed you, and every unchangeable aspect of your life, to fit the mission He has in mind for **YOU** and no other.

The "giants" in your life will best be conquered as you accept who you are and trust God. Wisely and lovingly, He has equipped you with everything He knows will work best in fulfilling the plan He has for **your** life.

PONDER: What unchangeable aspect of my life do I fight against? Dare I thank God for His purposes in making me as He did? How differently would my story turn out, if I could simply accept myself and trust God?

PRAYER: Lord, I accept _____ and give this, and every part of myself, to You for Your Glory!

August 26

Is It All Just A Show?

"He noticed a fig tree in full leaf... but there were only leaves..."
Mark 11:13

It seems a bit strange that Jesus would curse a fig tree so early in the growing season for not bearing fruit. But understand that a fig tree in full leaf means one thing: fruit is now only weeks away!

Along with leaves, fig trees also grow little green knobs, which are often eaten by hungry passersby. Those little knobs, referred to by the Arabs as "taqsh," eventually fall off, giving way to figs. A leafy tree with no taqsh will <u>not</u> bear fruit that season.

How often do we look just like that fig tree? We put on a good "show." We are careful to do and say all the things we believe Christians should do. As a result, our "leaves" are in full bloom, but, when Jesus comes by, looking for evidence of the fruit of His Spirit in us, it's sadly lacking.

It must break His heart because hungry sojourners will not find in us what they had hoped would satisfy their deep soul hunger.

PONDER: How about my life? Is it mostly "show," or is the Fruit of the Spirit increasingly evidenced in all I do, say, and think?

PONDER: Lord, the temptation to care more about what things <u>look</u> like than how they really <u>are</u> is so great. Help me look honestly and acknowledge what really is! And may the genuine fruit of Your Spirit show forth in my life.

August 27

If We Won't, Who Will?

"...You must influence them; do not let them influence you!" Jeremiah 15:19b

These words were spoken to Jeremiah in the midst of intense suffering and discouragement. Few in our culture are called to endure rejection and abuse like Jeremiah faced. But the admonition has never been more urgent: we must be the <u>influencers</u>, not the influenced.

People are messed up, wounded, and trapped in sinful habits and ideas. Jesus <u>weeps</u> for them and looks to <u>us</u>, His Body, to go and create friendships, to love them and impact their lives.

It's easier, of course, to spend time with those whose lifestyles, moral and political convictions, and faith are compatible with ours. Christian brothers and sisters are typically more gracious and certainly less offensive.

We don't know "what to say" or "how to respond" to the opinions, language, and moral choices of unbelievers.

Perhaps we're also afraid we will be influenced by them, so we hide among Christian friends and family, hoping our fleeting appearances at work or school will satisfy God's admonition to be salt/light/sweet perfume among unbelievers.

PONDER: If I am to fulfill this command of God, it will require <u>intentionally</u> seeking to build relationships with those who don't share my faith, for the express purpose of influencing their lives for Jesus. It will also require an intimate, moment-by-moment relationship with Christ, in which I allow <u>Him</u> to inform and shape my responses to each individual person, in each unique situation.

PRAYER: Lord, make this the intense desire of my heart!

August 28
Generosity—God's Trademark!

"…Give as freely as you have received!" Matthew 10:8b

What have I received? How have I received it? The answers to these questions are to provide the motivation for a life of generosity. If I see myself as a self-made person…

- That I've worked <u>hard</u> to be good and refused to indulge myself
- That I've <u>earned my money and possessions</u>, saved diligently, and lived frugally
- That I've trained and disciplined myself to cultivate my talents

…then I will have little motivation for generosity toward others. They should have to work hard, bite the bullet, toe the line, buck up, and shape up, just like I did!

On the other hand, if I comprehend…

- That *"Every good and perfect gift is from above…" (James 1:17,NIV)*
- That out of *"his abundance we have all received one gracious blessing after another…" (John 1:16)*
- That *"in him we live and move and have our being…" (Acts 17:28,NIV)…*<u>generosity</u> will increasingly become a way of life, whether with money, possessions, time, energy, forgiveness… whatever!

When we comprehend that **nothing**—absolutely **nothing**, including the very breath we breathe—would be ours apart from the mercy of God, grace and generosity will flow from our hearts. We'll embrace

God's instruction in *Ephesians 4:32*, *"...be kind to each other, tenderhearted, forgiving one another, just as God through Christ has forgiven you."*

PONDER: Would those closest to me describe me as gracious? Generous? Would God?

PRAYER: Lord, let me see my life from **Your** perspective and may that transform the motivation of my heart.

August 29

Come Quickly, Lord Jesus!

"He will come again, not to deal with our sins, but to bring salvation to all who are eagerly waiting for him." Hebrews 9:28b

Jesus Christ has already dealt with sin, once and for all. *"...once for all time, he has appeared... to remove sin by his own death as a sacrifice." (Hebrews 9:26)*

It is done! Finished! That was His victory cry on the cross, knowing He'd done <u>all</u> that could be accomplished, **all** that was necessary, to purchase salvation for the children of earth. God's wrath against sin was satisfied for any who would trust Him enough to draw near.

The next step was to entrust this Good News to His newly established Church, so every human being on earth would have opportunity to accept the Father's invitation: *"Come... drink freely from the water of life." Revelation 22:17b*

All who receive this glorious news, who embrace what Christ did for us on the Cross of Calvary, fall in love with the Savior. Our hearts long to know Him better, to see Him in all His glorious splendor.

And we will... <u>someday</u>!

Jesus left absolutely no doubt that He is coming back one of these days to take us to be forever with Him.

PONDER: Do I eagerly wait for that day? Does the thought of Christ's return bring **joy** and **<u>hope</u>** to my heart or anxiety and dread?

PRAYER: Lord, wean my heart from this earth and help me long for Your return.

August 30

Could Calamity Be My Friend?

"But when you had eaten and were satisfied, you became proud and forgot me." Hosea 13:6

It's a paradox of human nature. We are very God-conscious and aware of our frailty when we are in trouble, under siege, in ill health, or otherwise endangered. Once our calamity has passed, however, we easily resume life as if we are once again masters of our own fate.

How it must grieve our Lord when He supplies us with good things *("every good gift comes from above," John 1:17)*, and we let those things usurp the place of the One who gave them.

To allow us to continue down such a road would ultimately lead to our eternal destruction, a choice which would delight Satan and his angels immensely, because it would certainly break the heart of God Who longs to give us eternal life.

Sadly, the one thing that might rekindle a consciousness of our desperate need for God would be getting back in touch with our own sense of helplessness and the fragile nature of life itself. Wouldn't God be merciful, therefore, to allow into our lives any trials, sorrows, and heartaches which would serve to bring about such an awareness?

PONDER: Could the difficulties I am facing in this moment be God's "mercy" to me, calling my heart back to the only One who can ultimately satisfy my soul's desperate longings?

PRAYER: Lord Jesus, forgive me for allowing Your "gifts" to become more important than Your "Self."

August 31
Like A Marble Fudge Cake

"I'm not asking you to take them out of the world, but to keep them safe from the evil one. They do not belong to this world... Make them holy... teach them your word, which is truth... I am sending them into the world." John 17:15-18

Ever eat a slice of marble cake? My apologies ahead of time to those of you who love plain, white cake, but in a marble cake, there's just too much white and not enough chocolate for my taste. When I eat marble cake, I arrange each morsel to include a bit of fudgy goodness.

That makes every bite taste so much better!

How do bakers keep the chocolate **<u>separate</u>** from the white cake? They pour it **<u>into</u>** the batter, but don't mix it up. To make sure the chocolate retains its flavor and color, they **<u>swirl</u>** it gently. Thus, it becomes **<u>part</u>** of the cake, yet very separate, well-defined, and delectable. For chocolate lovers like me, it's the **<u>BEST</u>** part.

Jesus desires that we be "separate"—but not "separated"—from the world. He wants us **<u>IN</u>** the cake, but still deliciously distinct.

PONDER: Have I allowed God to weave my life into and throughout the world around me? Could anyone whose heart longs for "chocolatey delight" get close enough to my life to "taste and see" for themselves that the Lord is good?

PRAYER: Lord, show me what being in, but not of, the world should look like in my life.

September

September 1

Where Does My Help Come From?

"…Only in returning to me, and resting in me will you be saved. In quietness and confidence is your strength. But you would have none of it. You said, 'No, we will get our help from…'" Isaiah 30:15,16a

We are so prone to seek help, wisdom, peace, protection, and security from anyone or anything promising to provide it. And though what they offer may bring us a temporary sense of relief, true peace, lasting satisfaction, and authentic healing evade us. We find ourselves still full of uncertainly and anxiety about our lives, our families, our health, our nation, and our world.

Our desperate, frantic search for <u>any</u> source of comfort and security apart from <u>God</u> should signal "alarm" that our hearts have abandoned Him as our ultimate Provider and Source of Life.

We know we <u>should</u> trust the Lord. We <u>say</u> that we do. But our inner turmoil and anxiety betray our words. Many of us are <u>not</u> "at rest."

We don't have any idea what "resting" in God would look or feel like because we've seldom, if ever, experienced that kind of peace.

True peace comes only in the quiet, confident assurance that my God is <u>big</u> enough, <u>strong</u> enough, and <u>wise</u> enough to handle <u>everything</u> without my help—that I <u>can</u> trust Him, and I <u>choose</u> to!

PONDER: Have my actions or reactions said to God, *"No, I will get my help from…?"*

PRAYER: Lord, I acknowledge and seek You **alone** as the **Source** of all I need!

September 2
What Was God Thinking?

"Then he [God] turned the Egyptians against the Israelites…"
Psalm 105:25

At first glance, we might be shocked at this verse. Why would God purposely turn anyone against His chosen people?

God had made a promise to the Israelites: a land flowing with milk and honey. The Egyptian side-trip was only a means of preserving them during a time of famine and distress, **NOT** their final destination. Sadly, Israel had "settled in" and become comfortable with less than God wanted for them.

They had no motivation to pursue God's promised land.

So, God provided the motivation. When the Egyptians rose up against them, making their lives unbearable, the people cried out to God for help. Only then could God deliver on His promise.

Too often, we associate ease and prosperity with God's blessing and troubles and trials with its absence. That's because we see through a distorted lens. We are not capable of grasping what God knows. We cannot fathom His ways.

What if, as in the case of Egypt's oppression, God chooses to use our trials as a means of unsettling and motivating us to seek Him and His purposes over our own desires?

PONDER: How do I view trial? Do I fight against it, or am I willing to ask God to use it in my life, opening my heart to whatever He is doing?

PRAYER: Lord, keep me intent on seeking after You and Your designs for my life. Don't allow me to settle into complacency.

September 3

Light And Darkness

"If the light you think you have is really darkness, how deep that darkness will be!" Matthew 6:23b

The folks Jesus is addressing somehow really <u>think</u> they have the light. Jesus says otherwise... that what appears to <u>them</u> as "light" is actually darkness. How is it possible to be so deceived?

"Darkness" is where sin thrives and Satan resides. However, according to *II Corinthians 11:14*, Satan is able to transform himself into *"an angel of light."* He hides his true nature in a nefarious ruse to entrap us, cleverly disguising lies to look like truth and cloaking his dark agenda in what often appears to be spiritual enlightenment.

Our greatest defense against Satan's deception is to **know** the Word of God. *"Your word,"* declares the Psalmist, *"is a lamp for my feet and a light for my path." (Psalm 119:105)* Any departure from the Truth of Scripture opens us to Satan's deception.

God says there's only one source of true light. According to *John 1:9,14,* the true light is the *"Word"* that *"became flesh and lived here on earth among us."*

"I am the light of the world," Jesus declared. *"If you follow me, you won't be stumbling through the darkness because you will have the light that leads to life." John 8:12*

PONDER: Am I trying to live in "light" while rejecting any part of God's revelation of Himself through Christ?

PRAYER: I turn my eyes on You, Lord Jesus, the True Light. Open my heart to discern the enemy's lies.

September 4

Grasp Them Loosely

"Those who use the things of the world should not become attached to them. For this world as we know it will soon pass away. I want you to be free from the concerns of this life." I Corinthians 7:31,32a

Paul is talking here about Christians who become "absorbed" with the things of this world. Not becoming "attached" to our possessions is one of the great challenges we face as believers.

In our culture, we have an abundance of things to "use." A subtle, but unmistakable message comes through loud and clear: the more things you have, the more significant you are! Unfortunately, even some Christ-followers buy into that philosophy, allowing their hearts to embrace this world's toys and pleasures.

PONDER: How in love am I with the "things" in my life? How much of my time and attention are consumed with obtaining them? Maintaining them? Protecting them?

Upon waking, what captures my first thoughts? In my leisure moments, what draws my attention most often?

Would I be willing to give or loan my "things" to someone, if the need arose? If prompted by God, could I lay them down and walk away? Am I really *"free from the concerns of this life?"* Does it make any difference to me that *"…this world as we know it will soon pass away?"*

PRAYER: Lord, help me hold all the "things" of this life with a loose grasp, knowing that only what lasts for eternity is worthy of my affection.

September 5

Run Toward Your Giant

"David replied to the Philistine giant Goliath, '…Today <u>the Lord will conquer you</u>, and <u>I will kill you</u>… and the whole world will know that there is a God in Israel!'" (I Samuel 17:45a) (emphasis mine)

What would give a ruddy teenager the courage to face a nine-foot giant, armed only with a shepherd's staff and sling? The power of God, that's what! David would <u>kill</u> the giant, but <u>only</u> because the <u>Lord</u> would <u>conquer</u> him *FIRST!*

How did David know what God would do? At some point in his past, he had <u>chosen</u> to <u>trust</u> God, and God had not let him down. Each time David trusted and God rescued, David's confidence in God grew to match the next challenge.

PONDER: What are the "giants" in my life? Temptations? Problems? Obstacles? Where am I looking for answers, strength, wisdom? Do I cower in the face of my "giants" like the Israelites or run to meet them as David did *(I Samuel 17:48)*? When will I begin putting my confidence in the Lord of Heaven's Armies to fight my battles?

PRAYER: O God, I recognize with the Psalmist that *"…all human help is useless" (Psalm 108:12),* but in <u>You</u>, *"I can do all things…!" Philippians 4:13*

Starting today, I <u>choose</u> to believe that <u>You will conquer my personal "giants" for me</u>, so that I can "slay" them in Your Name and in Your power. I will <u>trust</u> You. I rise now and run to meet them in Your strength.

September 6

Who Loves You More?

"'For I know the plans I have for you,' says the Lord. 'They are plans for good and not for disaster, to give you a future and a hope.'" Jeremiah 29:11

God <u>loves</u> you, whether you love Him back or not. Whether or not you want Him, God passionately desires <u>you</u>! He longs to bless and heal and prosper each of us, but so often, our attitudes and choices make it impossible for us to experience the good things He has in mind.

Throughout Scripture, God pleads, *"Be reconciled to God!"(II Corinthians 5:20) "Seek the Kingdom of God above all else and… he will give you everything you need." (Matthew 6:33) "Acknowledge him,"* in all your ways, so He can direct your paths. *(Proverbs 3:5,6) "Draw near to God, and He will draw near to you." (James 4:8a)*

Jesus weeps over <u>us</u> as He did over Jerusalem. *"How often I have wanted to gather… [you]… as a hen protects her chicks… but you wouldn't let me." Matthew 23:37*

Can it be that we don't <u>really</u> trust His love? We're suspicious of His intentions?

Leaning on our <u>own</u> understanding, we set out on our <u>own</u> paths, to create our <u>own</u> happiness, with our <u>own</u> resources, eventually ending up in a predicament of our <u>own</u> making. **Then** we rail at God, blaming Him for not being good, not helping us, not providing like He promised.

PONDER: Do I trust God's love for me?

PRAYER: Oh, Lord, there is no one, including myself, with better intentions for me than You. Help me live and rest in that awareness!

September 7
Can "Bad" Ever Be "Good?"

"They were severely beaten... thrown into prison... next morning, the city officials... came to the jail and apologized... and begged them to leave..." Acts 16:23,35,39

Paul and Silas, in response to a vision, rerouted their journey and ended up in Philippi, where within days, they were stripped, severely beaten, and imprisoned. In spite of their injuries, however, *"around midnight, they were praying and singing hymns to God…" (v. 25)*

Rather than focus on their pain and loss, the disciples sought to bring glory to Christ. Suddenly, an earthquake shook their shackles loose and opened the prison door.

Terrified and believing his prisoners had escaped, the jailer drew his sword to end his life. Little did he know the God of the Universe had just gone to great lengths to make sure he would be introduced to the Savior, Jesus Christ. That very night, he and his whole family believed the Word and were baptized.

Curiously, the next morning, Paul and Silas were on their way again. Hmmmm…

PONDER: Is it possible that one of <u>my</u> life's difficulties might put me strategically in the path of someone seeking the Savior, someone who, apart from that specific encounter, might never know His love and forgiveness? Where is my focus in the midst of the difficult things in my life? Would I be able to recognize if God was planning to work a miracle through one of <u>my</u> trials?

PRAYER: Lord, help me keep my heart open to see how You might use my life situations for Your Glory.

September 8

I'd Rather Do It Myself

"What if the Lord had not been on our side?" Psalm 124:1a; "God opposes the proud, but favors the humble. So humble yourselves before God." James 4:6b,7a

I can't imagine trying to do life without God on my side. Yet, by refusing to acknowledge my helpless spiritual condition apart from Him, I set myself in direct opposition to God.

Why is it that we humans have such difficulty admitting we cannot "do it ourselves?" It galls us to have to own up to inadequacy in any area of our lives! We like to think that if we just apply a little more effort, we can somehow qualify for God's stamp of approval.

The problem? We've lost sight of what God is <u>really</u> like—His <u>holiness</u>, His <u>purity</u>. We've been comparing ourselves with each other. We've never seen how we stack up in <u>His</u> eyes, how we compare to <u>His</u> holy standard of perfection.

One glimpse of our own hearts in the presence of Almighty God and we would find ourselves <u>begging</u> for mercy!

PONDER: Am I willing to look at myself through God's eyes? Am I willing to admit I can't do this without Him?

PRAYER: Expose my heart in Your presence, Lord. Help me grasp what <u>You</u> have always perceived. Make me so desperate for deep friendship with You that I will let go of my need to be in control, to be "adequate," to depend on myself. Help me see how "lost" I am without You!

September 9
A Deadly Poison

"If you claim to be religious, but don't control your tongue, you are fooling yourself, and your religion is worthless." James 1:26

What power lies in the tongue! With the very same tongue, we can bestow blessing, encouragement, and hope. Or we can blister, humiliate, wound, and slander.

Scripture makes it clear that the tongue will never be tamed by sheer willpower alone. That's because what comes out of the mouth erupts from the heart. Censuring and disciplining our words is not the answer, because it's the content of our hearts—the stuff that simmers below the surface—that determines what escapes by way of the tongue.

Suppose a cup of coffee I'm holding is jarred. It won't be milk or lemonade that splashes into my lap. In the same way, angry outbursts, biting words, gossip, foul language, and slander escape my lips because those are the attitudes already present in my heart.

Without a change of heart, there'll be no real control of my tongue. Though we humans are often good at reforming certain "behaviors," we simply cannot change the motivations of our hearts. That's **God's** job and requires **God's** power!

PONDER: Does my tongue produce only what honors God and blesses others? Or is it sometimes used in ways that hurt, manipulate, and destroy those around me?

PRAYER: Lord Jesus, help me acknowledge and "own" the truth about how I use my tongue. Help me see that only You have the power to change it.

September 10

Advertising God's Goodness

"…Joyful indeed are those whose God is the Lord." Psalm 144:15b

What a beautiful advertisement for the God of the Bible! A joyful countenance is a rare quality these days, and anyone possessing it will almost certainly attract attention.

What does a joyful heart tell others about the God we serve? It declares He is good. It affirms His loving kindness. It telegraphs His abundant provision for those who put their trust in Him.

Too many people I know who claim the name of Christ are not joyful, but rather stressed, worried, and fearful. Some are even bitter and angry. What does that imply about God?

Remember that joy and happiness are not synonymous. Joy reflects an inner confidence, the assurance of knowing who God is and how I am related to Him. It finds its source in the Lord, not in circumstances, and thus becomes an anchor to the soul that puts its trust in Him.

No unhappy or tragic situation in one's life can alter that assurance, so joy can shine, even through tear-filled eyes.

PONDER: What does <u>my</u> countenance, <u>my</u> attitude, tell others about God? What does it divulge about my relationship with God, my trust and confidence in His goodness, His love, His provision?

PRAYER: Oh, Lord, forgive me for the times I've ever given people the impression that You cannot be trusted. Help me choose to rejoice in every circumstance and thus show others, through my life, that You are, indeed, good and trustworthy.

September 11
Whom Shall I Fear?

"Make the Lord of Heaven's Armies holy in your life. He is the one you should fear. He is the one who should make you tremble. He will keep you safe." Isaiah 8:13,14a

With rumors of renewed terrorist plots and activity swirling around the anniversary of 9/11, fear and trembling niggle at the minds of even the most stouthearted. Suicide bombers, bolstered with promises of heavenly bliss and no compunction against killing innocent civilians, have managed to cripple us with fear even when they're not actively striking at targets.

It's very natural for us to fear those who can destroy our bodies. However, Jesus said there is **One**—the Lord God, Almighty—Who has the power to destroy <u>both</u> body <u>and</u> soul in everlasting Hell (*Matthew 10:28*), a far worse fate than mere physical death.

Thankfully, this One Who has the power to destroy us is the very same God Who loved us so much He gave His one and only Son Jesus to die for our sins.

PONDER: Do I fear God's condemnation? Have I received reconciliation through Christ's atonement?

PRAYER: Thank You for making a way, through Jesus, for me to be welcomed as Your beloved child instead of cowering in fear of your wrath against sin.

September 12

God Says It Must Go!

"…You are growing old and much land remains to be conquered… the following area has not yet been conquered…" Joshua 13:1b,4

In chapter 10, Joshua and the Israelites completed a conquest of *"the hill country, the Negev, the western foothills and the mountain slopes."* They were victorious, for *"the Lord… was fighting for his people" (v. 40,42)*. Afterwards, they returned to camp.

Now, sometime later, God points out <u>new</u> areas, not yet under their control. God asks them to do battle <u>again</u>, and He promises to *"…drive these people out of the land ahead of the Israelites…" (13:6)*

This is so like our own lives. Initially, we "attack" certain un-Christlike areas with great enthusiasm, experiencing God's miraculous victory. But there remain pockets of resistance we are inclined to tolerate because they're not as noticeable or offensive to our gaze or, perhaps, because we've become fond of, or accustomed to, their presence. We coddle and indulge, rather than destroy, them. God's words to Israel are for us!

PONDER: Is there anything in my life God has clearly called "enemy" that I've not yet yielded to His ruthless, cleansing power? Will I agree with God that it must go, then trust and obey His instructions as to its demise?

PRAYER: Dear Lord, some things in me die hard. I choose now to deal with them mercilessly, and, in Your Spirit's power. Help me walk into the freedom and victory You purchased and secured for me when You died and rose triumphantly over sin and the grave.

September 13
But I'm A ~~Good~~ Person!

"Then Jesus told this story to some who had great confidence in their own righteousness and scorned everyone else..." Luke 18:9

Jesus told of two men, one very religious, the other a great sinner. The religious man, a Pharisee, was well respected by church leaders and careful to do everything required in the Scriptures, not allowing anything in his life that might be misconstrued by others as evil. He felt pretty confident as he stood to pray.

The sinful man had broken so many commandments, and done it so openly, he didn't dare show his face in church. But his sin had become too heavy to bear. Condemnation within screamed so loudly he couldn't hear anything else. Finally, he made his way to the one place he thought he might find mercy and grace.

Both men prayed, and to the same God. But only one went home in right relationship with Him.

Great confidence in his own righteousness not only kept the Pharisee from the brokenness and humility necessary to encounter God, but also caused him to look with disdain on others.

PONDER: Is trusting in my own righteousness keeping me from recognizing how utterly lost I am apart from God's mercy? What is my attitude toward those who've messed up royally in life? Do I offer grace as freely as I have received it?

PRAY: Oh, Lord, be merciful to me, for I truly am a sinner! Without Your grace, I am hopelessly and eternally lost.

September 14

Why Does God Make It So Hard?

"As soon as their feet touch the water, the flow of water will be cut off upstream, and the river will stand up like a wall." Joshua 3:13

The Children of Israel are ready to cross the Jordan River into the Promised Land. It is harvest season, and the Jordan is flooding its banks, a frightening picture for anyone who's ever experienced the devastation of a raging river.

No doubt the Israelites remember 40 years earlier, when they'd waited <u>all night</u> in *<u>terror of the Egyptians</u>*, with only a dark cloud between them, as God blew a strong, east wind over the Red Sea, creating a dry path on which to cross.

This time, there is no east wind. God says to step right into the fast-moving water! And they're supposed to believe it will suddenly quit flowing! Why does God always make it so hard?!

PONDER: Could it be God wants my <u>trust</u> more than anything? If I <u>really</u> believe God can, and will, do whatever He says, that God is good, His plans are good, and He always knows what's best… if I am <u>truly</u> convinced He loves me and would never do anything to harm me… why would I struggle with trusting Him with <u>*anything*</u> He asks of me?

PRAYER: Lord, You said even faith is a gift of God. Please give me more faith. But help me never forget what Jesus said: even a <u>*tiny*</u> bit of faith in a <u>*great big God*</u> is more than enough!

September 15

Who Might Be Listening?

"Around midnight Paul and Silas were praying and singing hymns to God, and the other prisoners were listening." Acts 16:25

The apostles have just been beaten severely and thrown into prison. Their crime? Casting a demon out of a slave girl. It just so happens that the girl is no longer useful for the profiteering her masters have enjoyed at her expense. Her owners stir up a mob, the authorities get involved, and the rest is history.

It's midnight. Paul and Silas, bloodied by their beatings, are in the inner dungeon, their feet clamped in stocks. And they begin to sing!

Scripture tells us that the other prisoners listened. I'm sure they'd never heard singing in prison before, at least not songs of praise to God, and they found themselves irresistibly drawn to this worship music sung by two men who had no earthly reason whatsoever to sing. We aren't told, but my hunch is that God used those songs to draw many of society's vilest offenders to Himself that night.

No doubt the jailer heard as well because, in the following verses, we learn that he and his entire family became Christ-followers.

PONDER: Who's listening or watching me? What do they hear? Praise and worship? Confidence in God to care for my needs and work things out for good? Or complaint, bitterness, and self-pity?

PRAYER: *"May the words of my mouth and the meditation of my heart be pleasing in Your sight, O Lord, my Rock and my Redeemer." Psalm 19:14*

September 16

Such Foolishness!

"...Dagon had fallen with his face to the ground in front of the Ark of the Lord! So they took Dagon and put him in his place again. But the next morning, the same thing happened..." I Samuel 5:3,4

The Philistines had captured the Ark of God and placed it in the temple of their "god" Dagon. Next morning, they came into the temple to find their "god" prostrate before the Ark of God's Presence.

So, they picked up Dagon and put him back on his feet, only to have the same thing happen again. This time, Dagon lost his head and his hands.

The Philistines finally realized they couldn't keep the Ark because everywhere they put it, disturbing things took place. So, they finally sent it "home" to the Israelites, then went right back to worshiping Dagon, whom, just days before, they'd had to help back onto his feet.

It seems like the height of folly to worship something they had to prop up with their own hands! Yet are we so unlike them?

Anything we value more than God becomes an idol in our hearts. We hang onto, and go to great lengths to preserve and protect, those things we've allowed to rule our affections.

PONDER: How many worthless "idols" have I set up in my heart? What will it take for me to recognize that only God is worthy of my worship?

PRAYER: Lord, point out anything that has taken Your place in my heart. Help me tear it down.

September 17

For The Sake Of The Team

"So encourage each other and build each other up..." I Thessalonians 5:11

Teammates share the same goals, struggle against the same opponents, overcome the same obstacles. The goal is a "W" for the team! Self-absorption, negative criticism, and put-downs destroy T-E-A-M.

When team members put themselves "out there," we cheer them on; we encourage every effort; we do what we can to make up for their weaknesses, knowing they will do the same for us. Together, we accomplish what we could not do alone.

We understand these concepts on the football field, but what about our marriages, our families, jobs, and churches? How do we fare as "team members" there?

One of the most intimate and critical "teams" in our lives is our marriage. What is the goal here? Who is supposed to "win"—one of the partners, or the marriage itself, the family unit?

Are we in competition with each other? Why then is it "okay" to put down, marginalize, demean, or neglect my spouse? I should be my spouse's biggest cheerleader, doing all I can to make sure he/she is fulfilled, encouraged and honored, and that his/her backside is "covered!"

PONDER: How do I view my spouse? ...as my teammate or competitor or, worse, as my opponent? Do my words, attitudes, and actions build up, encourage, and strengthen? ...or wound, hurt, and tear down?

PRAYER: Lord, help me get my eyes off myself! Help me "leave it <u>all</u> on the field" for the sake of the "TEAM."

September 18

Is There Any Place God Is Not?

"…Surely the Lord is in this place, and I wasn't even aware of it!"
Genesis 28:16

"Jehovah Shammah" is a favorite name for God found in Scripture. It literally means "The Lord is There."

"Where?" Well… where do I **need** Him to be? There is <u>no</u> place He is <u>not</u>.

In today's verse, we see Jacob, fearfully fleeing his brother's vengeance, traveling alone to a distant land, wondering about his future. How surprised he is to discover the Lord's presence in that place, though he'd not been aware of it.

Rarely do we humans see ladders ascending to Heaven, burning bushes, or angels in fiery chariots with drawn swords. The Lord asks that we walk by faith, not by sight.

But His Word is full of descriptions of His character and His promises. If we will but believe and rest in what He says is true, we will "**know**" in our spirits what we cannot perceive with our senses or understand with our minds.

PONDER: Am I more apt to rely on my ability to comprehend or in my feelings than to trust in the promises of God? Do I believe God's description of Himself, that He is "there," working on my behalf, even when I "feel" nothing?

PRAYER: Lord Jesus, help me remember and trust Your Word. Even when it seems I am alone, help me trust in Your name, Jehovah Shammah, and rest in Your promise to be "There," wherever I am, wherever I need You to be.

September 19

What Am I Missing Here?

"... They were totally amazed, for they still didn't understand the significance of the miracle of the loaves. Their hearts were too hard to take it in." Mark 6:51,52

The disciples had just watched Jesus feed 5000 men and their families with only five small loaves and two fish. Later that night, distressed by the violent wind and waves that threatened their small boat, the 12 are terrified when they see Jesus walking on the water toward them. The minute he steps into the boat, the wind stops.

These are seasoned fishermen. They've weathered storms like this before. They know wind doesn't just stop like that! They are totally amazed, nonplussed.

So, what lesson had they failed to comprehend in the miracle of the loaves?

Perhaps the key is found in Christ's own words as He approached their craft. *"Take courage. I am here!" (v. 50b)*

Why would the disciples stew about having enough to eat when Jesus was in their midst? Why would their hearts quake in fear when the Lord of the Universe had just come alongside and was stepping into their boat?

PONDER: Do I REALLY believe Christ's Presence is the key factor in determining the ultimate outcome of whatever distresses me at the moment? How do my responses prove or disprove that?

PRAYER: Oh, God, remind me that You are aware of everything that concerns me. You are there, in the midst of it all, calling me to trust You, assuring me of Your presence, and stepping into the circumstance with me to calm the storm.

September 20
If Ever I Loved Thee?

"I'll love Thee in life, I will love Thee in death... And say, when the death dew lies cold on my brow, 'If ever I loved Thee, My Jesus, 'tis now!'"

This seldom-sung verse to an old hymn came to mind recently when a dear friend of mine died. My friend was a Christ-follower, having recently trusted Jesus for salvation. Though it saddened her to leave loved ones behind, she was confident that, when she departed this world, she would step into the presence of her Lord. Death for her was not the end, but a transition to something much better!

Christ had freed her from the fear of standing before her Maker. The tendency, at life's end, is to review our "performance" which, because we're human, always comes up lacking.

How good is "good enough?" If that's what we're striving for, then fear, doubt, and anxiety will accompany us to our grave.

"All have sinned and fall short..."(Romans 3:23) That's why Christ sacrificed Himself—to become "The Way" back into relationship with God.

Those who put their trust in Jesus enjoy "rest" from their striving. God's peace will be their escort through death's door.

PONDER: What characterizes my relationship with God—striving, self-effort, and insecurity? ...or rest, peace, and confidence?

PRAYER: Lord Jesus, thank You for providing a full and adequate atonement for my sin. I cling to You, resting securely and confidently in your perfect gift of righteousness on my behalf. Hallelujah! What a Savior!

September 21
No Thanks, I'm Full!

"A person who is full refuses honey, but even bitter food tastes sweet to the hungry." Proverbs 27:7

Could this proverb tell us anything about how to protect those we love from destructive temptations?

Who doesn't want his/her spouse to remain faithful? We all come to our wedding day with starry eyes, proclaiming "you're the only one for me," making promises of "til death do us part." How could a couple so devoted to each other ever be seduced into infidelity?

We all want our children to obey and honor us. All parents remember those sweet days when Daddy was a hero and larger than life, when Mommy could barely get out of the toddler's sight without tears. How is it possible that such a precious child could ever come to view his/her parents with disdain?

The factors involved in such disloyalties are varied and complicated, but today's Scripture offers an important secret to keeping our spouses and kids loving us and the relationship we share.

Does my spouse have unmet longings and needs that produce a "craving," making him/her vulnerable to temptation? Does the amount of time, attention, and acceptance I give my kids leave a gnawing hunger inside them that makes even "bitter food" taste sweet?

PONDER: What keeps me from discovering and filling the "hunger" of those I love? Is it my own self-centered desires?

PRAYER: Lord, help me fill my loved ones so "full" that even "honey" would not tempt them.

September 22
Can't Take His Eyes Off Of You!

"...the one who watches over you will not slumber. Indeed, he who watches over Israel never slumbers or sleeps. The Lord Himself watches over you! The Lord stands beside you as your protective shade." Psalm 121:3-5

Who can fathom not ever getting tired, never needing sleep? This God of ours is far beyond our ability to comprehend! How comforting to belong to a God whose supply of strength and energy is absolutely limitless. When we lay our heads on our pillows at night and close our eyes to sleep, God remains awake, totally active on our behalf. What a promise! What a God!

Additionally, God declares that He is fully present with every person as if each was the only one in the universe. How is that possible?

Our human minds, limited as they are by time and space, struggle to comprehend an everywhere-present, all-knowing God. Yet, here, in this passage, God reveals His intimate attention to each person throughout the whole earth.

He sees <u>me</u>, yet He has His eye on <u>you</u> at the very same time. No wonder Jesus exhorts us not to be anxious. With such an awesome caregiver, why worry... unless, of course, we don't really trust Him.

PONDER: What is it I worry about? What keeps me from trusting this God Who never takes His eyes off me?

PRAYER: Lord, thank You for showing me Your exquisite, intimate, personal love and attention. Forgive me for not trusting You. Help me <u>**rest**</u> in Your care.

September 23

My Hiding Place

" ...Saul hunted him day after day, but God didn't let Saul find him." I Samuel 23:14b

Sometimes, as with David, the odds are stacked against us. The outcome looks bleak, and we may be tempted to give in to despair.

Surely, the king and his army could find David in a land as small as Israel. Not necessarily! Because the safest place in all the world is right where God wants us, in the center of His will.

David is obviously trying to live in God's will.

Just verses earlier, David asks the Lord whether or not he should rescue the people of Keilah from the Philistines. God says, "Go," but David's men are afraid, so he verifies again with the Lord before they engage the enemy.

Later, David twice inquires of the Lord whether or not he will be betrayed to the king. God answers affirmatively, so he takes refuge in the wilderness.

So, why all the problems?

Scripture never promises a life with no difficulties. Rather, we are assured God is ultimately in control of our destiny. Nothing can touch us without His "okay." Anything He does allow will be for our ultimate good and His glory. *(Romans 8:28)*

PONDER: Who or what am I trusting in to keep me and my family safe? Is my heart "at rest" in God, or am I frantically scrambling to control things myself?

PRAYER: You, Lord, are my Stronghold, my Hiding Place, my Refuge, and I run to You.

September 24
Is It Really Worth It?

"...your children will pay for your faithlessness... the entire family is affected—even children in the third and fourth generations." Numbers 14:33, and 18b

"I'm not hurting anyone but myself!" How often have we heard those words, or said them ourselves in a petulant effort to justify some irresponsible or sinful behavior? After all, **"It's my life!"** Right?

But, whether I like it or not, what I do impacts more than just "me." My life has a ripple effect on all those in my path. I may hide my behaviors, habits, thoughts and attitudes. I may think I'm getting away with them. But God warns that we will reap what we sow!

Sadly, those we love most may be the ones who end up paying the highest price for the choices we make.

The damnation of our <u>own</u> souls is not all that is at stake here! Can I bear the thought of my children and grandchildren living out the consequences of my disobedience to God?

PONDER: What am I hiding from God and others? What in my life is more important to me than yielding to Christ and obeying Him? Is it worth the price my children and grandchildren may pay physically, emotionally, or spiritually for my indulgence?

PRAYER: Lord, I give You full access to every part of my life. Purify me. Change me. Free me. May those who follow after me experience the blessings You promised to a thousand generations of those who love You.

September 25

Is This A Test?

"Turning to Philip, he [Jesus] *asked, 'Where can we buy bread to feed all these people?' He was testing Philip, for he already knew what he was going to do." John 6:5b,6*

Philip immediately begins to calculate all the available resources and concludes there's no way he can do what Christ has asked, even if he and the other disciples worked for months to accomplish it.

Why is it that, like Philip, our first response to any overwhelming situation is to look to ourselves and our own resources? Panic or despair usually ensues because we are "woefully inadequate" when it comes to doing the impossible!

The Lord was actually testing Philip. Jesus <u>knew</u> what He Himself would do. He would turn to His Heavenly Father, asking and expecting <u>God</u> to do what would otherwise be totally impossible!

But… what would <u>Philip</u> do? What will <u>we</u> do?

How like Philip we are, assessing what's possible through the lens of our limited human resources, forgetting that we live in the presence of One who promises, *"Nothing is too hard for me!" (Jeremiah 32:27)*

Meanwhile, God waits. Hopefully… expectantly. God waits, eager for the chance to *"show Himself strong on our behalf,"* to do for us what we cannot do for ourselves. *(II Chronicles 16:9)*

PONDER: What am I facing right now? Is it too big for God?

PRAYER: Forgive me, Lord, for not looking to You <u>first</u> in every situation. Keep me aware of Your presence. Help me trust Your <u>power</u> to do what I cannot do.

September 26

Please God! Please, Please, Please!

"…God told Balaam, 'Do not go with them…' But Balaam responded to Balak's messengers… 'Stay here one more night, and I will see if the Lord has anything else to say to me.'" Numbers 22:12,18,19

Terrified of the Israelites and their God, Balak, king of Moab, sends messengers to Balaam, a Moabite prophet, pleading with him to curse these people in order to give him an advantage over them in war.

Balaam must be somewhat familiar with the God of Israel and seeks the Lord's instructions before responding to the king. God is <u>very</u> specific. *"Do not go… Do not curse these people…"*

But when Balak's messengers return with even more money and lavish gifts, Balaam hopes God has somehow changed His mind and inquires <u>again</u> of the Lord. This time he gets the message he wants, but he finds himself the unfortunate recipient of God's anger.

God has made Himself abundantly clear in His Word. Through Scripture, He reveals His character, His holiness, His will for every person who responds to Him in faith. He spells out the behaviors and attitudes that honor Him and those that don't.

How dare we seek God's blessing on our lives while coddling sinful tendencies, words, and actions the Lord has already, very specifically, condemned!

PONDER: Am I guilty of the sin of Balaam?

PRAYER: Search me, O God. Know my heart. What You have revealed in Your Word will be my authority. Help me humbly forsake all that grieves Your Spirit.

September 27

Who Determines Right And Wrong?

"In those days... people did whatever seemed right in their own eyes." Judges 17:6; 21:25

A couple of stories, found in the Book of Judges, depict the perversity that can infect people's thinking when they decide they are capable of determining right and wrong for themselves.

In one story, a Levite, in order to save his own skin, offers his concubine to a perverted mob of sexual deviants from the tribe of Benjamin. After they rape and murder her, he cuts her into 12 pieces and sends her parts to each of the tribes of Israel, who then go to war against their Benjamite relatives, wiping out all but 600 men.

Afterward, they are remorseful, realizing this tribe is now on the verge of extinction, so they try to find wives for the men who remain. Earlier, however, they had vowed in anger not to allow their own daughters to marry men from Benjamin's tribe. So now, in order to keep from having to break their vows, they encourage the Benjamites to **kidnap** their daughters instead.

People's thought processes don't usually start out as twisted and perverse as this, but whenever we reject moral absolutes and God's authority in our lives, our thinking will become more and more convoluted, leading us down a road we never dreamed we'd travel.

PONDER: Do I reserve the right to determine right and wrong for myself, or is God's Word my standard?

PRAYER: Lord Jesus, protect me from my own futile thinking.

September 28

How Can We Know?

"How do you know what your life will be like tomorrow? Your life is like the morning fog—it's here a little while, then it's gone."
James 4:14

We feel so immortal, don't we? Of course, we <u>know</u> we're not, but it never really <u>feels</u> like we're not, so it's difficult for us to get the hang of thinking, talking, planning, and living as if today just might be our very last day on this earth.

For some people, the doctor is the one who brings them to this reality. After a devastating conversation in his office, they will never again look at life with a "ho-hum, it'll be here tomorrow" attitude. We tend to pity those folks. They're going to die. But we? Well… we get to keep on living.

But how can we <u>know</u> if we'll even be allowed to take our next breath? Or make it home from work tonight? Or wake up in the morning? We could find ourselves standing in the presence of God before we have time to think our next thought!

Those of us not forced by life's circumstances to stare death in the face may actually be the pitiable ones after all. We may be the folks least prepared for death when it comes.

PONDER: Am I ready to die? Am I confident of my eternal destination? Am I afraid to face thoughts of my own mortality?

PRAYER: Lord, give me courage to wrestle with this honestly… in Your presence… <u>NOW</u>! While I have the opportunity!

September 29

Even Manasseh? (Part 1)

"...while in deep distress, Manasseh sought the Lord his God and sincerely humbled himself before the God of his ancestors. And when he prayed, the Lord listened to him and was moved by his request..."
II Chronicles 33:12,13

Manasseh was the most evil king in Jewish history. His wickedness included idol worship, witchcraft, sorcery, setting up a carved idol in the temple of God, and sacrificing his own sons in the fire.

Scripture tells us that Manasseh led the people of Judah *"to do even more evil than the pagan nations that the Lord had destroyed when the people of Israel entered the land."* Manasseh aroused the anger of the Lord, who finally allowed the Assyrian army to overrun Jerusalem and take him captive.

I'm not sure why stories about Manasseh seldom include his "turn-around," how he humbled himself and sought the Lord. Why, when we hear about Manasseh, is the focus only on his wickedness?

Perhaps we're just not comfortable with what happened next. We tend to think someone so evil doesn't deserve a second chance. But *"The Lord listened... and was moved..."*

The centerpiece of Manasseh's story **should** be the incredible mercy and grace of our God!

PONDER: Am I more prone to pass judgment on sinners and hold them at arm's length than to extend the kindness of God?

PRAYER: Lord, forgive me for looking self-righteously at people I consider evil. Rather than condemning, help me be kind and gracious to them, as You are!

September 30

Even Manasseh? (Part 2)

"Manasseh finally realized that the Lord alone is God!" II Chronicles 33:13b

How many times have we read this verse and not grasped its magnitude? This is **Manasseh** we're talking about, the most evil king in Jewish history, who, for 55 years, ruled over Judah, doing *"what was evil in the Lord's sight, following the detestable practices of the pagan nations that the Lord had driven from the land ahead of the Israelites."*

To whom might we compare Manasseh in sheer wickedness? Adolf Hitler? Saddam Hussein? Jeffrey Dahmer? Our skin crawls at the thought of such men!

Apparently, God does not have the same reaction to them as we do. God <u>hates</u> sin, yes! But His heart is still broken by their lost souls. It was for **sinners** that Jesus came and died. He absorbed God's wrath against sin on Calvary's cross, and declares that *"...anyone who calls on the name of the Lord will be saved."* Acts 2:21

<u>Anyone</u>? Even Manasseh? Yes! And even <u>you</u> and <u>me</u>, despite <u>all</u> our sins! *"We are made right in God's sight when we trust in Jesus Christ to take away our sins. And we all can be saved in this same way, no matter who we are or what we have done. For all have sinned..."* Romans 3:22b,23a

PONDER: Have I ever wondered if my sin was just <u>too</u> great for God to forgive? Can I trust God's Word, which tells me otherwise?

PRAYER: Lord, have mercy on me, a sinner!

October

October 1
From Start To Finish

"This Good News tells us how God makes us right in His sight. This is accomplished from start to finish by faith…" Romans 1:17

Why is it so difficult to acknowledge? We have absolutely **NOTHING** to bring to the table, **NOTHING** to add to the equation, **NOTHING** with which to bargain or finagle for position before God.

Even when we finally recognize our salvation comes <u>only</u> from trusting Jesus, a sense of "responsibility" often kicks in again. We find ourselves striving to live a life holy enough to somehow satisfy God.

Scripture makes it very clear: <u>God makes us right with Him by faith</u>— **PERIOD!** Jesus is the Alpha and Omega, the Beginning and the End. That doesn't leave room for any contribution on my part.

Does this mean that I don't have to obey God's Word or live a life of purity and holiness? No, it doesn't. So what are we saying?

Only Jesus has lived a perfect life. To think that, with enough effort on my part, I could ever achieve sufficient holiness to satisfy God is the height of human arrogance. Only Christ's life, lived in and through me, will ever satisfy the righteous requirements of God's law.

PONDER: Do I feel obligated in my efforts to please God, or am I resting in what Christ has accomplished <u>**for**</u> me?

PRAYER: Thank You, Lord, for being my Salvation **AND** my Righteousness. Teach me how to rest in grateful trust that You are **ENOUGH!**

October 2

Honor Your Spiritual Leaders

"…honor those who are your leaders in the Lord's work… Show them great respect and wholehearted love because of their work…"
I Thessalonians 5: 12,13

October is traditionally known as "Pastor Appreciation Month," a time when parishioners shower cards, gifts, and acts of kindness on their spiritual leaders. As a former pastor, I can affirm that those expressions of love are welcomed and appreciated greatly.

However, when offered by one with a critical spirit, one who sows discord in the church, or one who has little interest in receiving from God through the ministry of His servants, that gift loses its impact.

The greatest gift you could <u>ever</u> give your pastor is a tender heart, open to God's Truth revealed by His Holy Spirit. To hear you say, *"Thank you, Pastor, for your ministry today. God used you to speak specifically to my heart in this area of my life, and I'm choosing to obey,"* will gratify your leader more than anything you could do for him/her.

We do want to offer tangible expressions of our love and appreciation, but let's also resolve to give our leaders what will bless them most: a heart that listens for the voice of God through their ministry and a desire to express to them when and how that is taking place.

PONDER: When is the last time I told my spiritual leader how his/her ministry has specifically impacted my spiritual growth?

PRAYER: Lord, give me an open heart… a grateful heart… an expressive heart.

October 3

Never Alone!

"But I know you well—where you stay and when you come and go..." Isaiah 37:28

Wow! This is God speaking—the God Who sits enthroned in the heavens—the One who spoke this world into existence. He says He knows me well. He knows my address. He saw me get up this morning and knows exactly where I am this very moment!

For those trying to "fly under the radar," that might <u>not</u> be a very comforting thought. It means even when I "feel" I'm all alone, nothing escapes His notice. God observes when I sit at my computer, surfing the web, gazing at its images. He's aware of my choices, and my motives, whether I'm at the refrigerator door, the cash register, or the wheel of my automobile.

On the other hand, for those whose hearts long to please Him, God's intimate knowledge of our comings and goings offers great comfort. I find joy in knowing I don't face hardship, sorrow, or death alone. Even when I <u>feel</u> alone, I'm not! And when I doubt anyone cares, I'm wrong! God cares enough to intimately watch <u>all</u> that concerns me. What else really matters?

PONDER: Is God's thorough knowledge of my life a source of joy to me or discomfort? Why? How does God <u>want</u> me to respond?

PRAYER: Lord, help me bring everything into the Light, knowing You see it anyway. I rejoice in the wonder that God knows and cares for me so deeply!

October 4

Leave Them Behind— And Go Free!

"What sorrow for those who drag their sins behind them with ropes made of lies." Isaiah 5:18

Scripture declares emphatically and repeatedly that there is forgiveness of sin for **anyone** who repents and receives God's free gift of salvation offered to us through Christ. *I John 1:9* minces no words: **IF** we confess, He **WILL** forgive!

So why do we feel… and think… and live… as if we're still guilty? Why do we beat ourselves up over sins we've already laid at the feet of Jesus? Because we choose to believe Satan's lies!

Rather than trust God, who declares our sins have been removed from us as far as the East is from the West and buried in the ocean's depths (*Psalm 103:12; Micah 7:19*), we listen to the voice of our enemy, whose whispers evoke condemnation and demand penance.

Our holy, yet merciful, God has declared us "not guilty" through our faith in Christ's atonement! When our standard of justice won't let us off the hook for "crimes" He's freely pardoned, haven't we, in effect, set ourselves up as a more righteous judge than He?

PONDER: What message am I giving God when I cannot let go of what He's declared "forgiven?" How must that make Him feel?

PRAYER: Lord Jesus, forgive me for allowing the devil's lies to bind me to sins You've already forgiven and forgotten. Your sacrifice was totally sufficient, Your Word absolutely trustworthy! I choose now to rest in what You've accomplished for me at Calvary.

October 5

How Do I Love Like That?

"...love the Lord your God with all your heart, all your soul, and all your mind... love your neighbor as yourself. The entire law and all the demands of the prophets are based on these two commandments." Matthew 22:37-40

Imagine a world where everyone loved God and others like Jesus instructs. No one would ever hurt anyone on purpose. We could leave our doors unlocked because no one would consider stealing from someone they truly love.

Policemen would be scarce, only needed in case of accidents. Folks would never assume another person meant to do them harm, so lawyers would have very little, if anything, to do.

We'd never need to conceal our hidden motives because there wouldn't be any! We could each be real and authentic without fear. What a world that would be!

Tragically, because of the sinful, fallen nature of mankind, that scenario will only be fully realized in Heaven.

Yet Jesus <u>clearly</u> indicates its <u>possibility</u> in the lives of His followers <u>here</u> and <u>now</u>—not because, within ourselves, we are capable of such purity of motive, but because, as we yield to His control, He is able to do in and through us what we cannot possibly do ourselves! *(Romans 8:3,4)*

PONDER: Do I love God most and best? Really? Do I love others as fervently as I love myself?

PRAYER: Lord, loving like that is totally impossible for me unless You do it <u>for</u> me, and <u>in</u> me, and <u>through</u> me. That's what I want!

October 6
In The Grip Of A Loving Father

"…I will strengthen you and help you. I will hold you up with my victorious right hand… I hold you by your right hand—I, the Lord your God. And I say to you, 'Don't be afraid. I am here to help you.'" Isaiah 41:10b,13

Remember the days when your children were learning to walk, toddling along beside you, stubbornly refusing your help?

Knowing how precarious their balance was at that point in their development, you insisted on holding their hand anyway, loosening your grip to give them the <u>feeling</u> they were achieving success on their own.

However, the minute you felt them begin to waver, your hand clenched firmly around their wrist, lifting them up over the uneven ground and back onto their feet.

God uses the experiences we share with our own children to inform our understanding of His tender love and concern for us. Just as our nearness and strength provide security and freedom for our children, God's presence and power should evoke a sense of peace in our hearts as well.

We need not be anxious. We may barely feel His Hand upon our wrist, but it is there, nonetheless. And even before we realize we are about to tumble, God has already gripped us tenaciously to lift us up and plant our feet firmly on solid ground again.

PONDER: Can I believe God's Word, even when I can't feel His touch?

PRAYER: Thank You that I am solidly in Your grip today!

October 7
It's A Lie, And We've Believed It!

"'...Repent, and turn from your sins... Put all your rebellion behind you and find yourselves a new heart and a new spirit. ...why should you die, O people...? I don't want you to die,' says the Sovereign Lord. 'Turn back and live!'" Ezekiel 18:30-32

Can you hear the <u>anguish</u> in God's voice as He <u>begs</u> His people to turn from their sins, and <u>live</u>? Why do we sometimes get the feeling God loves to punish people, that He's just waiting for them to mess up so He can crack His divine whip?

God hates sin, yes, but He <u>loves</u> people!

To satisfy God's wrath against sin, He clothed <u>Himself</u> in flesh and became human. Though Jesus <u>was</u> a good teacher, a miracle worker, One who came to show us what God is like and how to live, His <u>ultimate</u> purpose was to become the "once-for-all-time" sacrifice for sin, substituted for you and me, so we might be forgiven.

Now He <u>longs</u> for us to turn from our sins, turn back to Him, trust what He's done for us, and **live**!

From the beginning, Satan has lied and misrepresented God. Jesus said the devil is a thief who comes to *"rob, kill, and destroy"* those God loves. *(John 10:10)* Will I believe Satan, or trust God?

PONDER: How do I picture God? When I mess up, what do I imagine God feels about me?

PRAYER: Forgive me, Lord, for believing Satan's lies about You. Thank you for forever proving Your love for me at Calvary.

October 8
Appearances Can Be Wrong, You Know!

"You say, 'I am rich. I have everything I want. I don't need a thing!' And you don't realize that you are wretched and miserable and poor and blind and naked." Revelation 3:17

Some of us work mighty hard, disciplining and denying ourselves to be good people, to make something of ourselves. We admire and surround ourselves with others who've done the same, and we have little patience for those who can't seem to "get it together."

We read Scriptures that admonish us not to lie or steal or kill, and we feel pretty comfortable as we hold our lifestyles up to the commandments. ***"Doin' good!"*** we think, as we check off another benevolent deed or religious obligation.

We don't realize that God isn't impressed. He doesn't see things the way we do. *"...People judge by outward appearance, but the Lord looks at the heart." I Samuel 16:7*

God knows the **"why"** behind my every word or deed. What may appear to others as "worthy" and "sacrificial" may actually arise from "ulterior" motives. Nothing is hidden from His sight. *"...I, the Lord, search all hearts and examine secret motives." Jeremiah 17:10*

PONDER: What if God were to broadcast the **true** motives behind every good work I do? A day is coming, when *"...all that is secret will be made known..." Luke 12:2*

PRAYER: *"Search me, O God, and know my heart... Point out anything in me that offends you, and lead me along the path of everlasting life." Psalm 139:23,24*

October 9

Moses At The Rock—And He's Angry!

"You failed to demonstrate my holiness to the people..." Deuteronomy 32:51

Moses was mad when he struck that rock. He'd "had it up to here" with those people! God had shown His power over and over again, yet they still complained at the first sign of trouble.

Moses immediately sought God's intervention. God told Him what to do: "<u>speak</u>" to the rock, and water would gush forth. Instead, Moses "<u>struck</u>" the rock… twice and "<u>shouted</u>" at the people!

Human patience has its limits. We don't blame Moses for being exasperated. But, even in our moments of exasperation, what we say and do <u>must</u> reflect <u>God's</u> heart, not our own. Scripture is clear: *"...man's anger does not bring about the righteous life that God desires." James 1:20 NIV*

We are Christ's ambassadors. How we interact with people, even difficult people, will reflect on the character of God.

Do we ever rail against sinners in the name of Jesus? Might people come to view God as angry or vengeful as a result of the way we speak to, or about, those who challenge or repudiate our beliefs?

Do we ever justify unkind words or acts toward people we feel are destroying society with their wickedness?

PONDER: What kind of God do my words and actions portray? Do I use God as an excuse to vent my own personal revulsions?

PRAYER: Keep me aware of Your ability to love people, even when You hate what they do. And help me do the same.

October 10

Moses At The Rock—God's Reputation...

"You failed to demonstrate my holiness to the people..." Deuteronomy 32:51

It is time for Moses to die. He will not enter the Promised Land. He had misrepresented God to the people, and God says that breach will keep him on this side of the Jordan.

Wow! To us, it seems like such a trivial matter. The first time God brought water from the rock, He'd told Moses to "strike" it. Wasn't it natural for Moses to assume God would work in the same way? And God <u>did</u> provide water <u>both</u> times, didn't He? So what's the problem?

It's far more complex than our finite minds can fully comprehend, but a few things stand out:

1. **Moses failed to really "listen" to God's instructions, which had changed.**
2. **Moses was angry with the people and used God's Name to vent His frustration.**
3. **Moses asked, "Must we (Aaron and himself) bring you water from this rock?" He'd "read his own press" and believed it. As a result, he diverted glory away from Almighty God.**

God's reputation is not to be trifled with. He is holy. How we represent Him matters!

PONDER: Am I careless with God's reputation? Does my life give an accurate portrayal of what He is like?

PRAYER: Oh, God, forgive me for assuming I can take Your name and live however I want. Whatever I do or say or even think, may it be as a representative of my Lord Jesus Christ and for His Glory alone!

October 11

Moses at the Rock—What Might Have Been...

"...When the people of Israel rebelled, you failed to demonstrate my holiness to them at the waters." Numbers 27:14b

As Moses looked out over the Promised Land he would never enter, memories of his frustration with the Israelites, who had repeatedly provoked and aggravated him, spoken against him, and challenged his authority, must have surfaced once again.

ONE time...! Instead of speaking to the rock as God had instructed, he'd struck it in rage. Water had still flowed, but the message was lost! He'd distorted God's "object lesson." God Himself is the **Living Water**, the **Source of all Life** that flows from the **Rock of Salvation**.

Oh, the regrets that must have filled his heart as He glimpsed the beautiful promise he'd forfeited by his rashness.

Unlike Moses, most of us will probably never catch a glimpse of what God wanted to do **for** us, give **to** us, or accomplish **through** us but was unable to, because of our failure to demonstrate His holiness in the difficult situations of life.

What a shame! What a loss! ...not only to ourselves, but especially to the Kingdom of God!

PONDER: When people sin against me, don't I have a right to get angry? To carry a grudge? To get even? But what might I be missing by standing on **my** rights? How might others be affected by my attitudes? Is God's Holiness being demonstrated through my response?

PRAYER: O God, may Your Holiness be more important to me than my rights, my reputation, or my comfort.

October 12

How Can I Even Know?

"Put me on trial, Lord, and cross-examine me. Test my motives and affections... Search me, O God, and know my heart; <u>test</u> me and know my thoughts. Point out anything in me that offends you and lead me along the path of everlasting life." Psalm 26:2; 139:23,24

How can we possibly know what is in our hearts, if we are never put into circumstances that bring it to the surface? How can we see whether we're growing or stagnating in our walk with the Lord, unless God allows us a good look at ourselves by exposing us to situations in which our reactions occur before we have time to think?

In revealing our true selves, God is not scolding or shaming us. He is not shocked or disappointed. How could he be? He's known every ugly thing about us from the beginning. And the amazing truth is He has loved us <u>anyway</u>!

The fact that He is just now allowing <u>us</u> to see what He's always known means we must be ready to face whatever it is and make necessary changes.

PONDER: Can I identify any recent situation in my life as a possible "test?" How did I respond? In trust and faith? With love and compassion? Or in anger and retaliation? In fear and anxiety?

PRAYER: Lord God. Forgive me for fighting against Your ways. Help me view life's trials and difficulties as tools, that, in Your loving hands, can be used to make me more like Christ.

October 13
Am I A Christian, True Or False?

"You can identify them by their fruit, that is, by the way they act... A good tree can't produce bad fruit, and a bad tree can't produce good fruit." Matthew 7:16a,18

Jesus is giving us a way to evaluate the authenticity of our faith, to know whether or not we really belong to Him and are living in Him.

It's so much easier to say "Jesus is Lord" than to surrender to His Lordship. However, it's **only** as we **yield** to **His control** that the fruit of His Spirit—love, joy, peace, patience, kindness, goodness, faithfulness, gentleness, self-control—grows in our lives. *(Galatians 3:22,23)* And that, my friends, is the evidence of our salvation.

If I belong to Jesus, I have a new nature—His Divine Nature. I simply cannot be comfortable any longer with attitudes and actions that grieve His Spirit. It's not that I will be perfect. There is no human, except Jesus Christ Himself, capable of that.

But with Jesus living in me, my spirit is grieved by what grieves Him. When I sin, I might try to ignore it for a time, but His Spirit will always pursue me, drawing me back toward repentance.

PONDER: If I'm honest, what kind of fruit grows on the tree of my life? Is it Christlike?

PRAYER: Lord, good fruit can only come from a heart that has been washed by Your blood and is controlled by You. Make me Yours, Jesus. Produce the Fruit of the Spirit in me.

October 14

How Can You Eat At A Time Like This?

"You prepare a feast for me in the presence of my enemies. You welcome me as a guest, anointing my head with oil. My cup overflows with blessings." Psalm 23:5

David is obviously speaking from personal experience. Can you imagine sitting down to a feast, surrounded by your enemies, and enjoying it? Yet David declares that, though pursued by people who weren't content just to malign and slander him, but vowed to kill him, he found himself the honored guest at a lavish banquet prepared by the Good Shepherd.

For most of us, the feast would go uneaten, the cup unfilled. With enemies lurking nearby, our focus would be totally consumed with our own self-preservation. Any meal at that moment could mean only one thing—a very bad case of indigestion!

Yet this "feast" is available for anyone willing to tear his/her eyes away from the menacing enemies threatening to devour and destroy and fasten his gaze on the Shepherd who offers anointing and blessing.

If we will <u>choose</u> to sit down at His banqueting table, even in the toughest of times, we'll realize anew God's goodness and unfailing love.

PONDER: In my most difficult moments, who/what gets my attention? Have I ever missed the "feast" Christ has prepared for me because I couldn't tear my mind from the situation at hand?

PRAYER: In You, Lord, I have everything I need: protection, provision, peace. Help me keep my eyes on You and trust You completely.

October 15

Is God Really God?

"He [Abraham] was fully convinced that God is able to do whatever he promises." Romans 4:21; "Who is God except the LORD?" II Samuel 22:32a

Why would we ever choose to use the words "too difficult" or "impossible" in a sentence referring to God? Think about it. If something is too difficult for our "god," then he/she is <u>not</u> **GOD** at all, just a glorified version of our best selves!

By definition, God must be One for whom nothing is impossible, nothing can be hidden, and nothing is unknown. No one is greater than He. None could possibly have preceded Him in existence. To be anything less disqualifies Him from being God.

God has chosen to reveal Himself to us in Scripture. This self-revelation is sometimes difficult for us to reconcile with our human understanding. There's so much about Him we don't understand or even comprehend. That bothers us. But why? God <u>must</u> transcend us, or He is not God!

"'My thoughts are nothing like your thoughts,' says the Lord. 'And My ways are far beyond anything you could imagine.'" Isaiah 55:8

IF I COULD FULLY COMPREHEND GOD, I WOULD <u>BE</u> GOD.

So, how is it that I feel so free to stand in judgment of Him? What makes me comfortable with ignoring Him or dismissing Him?

PONDER: Have I ever "judged" God? Mistrusted God? Ignored Him? Dismissed Him altogether?

PRAYER: Forgive me, Lord, for my foolish pride that allowed me to judge You. I spoke of things I did not know.

October 16

At The End Of Your Rope!

"...all our busy rushing ends in nothing. We heap up wealth, not knowing who will spend it. And so, Lord, where do I put my hope? My only hope is in you." Psalm 39:6,7

Life! Its pace gains momentum like a snowball rolling down a hill. We find ourselves straining to keep up, stressed with its demands and pressures, wondering if there is any way to "stop this train!"

We make commitments to ourselves, our families… even to God. *"From now on, I'm going to…"* But that's countercultural, like swimming against a swift current. Almost before the words are spoken, we've broken our promise.

The Psalmist must have experienced similar frustrations. He'd apparently tasted the futility of his own efforts to make sense of life without God at its center. Ultimately, we must reach that same conclusion.

After having tried everything to fulfill our longings, meet our needs, and fix the broken places of our hearts, we finally cry out in desperation, *"Where in the world can I put my hope? Who can I turn to? I've tried everything I can think of. Nothing has worked. MY ONLY HOPE IS GOD!"*

My friend, God is waiting—at the end of your rope—for that moment! Oh, that we would recognize our desperate need of Him **before** experiencing such anguish, but that seldom happens.

PONDER: Could the difficulties in my life be God's way of drawing me into His arms?

PRAYER: Lord, forgive me for seeking "hope" apart from You.

October 17
Eagerly Waiting Or Dreading The Day?

"For all creation is waiting eagerly for that future day when God will reveal who his children really are." (Romans 8:19)

Someday, perhaps soon, at the close of the age, God is going to set the record straight. Those who are His children will be invited to join Him forever in His New Heaven and New Earth. Those who have rejected His gift of salvation provided through the death and resurrection of His Son Jesus Christ, will follow <u>their</u> leader, Satan, into everlasting damnation.

Do those thoughts bring you peace and hope… or fear and trepidation? In that day, it won't matter what I think, what my denomination or religion taught me, or what I always thought "seemed" right. **Only God's opinion will count!**

Those who've rejected God in this life will wish for some place to hide from Him. There'll be no argument—no justification. All will know, even as we are known… standing without excuse… in <u>God's</u> presence.

How different for those who've embraced Jesus Christ in this life. Hope springs within us at the <u>thought</u> of Christ's return! We may tremble at the "unknown," but we do not fear **Him**. Our peace comes not because we've somehow <u>earned</u> His favor. Our salvation is in Christ ALONE.

PONDER: What emotions stir within me when I think of standing before God at the Judgment?

PRAYER: Lord God, thank You for providing the Way back to You through Christ and for pouring **HOPE** into each heart that will trust Your gracious provision!

October 18
God's Word — My Most Powerful Tool!

"…he used the Scriptures to reason with the people." Acts 17:2

As we seek to disciple our children and others in the faith, our greatest tool is God's Word. Our goal is to introduce them to what God specifically says in His Word on any given topic.

At times, there will be no clear command. Helping them see what God declares about Himself, about His character and His heart, will enable them to understand how to honor God, even when no specific instruction is laid out for them.

The more of God's Word we introduce them to, the more likely they will be able to live victoriously in the power of God's Spirit.

Sometimes, especially as parents, we refer to God's Word in our conversation, i.e. "The Bible says…" rather than taking time to open the Word of God with them, allowing them to read it for themselves.

Even more important is helping them find and read the verses in their <u>own</u> Bibles. Then it will no longer be just <u>our</u> voices telling them what God says, or even seeing what is written in <u>our</u> Bibles. Reading and acknowledging God's Word, in their <u>own</u> Bibles, is difficult to argue with.

Once they recognize God has spoken directly to them, the impact is powerful and much harder to dismiss or ignore.

PONDER: How often have I simply said, "The Bible says…" rather than helping people view God's Word for themselves?

PRAYER: Thank You, Lord, for the Power of Your Word!

October 19

Have I Missed God's Heart?

"...let the one who has never sinned throw the first stone!" John 8:7

The woman caught in adultery braced for the barrage she knew was coming. But Jesus issued a simple challenge that changed the outcome of this story.

These were religious men, very zealous for the law, yet they'd totally missed God's heart, which He'd exposed clearly in *Ezekiel 33:11: "I take no pleasure in the death of the wicked. I only want them to turn from their wicked ways, so they can live."*

Jesus's challenge to these self-righteous Pharisees still reverberates today. **Only** a person who's **NEVER** sinned may condemn those still caught in sin's deadly grip.

Jesus was the **ONLY** One qualified to condemn this woman. He chose not to, because He came not to judge, but to save the world *(John 3:17)*.

Sadly, there are still a lot of "stones" being hurled at sinners these days, by folks so blinded by zeal they can't feel God's passion for restoring broken people.

PONDER: Do I see myself as worthy of and thus "deserving" a place in God's family? Am I smugly confident that God is impressed with how hard I've worked at being good? Is that why I feel justified when casting "stones" at those still caught in the web of sin's deceit?

PRAYER: Oh, God, let me never forget that I don't deserve to stand in Your presence. By rights, You should have condemned me, but You chose instead to offer mercy and grace. Help me do the same for others!

October 20

Forgive And Forget?

"…I will forgive their wickedness, and I will never again remember their sins." Jeremiah 31:34; Hebrews 8:12; "…forgiving one another, just as God through Christ has forgiven you." Ephesians 4:32

In our human effort to deal with pain and injustice, we often tell ourselves to *"Forgive and forget, just as God forgives and forgets our sins."*

That begs a question: is it really possible for an All-Knowing God to ever forget anything? Look back at the text. Is God saying He "forgets" our sins, or that He simply "refuses to remember" them, bring them up, or hold them over us? That is actually an even more incredible feat than simply "forgetting."

To **know** keenly what was done, to be vividly in touch with the cruelty and betrayal involved, yet choose **not** to remember or bring it up to the offender, to others, and even to ourselves—**THAT** takes more grace and power than if we could somehow forget altogether.

My friend, that's what God does for us! He knows **EXACTLY** what we've done against Him and the penalty we deserve. Yet He forgives us, and when we come to Him in humble repentance, He forbids Himself **EVER** remembering it against us again.

Then—He asks **US** to forgive in that same manner.

PONDER: Will I forgive as Christ has forgiven me? Will I refuse to dredge up the hurts and offenses of the past?

PRAYER: Lord, help me know I can do **"even this"** through Christ Who strengthens me.

October 21
Give To God First

"Take your son, your only son—yes, Isaac, whom you love so much—and... sacrifice him..." Genesis 22:2

God promised Abraham so many children he would not be able to count them all. After waiting many long years for Isaac, this first child of the promise, Abraham is now being asked by God to sacrifice him. God's request is in keeping with the principle of the tithe and the first fruits.

"Consecrate to me all the firstborn, whatever opens the womb among the children of Israel, both of man and beast; it is Mine." Exodus 13:2

"Honor the Lord with your possessions, and with the first fruits of all your increase." Proverbs 3:9

God asks us to give first, without knowing how or when He will meet our needs.

Our human tendency is to wait and see if there is "enough," or to observe how things go, before giving to God.

Abraham was asked to give his **FIRST** son, when **ONE** was all he had! He obeyed. God proved His Faithfulness by returning the one sacrificed and giving many, many more.

It'll be impossible for us to give God our "first fruits" unless: (1) We acknowledge that God alone deserves first place in our lives, and (2) We trust God, knowing that He will keep His promise to provide all that we need.

PONDER: What do my choices reveal about what I love most and who or what I trust in?

PRAYER: Help me love and trust You enough to put You first.

October 22

The Best Security System!

"… Wise choices will watch over you. Understanding will keep you safe…" Proverbs 2:10-12

How often have I paid dearly for my negligence, lack of information, foolish choices, failure to understand another's perspective? How many times in my life have I said (or thought), "If only…" or "I just wish I could go back and do it all over again!"?

Imagine living our lives in the wisdom God talks about here, a wisdom which would **keep us safe** from all the stupid things we do and say that derail even our best intentions!

Scripture tells us *"the fear of the Lord is the beginning of wisdom."* Wisdom is seeing and responding to life from God's point of view, which seldom, if ever, comes naturally to us. We have to <u>seek</u> to know and understand God's perspective.

Wisdom is <u>hidden</u> in His Word, but <u>readily available</u> for anyone and everyone who <u>desires it enough</u> to embark on a lifelong "treasure hunt." The problem is God's wisdom runs counter to our own intuition. All too often, even when we <u>know</u> what God desires, we trust our <u>own</u> instincts instead. And how's that working for us?

PONDER: How badly do I want God's perspective on life, in decision-making, in relationship dilemmas? Am I content to continue "as is?"

PRAYER: Lord, You've hidden Your unfathomable wisdom in Your Word, yet make it freely available to anyone who longs for it and pursues it. Help me **want** it badly enough to **search** it out and make it mine.

October 23
This Is God You're Talking To!

"Then the Lord said to Moses, 'Has my arm lost its power? Now you will see whether or not my word comes true!'" Numbers 11:23

The people of Israel have been whining about having no meat to eat. The Lord hears their complaints. To God this is personal rejection (*v. 20*). He responds with a vow to send meat every day for a month and make them eat it until they gag and are sick of it!

Moses is incredulous! What is God thinking? Even if the Israelites butchered all their flocks and herds, even if they caught all the fish in the sea, he says, there wouldn't be enough meat to feed these people for a whole month.

Wrong answer! You're forgetting something here, Moses! This is **GOD** you're talking to! Is anything too difficult for Him?

How it must break God's heart to know He can do so much, yet find those He loves so unwilling to trust Him?

PONDER: How about me? How big is God to me? How good is God, in my estimation? Do I pretend to trust while harboring complaints about my life and circumstances, deep in my heart? How important is "trust" in being able to live a life of contentment and joy?

PRAYER: O God, forgive me for selling You short so often! Help me recognize that I insult You when I fail to trust You. Open my eyes to see how big and how very good You are.

October 24

What About My Rights?

"Let's not allow this conflict to come between us... Take your choice of any section of the land you want..." Genesis 13:8,9

How hard was it for Abraham to make this offer, knowing his nephew Lot would choose the very best for himself (which, of course, he did)?

Did Abraham feel cheated afterward? Resentful? I have to admit that, most often, I grab and cling to, even fight for, what I believe I deserve. Even in the rare moments when I do the noble thing, my heart is often filled with regret and bitterness.

Whatever his motives, Abraham chose to yield his rights for the sake of the <u>relationship</u>. God honored him by multiplying and blessing what remained until it was far better and more satisfying, in the long run, than the fertile valley he gave away.

It really comes down to <u>trust</u>, doesn't it?

Generosity flows from a heart that knows its source is God Himself, the One who owns the cattle on every hill, the wealth in every mine, who knows how to make something out of nothing and promises to meet our every need.

PONDER: Am I a grabber, hanging on to and demanding my rights? Or do I trust the Lord to be the Source of all I need and want?

PRAYER: Lord, it's in moments like these, when my rights and desires are challenged, that I see my heart most clearly. Too often, it is just plain selfish and ugly! Please cleanse and change me.

October 25
The Power Of A Peaceful Heart

"A peaceful heart leads to a healthy body..." Proverbs 14:30

There are many factors involved in maintaining good health. In our culture, we must deal with the effects of our environment, the food we eat, our lifestyle, any medications we take.

There is also a correlation, according to Scripture, between the condition of our hearts and the health of our bodies. A heart at peace has a better chance at health!

What does a peaceful heart look like? How does it manifest itself? Let's first define a heart that is **not** at peace as one filled with anxiety, fear, guilt, anger, bitterness, resentment, worry, regret, pride, greed, envy, or insecurity.

Scripture warns these attitudes are part of our old sinful nature, inspired by Satan himself, whom Jesus describes as a thief, whose goal is to steal, kill, and destroy those God loves. It shouldn't surprise us, then, that attitudes like these tend to rob us of health, both physical and spiritual.

On the other hand, a peaceful heart manifests humility, gratitude, trust, confidence, gentleness, forgiveness, faithfulness, contentment, compassion, joy, and hope. These reflect the character of our loving Heavenly Father and are increasingly produced in our lives by His Spirit, as we learn to live and grow in vital relationship with Him.

PONDER: What attitudes best describe my heart? Is "peaceful" one of them?

PRAYER: Lord, I want a peace-filled heart. Help me let go of anything that would rob me of the peace I so desperately need and desire.

October 26

A Sweet Kiss!

"Unfailing love and truth have met together. Righteousness and peace have kissed!" Psalm 85:10

We humans are <u>not</u> very good at balancing love and truth. Some of us lean so heavily on the side of truth that love takes a back seat as we defend what we believe is right.

Others tilt way too far on the side of "love," diligently trying to make every philosophy, every belief, fit together so no one is alienated or offended.

In Christ, truth and love have met and "kissed." And through the mighty power of His Holy Spirit at work within us, God wants to "wed" the two of them into one uncompromising, yet consistently gracious, kind, and winsome response to every person, and in every situation, we encounter.

Without Christ's life in us, we will always be drawn to one over the other. <u>Only</u> in the character and life of our gracious and holy God do they come together. And <u>only</u> as He is allowed access and control of our lives will we be able to accurately reflect His heart in this matter.

PONDER: Which of these qualities has tipped the scale in my life? Am I a champion of "truth," even at the expense of the people I hurt along the way? Or am I so concerned about people's feelings that I am willing to compromise God's Word to accommodate everyone?

PRAYER: Lord, wed Your truth and love into Christlike responses that flow readily and consistently from my life.

October 27
God Sees And Knows All!

"He knows everything—doesn't he also know what you are doing? The Lord knows people's thoughts…" Psalm 94:10b,11a

It makes sense, doesn't it? If He is truly God, He <u>would</u> know our thoughts and everything we do. Yet most of us live as if we're somehow hidden from His view. Too often we're like a toddler playing "peekaboo." Since we can't see God, we assume He can't see us either.

How different would my life be were Christ to sit physically beside me at my computer, in my car, at my dinner table? Would I laugh at the same jokes, view the same scenes, drive the same speed? How comfortable am I, knowing that God is privy to my every thought?

In this passage, God is declaring that there is not a word He cannot hear, not an action He isn't aware of, not a thought He doesn't know. What does God do with that information?

Luke 12:2 informs us that *"the time is coming when… all that is secret will be made public. Whatever you have said in the dark will be heard in the light, and what you have whispered behind closed doors will be shouted from the housetops for all to hear!"*

PONDER: Do I live in conscious awareness of God's all-knowing presence? How can I intensify the sense of His nearness?

PRAYER: Let *"…the words of my mouth and the thoughts of my heart be pleasing to You, O Lord, my Rock and my Redeemer."* (Psalm 19:14)

October 28

It's A Matter Of Perspective!

"Joseph… said, 'God has made me fruitful in this land of my grief.'" Genesis 41:52

Joseph has been a slave in Egypt for over a decade, mistreated, maligned, and imprisoned. "Grief" is probably an understatement of the anguish he's endured.

Throughout his ordeal, he could not have known, or even imagined, what God was going to accomplish, what God was doing <u>even</u> <u>then</u>, in His magnificent plan to save Joseph's family, to preserve a nation and, ultimately, the Messiah's lineage.

Even as he says these words, Joseph still doesn't comprehend what he is part of, only that prosperity has come to him in the very place he has suffered so tremendously.

If we could fully comprehend God's perspective of our trials from "day one," how would that change our response? Would praise replace grumbling? Would anticipation outweigh drudgery? Would a song find its way into our hearts and onto our lips?

Yet God <u>has</u> graciously given us His vantage point: *"…we know that God causes all things to work together for the good of those who love God and are called according to his purpose for them." Romans 8:28*

So, what are we waiting for?

PONDER: Have I lost God's perspective? What is keeping me from trusting His promises? Do I not really believe His Word?

PRAYER: Lord, Jesus, forgive me for leaning on my own understanding rather than trusting Your promises. Help me see each situation through Your eyes, and may my responses confidently reflect the beauty of Your peace.

October 29
Every Tear I've Ever Cried!

"You keep track of all my sorrows. You have collected all my tears in your bottle. You have recorded each one in your book." Psalm 56:8 NLB

The mental image of Almighty God, the Creator of the universe, keeping track of each of the sorrows of my life, carefully collecting my tears in a bottle, overwhelms me!

And to think that He would then record each one in His book! How tender! How compassionate is this God of ours! And fiercely loyal to me! *"This I know, God is on my side!" (v. 9b)*

PONDER: How many times have I felt like no one cared… like I was all alone? Even then, God was keeping track of what I was going through, sweetly catching my teardrops when I was crying myself to sleep.

How is it possible that this God, whose presence fills the universe, notices and cares what I'm experiencing?

PRAYER: Forgive me, Lord, for allowing myself to believe Satan's lies to me, that I am alone and unloved… that no one cares. I choose to run to You and allow myself to be enfolded in Your embrace and comforted by Your tender mercies and unfailing love.

Help me to live in the confident trust that someday, in Your eternal presence, every tear will be finally and forever wiped from my eyes by the gentle finger of God Himself! This hope is possible only through the gracious sacrifice of the Lord Jesus Christ. It is in His Name I pray. Amen.

October 30
Still Trying To Be Good Enough?

"…no one will ever be made right with God by obeying the law." **Galatians 2:16**

Most of us spend all our growing up years believing that being good is what gets us the approval and rewards of those we are trying to please.

For those of us who were raised in religious families and churches, the same holds true. We learn early what to say and what not to say, what to do and what not to do. It doesn't take us long to put two and two together, and we spend the rest of our lives living out what we concluded as kids: that being accepted was all a matter of our performance or lack of it.

But Paul contradicts that theory in this profound statement. *"No one will ever be made right with God by obeying the law."*

Then how in the world does one become right with Him? *Romans 3:24* makes a very clear, bold statement: *"We are made right in God's sight when we trust in Jesus Christ to take away our sins."*

Galatians 5:4 declares, *"If you are trying to make yourselves right with God by keeping the law, you have been cut off from Christ…!"*

PONDER: Do I feel like I must "do" something to be approved by God?

PRAYER: Lord, I can never be good enough. That's why I need Jesus! Thank you for offering salvation as a **FREE GIFT** for all who will turn to You and admit they can't earn it.

October 31
Must I Always Learn The Hard Way?

"My child, never forget the things I have taught you. Store my commands in your heart. If you do this, you will live many years, and your life will be satisfying." Proverbs 3:1,2

Accepting advice and counsel is not easy to do, especially when we're young and sure of ourselves. However, now that I've become part of the group whose experience and wisdom is so often disregarded, it's more and more obvious to me why those of us further down the road are so prone to offer it.

Having done things "our way," having reaped the "benefits" of choices we've made, having realized the precious things we missed out on because we were too impatient or headstrong to wait on and obey the Lord, we often find ourselves longing for a way to warn and challenge the younger ones we love against heading down that same path.

The problem is <u>not</u> that we don't remember what it's like to be young. It's that we remember <u>all too well</u>! Wisdom is learned two ways: either the hard way or by listening to those who've already acquired it.

PONDER: Do I believe God knows best how to satisfy my life? Do I value those He's placed alongside me, whose experience and wisdom may help me avoid choices I might later come to regret?

PRAYER: Lord, help me know I need wisdom in my life. Help me seek it from You, Your Word, and from those You've lovingly placed in my life.

November

November 1
The Ultimate Lover

"For his unfailing love toward those who fear him is as great as the height of the heavens above the earth." Psalm 103:11

So—how much does God love us? Well, how high are the heavens? Only God knows the answer to that question, but we can get a little idea by listening to those within the scientific community who are diligently trying to figure it out.

By measuring the speed of light, scientists believe they have looked as far as 13.8 billion light years away. They estimate the Universe to be 28 billion light years in diameter, but know it is far larger than that.

This is not to comment on the accuracy of their work or conclusions, only to overwhelm us with the immensity of the Heavens God created. He declares them an instrument in comprehending the height, depth, length and breadth of His love for us.

The Apostle Paul, in *Ephesians 3:19*, prays that, though we will <u>never</u> be able to understand it fully, we might <u>experience</u> God's love and let it <u>change</u> us and make us *"complete with all the fullness of life and power that comes from God."*

PONDER: As I look into the Heavens and contemplate the size of the Universe in light of today's Scripture, what do they tell me about how much God loves me?

PRAYER: Lord, You are the Ultimate Lover! No one else in my life could possibly love me like You do. You have forever won my heart.

November 2
A Passionate Longing

"I long for the Lord more than sentries long for the dawn, yes, more than sentries long for the dawn." Psalm 130:6

Have you ever been assigned to an all-night job of some kind? Funny how when you <u>want</u> to stay up all night, it's exciting, but when you are <u>required</u> to, the night drags on forever.

Can you imagine any job more boring than standing guard on the wall of a city or fort in the last watch of the night during peacetime? Dawn couldn't come soon enough!

The Psalmist had obviously worked his share of all-nighters. He knew firsthand the restless longing for the break of day. Yet he declares in this passage, twice, that his longing for God was even more intense.

PONDER: As longings go, how would I describe my longing for God? What pushes my "hot button?" Is my relationship with God one that consumes me, or do I approach Him with a "take it or leave it" attitude—if I'm in the mood… if there isn't something more exciting to do or think about… if I'm not too busy, too tired, or…?

PRAYER: Heavenly Father, forgive me for my lack of spiritual desire. Forgive me for the times when I deliberately choose to forgo time with you for some other pleasure or obligation. Whet my appetite for spiritual things and woo my heart so that, like a starstruck lover, my thoughts will always run to You; my desire will always be for You.

November 3
The Death Of A Saint—Precious To God

"Precious in the sight of the Lord is the death of his saints." Psalm 116:15 KJV

Death will probably never seem precious to us! It robs and cheats us of those we love. But it is precious to God, and when we think about it, it makes sense.

From His perspective, God knows the deceased saint has finally cast off his/her frail body, prone to fatigue, pain, and disease, to exchange it for a brand-new, glorious body that will never, ever die.

God rejoices that the deceased believer is finally safely out of the reach of the evil one—FOREVER! The deceiver, the destroyer, will never again have any power to accuse, sift, or devour this loved one.

From His perspective, God finally gets to give His beloved child all He's been preparing for him/her. *"...eye has not seen, nor ear heard, neither have entered into the heart of man, the things that God has prepared for them that love Him." (I Corinthians 2:9 NKJV)*

Finally, death causes people to think about, and prepare for, the eternal. If the death of a believer we love stirs our hearts to seek God and receive His gift of salvation, then, from God's perspective, that is _especially_ precious.

PONDER: Do I see death as enemy #1, to be hated, feared, and avoided at all costs? Am I willing to allow God to help me view death from His perspective?

PRAYER: Thank you, Lord, for your take on death, which gives us glorious HOPE!

November 4

Oh, To Be A Child Again!

"Praise the Lord; praise God our savior! For each day he carries us in his arms." Psalm 68:19

Remember when you were little and your mom and dad (or brothers/sisters) carried you everywhere? Me neither. But life must have been simple back then, with somebody else responsible for what I ate, what I wore, whether I was dressed, fed, bathed… or not.

For the life of me, I cannot figure out why I was always so anxious to grow up and be big enough to do everything myself! These days, I often feel overwhelmed. Sometimes life is just plain hard! In those moments, it would feel good just to rest in someone else's arms and be a child again.

The Psalmist discovered an incredible secret and wants to share it with us! Our Creator God longs to be "Abba Father" to us— "Daddy God"—adopting us into His family, providing for us, guiding us, cleansing our hearts—yes, even "carrying" us.

There is a catch, however: we must quit pretending we have all the answers. We must humbly trust His provision and rest in Him!

PONDER: What areas of my life are out of control? What broken places in my heart have I been unable to fix? What keeps me from simply resting in the strong, loving arms of my Heavenly Father?

PRAYER: Lord, I realize I <u>do</u> need you. I'm done pretending. I can't do life on my own anymore. I need your forgiveness and cleansing. Heal my brokenness. Carry me! I trust in You alone.

November 5
How Much Do I Care?

"And the Good News about the Kingdom will be preached throughout the whole world, so that all nations will hear it; and then the end will come." Matthew 24:14

In our world today, there are still many un-reached people groups, persons who have yet to hear the name of Jesus and His incredible offer of salvation.

For those who long for His return, Jesus's words in this passage should motivate us. When all nations have heard, the end will come. Then and only then will Jesus return!

What can we do to hasten that day? Does Christ's Second Coming score more than a 'blip' on the radar screen of our longings? Have we ever allowed God to break our hearts with His passion for those who have never heard?

It's too easy to become so preoccupied with <u>my</u> life, <u>my</u> cares, <u>my</u> loved ones, <u>my</u> career, or even <u>my</u> spiritual life, that I give little thought to whether or not there are people out there somewhere in the world—people like me—who still live in darkness and fear, without even a glimpse of hope.

PONDER: Does God have ready access to my money, my time, my plans, my prayer life? What might He do through me, if I let Him?

PRAYER: Lord, fill me with Your compassion for lost folks. Place in me Your longing for the people of the world who have yet to hear of Your love and mercy. Then move me to action on their behalf.

November 6

If It's All God's Anyway…?

"All the believers… felt that what they owned was not their own, so they shared everything they had." Acts 4:32

How does one come to grips with the reality that, despite the world's system of declaring ownership, you and I would have nothing, if not for the grace and provision of God?

The very <u>breath</u> we breathe comes from Him. Our health, strength, time, energy to work, creativity to produce—all are gifts from the loving hand of a merciful God Who owes us <u>nothing</u>, except retribution, yet chooses to lavish love on us anyway.

Everything we have is on temporary loan from God. Our very life belongs to Him. If it's all His, then its use should be determined by **<u>His</u>** priorities, not ours, right? Do I even <u>know</u> God's priorities, or do I just assume they are the same as mine?

When making decisions about where to spend "my" time, "my" energy, or "my" money, perhaps the best question would be, "How does God want **<u>His</u>** money spent? Where does God want **<u>His</u>** energy used today? What would God like to do with **<u>His</u>** car, house, tools, etc. today?"

PONDER: Are my answers to those questions different from the way I already live? If so, what does God want me to do about it?

PRAYER: Lord, forgive me for grasping the things you've given me as if they were actually mine. I acknowledge You as their true Owner and seek Your heart in all decisions concerning their use.

November 7
Pfew! Something Stinks Here!

"...You've made me stink among all the people of this land..."
Genesis 34:30

Their sister had been raped, and they were understandably enraged. The town leaders were not interested in righting this wrong, so justice would be up to them.

After immobilizing the men of Shechem through crafty scheming, Simeon and Levi killed every adult male, and, with the help of their brothers, they looted the village and took the women and children captive.

When Jacob realized what they had done, he knew they had forever tarnished his good name and reputation in that place. Before moving on, Jacob insisted his sons purify themselves and get rid of all their pagan idols.

This story reminds me of *Ezekiel 36:22,23*, where God tells the Israelites they have profaned **His** Holy Name. Apparently, it's possible for God's children to bring shame on their Father's name, just like Jacob's sons did.

In our zeal to see right prevail and wrong exposed, to ensure God's people are protected and vindicated, is it possible to lose sight of the honor and holiness of the Name we bear?

How should the long-suffering of God, the everlasting kindness, mercy, and grace with which the Lord has treated <u>our</u> sinfulness, inform and shape the ways in which we address the wrongs of others?

PONDER: If people's understanding of God could <u>only</u> come from <u>my</u> attitudes, words, and actions, would they get an <u>accurate</u> picture of what God is really like?

PRAYER: Lord, make me a faithful ambassador of Your Holy Name.

November 8

You Want Me To Do What?

"He... made a clay paste... rubbed the paste on the blind man's eyes, and said, 'Go, wash at the Pool of Siloam [Siloam means 'Sent'].' The man went and washed—and saw." John 9:6,7

Why didn't Jesus just heal him? Why send him down a narrow path of uneven, stone steps to wash mud from his eyes? The trek to the Pool of Siloam was not an easy one, even for a sighted man.

We're told only that the man <u>went</u> and <u>washed</u>—and **SAW**!

When did the miracle take place? When he washed, or when Jesus spoke? As the man groped and stumbled his way to the pool, what kind of thoughts went through his mind? Was he tempted to be discouraged, to doubt, to give up?

What if he had stopped?

How often our Lord asks us to step out of our comfort zone and head toward a destination called "Sent." We may even begin eagerly, but the way is fraught with uneven steps. We "skin our knees" and "stub our toes" and perhaps even question our sanity along the way.

From Christ's perspective, the blind man's miracle was already accomplished! What happened next would reveal whether the man really trusted Jesus or not.

PONDER: Has God spoken a clear, yet unfulfilled, Word to my heart? How am I doing? Still believing? Still moving forward?

PRAYER: Lord, help me know that trust and obedience are part of the miracle! Your Word is all I need for now.

November 9
Too Quick On The Trigger

"...the whole community... gathered... and prepared to go to war... First, however, they sent a delegation... to talk... When the leaders... heard... they were satisfied... [and] *replied, '... you have not committed this treachery...as we thought...'" Joshua 22:11-13,30,31*

A terrible tragedy was barely averted!

The tribes east of the Jordan built an imposing altar as a reminder to all Israel that they, too, worshiped the One True God. Israelites on the west misread their motives as rebelling against God's clear instructions. War nearly erupted.

"How silly," we declare from the advantage of perspective. "Why would they kill their relatives and friends over something like that?"

Why, indeed? Yet how many times have <u>we</u> jumped to conclusions and responded in ways that wounded others and brought unnecessary division and strife? Our human tendency is to assume we know **"why"** people do what they do. Our sense of justice compels us to respond. We seldom question our assumptions.

Two "takeaways" should guide our future interactions:

1. "The Lord, the Mighty One, is God! He knows the truth..." (v. 22) If only we would choose to consult the One Who knows, how much pain might be avoided in the Body of Christ?

2. **Talk to the offending party. How can we really know a person's motives unless we ask and then listen?**

PONDER: Am I quick to assign motives before asking God, or others, for truth?

PRAYER: Lord, make me *"quick to listen, slow to speak, and slow to get angry." James 1:19*

November 10

Show Mercy—Hate Sin

"Show mercy to still others, but do so with great caution, hating the sins that contaminate their lives." Jude 1:23

God is perfectly able to hate sin and still offer mercy. Calvary was His ultimate demonstration of that! His loathing for sin, combined with His fierce love for mankind, drove Him to offer Himself as the atonement for our sin.

We humans struggle with finding that balance. It's usually "either/or" for us. To those for whom compassion rules the day, calling people to forsake their sin seems harsh and uncaring. Conversely, hating sin is very often accompanied by a legalistic, unbending adherence to a set of rules, which can produce cruel results.

Neither reflects the heart of God. God hates sin, but He loves people! Sin is loathsome to Him because of what it does to people. Until Jesus came, there was no way to separate sin from the person who committed it. Both had to be condemned!

In taking our sin upon Himself, however, Jesus Christ forever removed our sin from us! When we choose to receive His amazing gift of salvation, God hides us "in Christ" so we may stand in His presence without fault or blemish. Hallelujah!

PONDER: Am I an "either/or" person? On which side of this issue does my heart usually reside?

PRAYER: Thank You, Lord, for showing mercy to me! Help me pass it on without ever minimizing sin's destructive power in people's lives.

November 11
Asleep In The Enemy's Lap

"When he woke up, he thought, 'I will do as before and shake myself free.' But he didn't realize the Lord had left him." Judges 16:20b

For the first time in his life, Samson was utterly powerless. He'd been told his strength was supernatural, a gift from God, but somewhere along the line, he'd forgotten or disregarded the true source of his abilities. Self-indulgence, flirtations with God's enemies, and disregard for the holy anointing on his life had pushed God away. Though he still **felt** confident and powerful, his might was gone.

How like Samson we are. Most days, we barely give God a nod, choosing instead from a myriad of worldly pleasures and activities. Though Scripture warns us vehemently to stay awake and alert, we've been lulled to sleep in the lap of our enemy.

To be sure, we still want Christ at our beck and call in times of crisis. However, we've grieved God's Spirit. Unbeknownst to us, we're now solely dependent on our own meager resources, and, when calamity comes, we'll find ourselves at the mercy of the situation we've created.

Even so, with God, it's never too late to begin again! Praise His Name!

Though Samson's choices had cost him everything he held dear, God was still just a prayer away, and in his last moments of life, Samson trusted God to deliver his most stunning victory.

PONDER: On what do I focus... or depend?

PRAYER: It's You I need and want, Lord. Only You.

November 12
Why Such A Struggle?

"…Why have you brought all this trouble… Lord? Ever since I came to Pharaoh… he has been even more brutal to your people. And you have done nothing…!" Exodus 5:22,23

Perspective is so difficult to come by. God had told the Israelites He would deliver them. In His original instructions, he'd also indicated that He would strengthen Pharaoh's resolve, that Pharaoh would not give in until after his own son was killed. God's Word <u>should</u> have been enough, but it wasn't.

God **<u>could</u>** have spelled it out in more specific detail, i.e:

"I'm not only going to <u>deliver</u> you from your enemies. I'm going to <u>annihilate</u> them. Because of the extra burdens you are being asked to bear right now, when you finally leave Egypt, your bodies will be stronger, healthier… better able to endure the journey ahead.

"The very suffering you're complaining about will evoke so much compassion and fear in the hearts of your Egyptian neighbors that they will gladly load you down with all their wealth and possessions.

"And finally, when you observe all I am about to do to your enemy, you will come to know that I am God alone, and there is nothing too hard for me!"

God seldom reveals all the specifics. What He wants <u>most</u> is our **<u>trust</u>**. We have His **<u>Word</u>**. That <u>should</u> be enough.

PONDER: What are the areas of my life I can't seem to trust God with?

PRAYER: Lord, I do believe You, but part of me struggles with that. Please, help my unbelief!

November 13
Chained To The One I Hate

"A bowl of vegetables with someone you love is better than steak with someone you hate." Proverbs 15:17

When one's heart is free from bitterness and hatred, even the simplest of meals can be a pleasant experience. But nursing a grudge, refusing to forgive, and permitting bitterness to fester will allow the person I hate to take up residence in my heart and go with me everywhere I go, spoiling even the most momentous occasions.

The mere thought, or mention, of his/her name can produce indigestion, tainting a juicy steak which, just moments earlier, had made my mouth water. This individual doesn't have to be physically present to ruin things for me. Let someone speak of, or praise, him/her in my hearing, and the effect is instantaneous.

Hatred makes me a prisoner. It chains me to the very one I loathe, sentencing me to relive the offense over, and over, and over again.

Jesus commands and enables me to "let it go." When I choose to forgive in the power of His Spirit, I will be set free, liberated, no longer in bondage to that person or event that has so long enslaved me.

PONDER: Has a name or face come to my mind as I've read today's thoughts? How much more of my life will I allow that person to contaminate?

PRAYER: Lord, I'm so tired! Bitterness is such a heavy load to carry. I lay it down now and choose forgiveness instead, in the Name of Jesus.

November 14
Do I Have To?

"…Who knows if perhaps you were made queen for just such a time as this?" Esther 4:14

Young Esther finds herself in a position she'd never anticipated or desired. Ripped from all she'd ever known, she's placed in the king's harem, with no hope of ever returning to her former way of life.
All dreams of marrying a Jewish man (did she already have a betrothed?), having Jewish babies, living among Jewish family and friends are gone… forever!

No doubt her new position includes certain perks. However, isolation from family and friends, strange customs and religious practices, and marriage to a much older man are far from what she'd have wished for her future.

Even more frightening, the king of Persia is intimidating, unpredictable, and easily persuaded to make new, irrevocable laws on the recommendations of ill-intentioned advisors.

As a result, Esther finds herself in a precarious situation. She's the only person capable of saving her people from annihilation, yet to do so may cost her life. She hesitates, but her uncle Mordecai reminds her that she may be **IN THIS PLACE… AT THIS TIME… FOR THIS VERY REASON.**

PONDER: Do I find myself in an unwanted, difficult situation? How might God want to use me to fulfill His purposes?

PRAYER: Lord, open my eyes to look outside myself, to see the people you've placed around me, the opportunities that are mine **ONLY** because I am here, in this place, at this time. And then, Lord, use me for Your Glory.

November 15

Hot Or Cold?

"…the love of many will grow cold. But the one who endures to the end will be saved." Matthew 24:12,13

Nothing ever goes from hot to cold in an instant. Even in the Arctic, when we put a pot to boil, there isn't a chance in the world the water will grow cold as long as the fire is burning.

Things grow cold <u>only</u> when the fire is allowed to go out. Even so, the cooling process is never a quick one. Rather, it is imperceptible, so gradual it's difficult to say when it begins and ends.

Of course, in some circumstances, the cooling-off process is desirable, or even necessary, to achieve a specific outcome, but **<u>not</u>** in our relationships, especially not our relationship with the Lord Jesus Christ!

In any friendship, inattentiveness, neglect, or preoccupation with life can be deadly. Unfortunately, their effect is so subtle, we may fail to appreciate the danger. Like tending a fire, close, intimate relationships <u>must</u> be carefully nurtured.

PONDER: How many of my waking, unoccupied thoughts turn to my Savior? What is it that consumes my attention most of the time? Does Jesus get my <u>first</u> thoughts or my last, my <u>best</u> time or what's left over, the <u>largest</u> portion or the least amount of my time, energy, and imagination?

PRAYER: Dear Lord, help me pursue You as the Lover of My Soul. Help me recognize those things that draw my heart away. Strengthen my desire to flee from them at any cost.

November 16
Learning To Live Loved!

"Take delight in the Lord, and he will give you your heart's desires."
Psalm 37:4

Both our vehicles were approaching 200,000 miles. Twice, while transporting clients, mine had overheated. My husband's was making threatening noises. We decided we shouldn't invest big bucks in either of them again.

However, I wanted to make sure we weren't jumping ahead of the Lord—that I wasn't acting out of a spirit of discontent. My prayer was, *"Lord, help me seek You first and trust Your provision for me, knowing that, at the right time, You will provide exactly what I need."*

I'd told God the kind of car I felt was necessary, but one day, I shamelessly asked, *"Lord, if I wait on You, will You please make my new car <u>red</u>?"*

When the day finally came, guess what God provided? As I drove home in my "new," red SUV, I thought how thrilled my deceased mother would have been, and then it hit me: my Heavenly Father was thrilled for me, too, even more so!

My heart was overwhelmed as I realized just how much it must have delighted my God to so carefully and meticulously orchestrate this provision for me.

PONDER: Do I think of God as an ogre, ready to pounce at my mistakes? Or as a loving Father, excited to bless me when I delight myself in Him?

PRAYER: Your Word is true, Lord. Forgive me for <u>**ever**</u> doubting You. Teach me to live loved by You.

November 17

What Do My "Thoughts" Reveal?

"So don't worry about these things saying, 'What will we eat? What will we drink? What will we wear?' These things dominate the thoughts of unbelievers, but your heavenly Father already knows all your needs." Matthew 6:31,32

What thoughts dominate my mind? God says my thoughts are a "dead giveaway" to what is really true about me. Worry, anxiety, fear… these dominate the minds of those who don't really believe God. Even BELIEVERS can find themselves in that category.

There is a difference between "believing **in** God" and "believing **God**." Many of us who believe "in" God, who've been born again and received eternal life still fail to believe <u>God</u> when He promises to take care of us.

There is also a distinction between "peace **with** God" and "the peace **of** God." When we believe in God and open our hearts to His salvation, we experience peace "with" God. But the peace "of" God is reserved only for those who will believe God, trust what He says, and rely on Him.

The thoughts that dominate our minds prove whether or not we really **trust** God. It matters little what we say with our mouths, if it isn't matched by a willingness to *"take every thought captive and make it obey Christ." II Corinthians 10:5*

PONDER: What do the thoughts that dominate my mind reveal about my confidence in God?

PRAYER: Lord, expose the worry and anxiety that rob me of Your peace and reveal my lack of trust.

November 18

How To Get Even With Your Enemy

"Don't retaliate with insults when people insult you. Instead, pay them back with a blessing. That is what God has called you to do, and he will bless you for it." I Peter 3:9

Pay them back with a "blessing?" Did I read that correctly? This may be perfectly natural for God, but it goes against the grain of everything within the human heart!

Actually, without God's power at work deep within us, changing our hearts and motivation, it's downright impossible. Yet here is Peter, under the Holy Spirit's inspiration, calling us to repay insult and injury with a "blessing."

Imagine, for a minute, what that might look like. Someone betrays us, cheats on us, slanders us… Our response? *"Okay! You're in for it now! I'm going to get you! I'm going to repay you… by asking God to bless and prosper you! …with a friendly smile and a wave whenever I see you! …with a plate of cookies for the holidays!"*

The writer of Proverbs says that by returning good for evil, we shame our enemies far worse than if we injured them somehow. Hmmmm…

We would never have thought of it, but that's how God operates all the time. And aren't we glad God paid <u>us</u> back with kindness when we thumbed our noses at Him?

PONDER: How like God am I? Am I willing to allow Him to work this miracle into my life?

PRAYER: Lord, I want to know the joy of responding like You do.

November 19

Worship That Pleases Me? Or God?

"David and all Israel were celebrating before God with all their might, singing songs and playing all kinds of musical instruments…" I Chronicles 13:8

Could there possibly be anything wrong with this scene? Why then, just moments later, does it turn tragic, as God's anger is displayed in shocking fashion?

God had <u>specifically</u> instructed them how to transport the Ark. However, when the Philistines had captured it, they'd carried it off, and returned it, on an ox-drawn cart. That made a lot of sense! Why not do it that way?

David is utterly stunned at what happens next. He immediately halts the worship service and parks the Ark of the Covenant.

Though David is now understandably afraid of God, he immediately recognizes the fault lies with the Israelites. They have obviously breached their covenant with God. So, he goes **back to the Word** to discover the problem: *"Because…[the] Levites did not carry the Ark the first time, the anger of the Lord our God burst out against us. We failed to ask God how to move it properly." I Chronicles 15:13*

The Ark is moved again. The same joyful, jubilant celebration occurs. But <u>**this**</u> time, God blesses their worship.

PONDER: Do I worship in ways that accommodate and please me? Do I combine what I love about the world with what I love about God and hope God is pleased?

PRAYER: Heavenly Father, help me search out <u>Your</u> heart, in <u>Your</u> Word. Teach me how to worship You as <u>**You**</u> desire.

November 20

A Healthy Pain!

"...Those who love their children care enough to discipline them..." Proverbs 13:24; "Blessed are those who fear to do wrong, but the stubborn are headed for serious trouble." Proverbs 28:14

How does anyone become fearful of doing wrong? We're certainly not born with this capacity. Human nature stubbornly pursues its own desires, thinks it knows best, and defies anyone to tell it otherwise.

Fear of wrongdoing comes only by association, and <u>that</u> only through experiencing the pain of consequences. The first opportunity to learn the connection between wrong behavior and that "pain" should come from loving parents.

If we truly love our kids, God says we'll be diligent to help them learn this lesson early in their lives. He's lovingly created a place on the human body with enough nerve endings to allow for acute association of painful consequences, yet with enough padding to protect from real harm.

The association of pain as a swift and direct consequence of disrespect, disregard, and disobedience to authority is the surest way to enable those we love to avoid the "serious trouble" that results from such attitudes and behavior as they move through life.

PONDER: In withholding discipline, am I actually loving <u>myself</u> more than my child, protecting <u>myself</u> from the emotional distress of inflicting "pain" on one I love?

PRAYER: Lord, help me love my child enough to do the difficult thing that is <u>needed</u> and <u>right</u>, rather than the emotionally expedient thing that sets him/her up for serious trouble down the road.

November 21

Is What I Tell Myself Always True?

"And you will know the truth, and the truth will set you free."
John 8:32

Which of us has not heard voices inside our head, accusing and making us feel worthless, disgusting, unlovable, ashamed, unforgiveable? Our minds and emotions are quick to agree, and they shape our thinking as we move into the day, make our decisions, interact with people, etc.

Stress, lack of sleep, physical illness, and hormonal imbalance are only a few of the influences contributing to our inability to recognize and debunk the lies constantly bombarding us.

Years ago, during overwhelming bouts with PMS and its accompanying feelings of self-denigration, I remember a wise person telling me:

"What you're feeling and believing right now is not necessarily true. **God's Word** *is absolute* **Truth**. *You need to get God's Word into your heart— whether you feel like it or not, whether it inspires you or not—in order to recognize Truth and discern lies when you hear them."*

Though my emotional state made it difficult to get inspired by anything, I turned to God's Word as though it were "medicine" for my soul. The change was not instant, but, over time, I learned to question and reject those voices that didn't line up with Truth.

PONDER: Am I a slave to the inner voices of self-doubt, worthlessness, shame, and fear?

PRAYER: Lord, help me get the Word into my heart so it can set me free. Help me challenge personal beliefs with Your Truth!

November 22

Is God Good — All The Time?

"Though a mighty army surrounds me, my heart will not be afraid. Even if I am attacked, I will remain confident." Psalm 27:3

How does one arrive at such confidence in the face of incredible danger and overwhelming odds? Such a declaration defies logic and flies in the face of human emotion.

The secret of the Psalmist's calm in the midst of the storm lies in his assurance that the Lord is his light, his salvation, his fortress, his protection from danger *(v. 1)*. Peace comes from knowing that the One in whom he trusts is **GOOD**, and whatever his God allows will be used for good purposes, even when all appearances suggest otherwise.

Most of us wait until we are in the midst of trauma and then interpret God's character through what we see happening around us. Trying to decipher God's trustworthiness through <u>that</u> grid will always lead to deductions based purely on the emotions at hand.

Our conclusions regarding the character of God **<u>mus</u>t** be based on facts, given by God Himself in His Holy Word, rather than on the unstable, volatile emotions of the moment. Choosing, like the Psalmist, to trust God's self-revelation will hold us steady in crisis.

PONDER: Have I settled the issue of God's goodness? On what am I basing my conclusions?

PRAYER: God, Your Word declares You are good and what You do is good. That doesn't always "<u>feel</u>" true, but I choose to believe it **<u>is</u>** true, because Your Word affirms it.

November 23

Forget Not To Remember

"Let all that I am praise the Lord; may I never forget the good things He does for me." Psalm 103:2

The Psalmist was apparently well aware that our "forgetters" are generally much better than our "rememberers." Perhaps he knew firsthand that unless we are intentional in our efforts to "forget not" the good things God does for us, the hard stuff of life will take center stage.

It's not that we <u>intend</u> to forget all God's good gifts. It's just that God's blessings include many things we take for granted, like waking up in the morning, breathing another breath, and the capacity to think and feel. We get so used to them that we don't consider them "blessings" anymore. They feel more like "rights."

PONDER: What "good things" from God have I taken for granted? Are my conversations (and my prayers) consumed with my problems or my praises? Is my life truly devoid of blessings, or have I just failed to "remember" them?

PRAYER: *"Let all that is within me praise the Lord!"* Yes, I <u>will</u> praise You, Lord, with my whole heart, even in the midst of circumstances I don't like or understand. I will intentionally recount (and record) the good things You <u>have</u> done for me! And as I do, I pray I will find it easier to trust (and praise) You in life's difficult places. In the name of the Lord Jesus, Your most incredible Gift to me. Amen.

November 24

Apathy Hurts God's Heart

"My people don't recognize my care for them." Isaiah 1:3b

Probably not much can break a parent's heart more than a child's ingratitude. To love so much it hurts, to give one's self sacrificially, to spend and be spent, for someone who doesn't seem to notice or care, must be very difficult.

In some ways, straight-up rejection would be easier to bear than indifference. One has to at least acknowledge you in order to hate you. Apathy and ingratitude communicate total disregard. You might as well be nonexistent!

Many parents try to motivate attitude change by withholding privileges or "trinkets," but who wants to be acknowledged only because of gifts given or withheld? We want to be known and loved for who we <u>are</u>! Because we've experienced such longings ourselves, it seems inconceivable that we would not be able to comprehend God's heartache as he describes the apathy of those He loves.

If even donkeys and oxen instinctively know and recognize their masters *(v. 3)*, why is it, God asks sadly, that people He made in His own image don't bother to acknowledge His love and care?

PONDER: Do I humbly identify all God has given me, or do I take it for granted? Is anything too small to be gratefully recognized as a gift from God?

PRAYER: Lord, I acknowledge You're the source of every good thing in my world. Make my life a continual offering of praise!

November 25

Did God Blow It?

"You made all the delicate, inner parts of my body and knit me together in my mother's womb." Psalm 139:13

Ever wonder why you are the way you are? Ever wish you were more like someone else, someone more popular or talented, someone whose life represents all you wish yours could be?

You and I are fearfully and wonderfully made by God. What did God envision when He first dreamed of creating us? Is He excited about what He's concocted?

We humans can understand such delight. One who bakes a cake wants it to be eaten and enjoyed, not simply admired. There is great pleasure for an artist in knowing his paintings have been appreciated and proudly displayed.

Imagine God's joy as He anticipates the unfolding of His purposes for our lives. Consider how He must grieve, then, when we waste or disregard the beauty and potential He's placed within us, rejecting His plan to pine unabashedly for someone else's lot.

PONDER: Do I begrudge the way I'm made? Do I feel, deep down, that God blew it when assigning parents, determining ethnicity, or handing out talents, beauty, or brains?

PRAYER: Lord, forgive me for judging You and Your purposes for my life. Help me trust that the plan You have for <u>me</u> is a <u>good</u> one, and one only <u>I</u> can accomplish. And thank You for designing me with <u>everything</u> I need to fulfill that special purpose.

November 26

I've Gotta Say "Thanks!"

"Those who live at the ends of the earth stand in awe of your wonders. From where the sun rises to where it sets, you inspire shouts of joy." Psalm 65:8

Did you notice the sunrise this morning? The sky, streaked with glorious shades of pink and purple, was so breathtaking that an almost involuntary "Wow!" escaped my lips before I was even aware I'd made a sound.

Immediately, my mind acknowledged the presence of the **Artist,** the Creator of such intense beauty. A spirit of gratitude and worship welled up in my heart.

I dare say many who marveled at the incredible beauty of this morning's colorful display are people for whom an acknowledgement of God as its Source would be unthinkable. Yet they, too, stood in awe of the exquisite exhibit before them.

Those who refuse to acknowledge God as Creator still feel the same pleasure, the same sense of wonder, at such a display, but they've no One to whom they can express the joyful appreciation that's been awakened deep within their souls.

How sad! To feel such gratitude yet have no One to praise would be like holding your breath underwater. Eventually, you <u>have</u> to take a breath, but if you do, life as you've known it will end!

PONDER: Do I give voice to the worship that wells within me as I enjoy God's artistry?

PRAYER: Thank You, Lord, for the joy of acknowledging my gratitude to **YOU** as the Source of all the beauty and grandeur of life!

November 27

Do I Know God's Heart—Do I Care?

"They call me the Most High, but they don't truly honor me." Hosea 11:7

Most kids don't set out to shame or embarrass their families. But each of us did, in one way or another. Our choices didn't always reflect our parents' training, hopes, and dreams for us.

The problem was our selfish, stubborn hearts. We talked ourselves into believing we were obeying their commands when we were actually just parsing words, trying to do what they "said" while still managing to get what we wanted.

When confronted, we probably argued and justified ourselves with, *"But I **did** what you **SAID**!"* Mom and Dad might have had to acknowledge that fact, but their hearts were broken with the realization that either we knew what they "meant," and chose not to do it, or we never knew them well enough to know or care about what was really important to them in the first place.

God's heart must break almost continually for the very same reason. He has spoken to us through His Word, and, while it's true that Scripture is silent on many of the issues we face in our modern culture, God has revealed <u>more</u> <u>than</u> <u>enough</u> about Himself for us to make the choices that align with His heart.

PONDER: Do I parse God's words, obeying the "letter" of the law, while ignoring its "spirit?"

PRAYER: Lord, I want to care about what's important to You, to <u>honor</u> the desires of Your heart, not just Your words.

November 28

Receiving Instruction—So Hard to Do!

"The wise are glad to be instructed, but babbling fools fall flat on their faces." Proverbs 10:8

One of the hardest things in life is to welcome instruction. From our earliest days, the independent, *"I can do it myself"* attitude shows up. Admitting we might need help runs counter to everything within us. Some of us see such an admission as "weakness," and, like the babbling fool in our passage today, will only learn when we've made a royal mess of things, run out of options, or fallen flat on our faces in humiliation.

How much better to walk through life with our eyes and ears open to learn from the mistakes and failures of others along the journey.

To their advantage, some people have been smart enough to **seek** the advice and counsel of those folks who've learned life's lessons the hard way. God calls that "wisdom."

But in this passage, we're not just talking about someone who seeks instruction, though that is a very noble pursuit. God is referring here to one willing to **BE** instructed, to **receive** even **unbidden** instruction with a **glad**, welcoming attitude. That's a whole different ballgame—one few of us want to play!

PONDER: How good am I at allowing myself to **be** instructed?

PRAYER: Heavenly Father, without Your Spirit's power, there is just no way I have the wisdom to receive instruction with gladness. Fill me with Yourself! Make me wise enough to see and respond to things the way You do.

November 29

God As I Want Him To Be

"Have any of these prophets been in the Lord's presence to hear what he is really saying? Has even one of them cared enough to listen?" Jeremiah 23:18

God's anger in this passage of Scripture is directed at false prophets, but there is a principle here worth pondering.

God could just as easily ask these questions about us. ***"Have any of those who've taken My Name been in My presence to hear what I am <u>really</u> saying? Has even one of them cared enough to listen?"***

If we are not waiting on the Lord for marching orders—constantly listening for His voice—we can easily succumb to the notion that God thinks like we do. We end up representing Him then, not how He <u>truly</u> is, but rather how we, in our humanness, assume or desire Him to be. We "create" a God more to our liking, one that better fits the mores of our society.

It's easy to talk about a God of love, but who in our culture wants to hear about moral absolutes or a coming and final Judgment upon sin? Most folks aren't comfortable with a God Who says we're <u>all</u> "sinners" and declares us unfit to share His glory unless we are "born again" by His Spirit.

PONDER: Is my view of God dictated more by what I <u>want</u> Him to be than how He's revealed Himself in His Word?

PRAYER: Lord, help me come to know and love You as You **REALLY** are!

November 30

His Life—In MY Body!

"Oh, what a miserable person I am! Who will free me from this life that is dominated by sin and death? Thank God! The answer is in Jesus Christ our Lord…" Romans 7:24,25a

The miracle of the cross/Resurrection for believers is that bondage to sin, which for so long dominated our lives, has been broken. New, victorious, joy-filled life is available! But try as we might, we will never be able to live this life apart from the indwelling Christ.

Some of us do try. In fact, we've been trying for as long as we can remember. Deep down, we're tired, frustrated, defeated, angry, and guilt-ridden. We don't want to give up on Christ, but we certainly aren't experiencing abundant life!

Jesus Christ is the answer, but not as an "example to follow" or a "life to emulate." Abundant living comes only as Christ is allowed to live His very life in and through our bodies.

No matter how hard we try, we can't pull it off, but when we crucify that part of us that demands its own way, Christ is free to live His life in our bodies, looking out at the world through our eyes, touching with our hands, speaking with our mouths…

PONDER: Have I been trying to "live for" Jesus, "imitate" Him, "copy" His behavior? Do I actually think that, with enough effort, I can succeed?

PRAYER: Lord, I'm totally weak, inadequate. Take every part of me and live Your life through my body.

December

December 1
Why Not Just Receive It?

"Jesus replied, 'If you only knew the gift God has for you… you would ask…'" John 4:10

Why is God the last One we turn to for filling our empty, thirsty souls? Why are we so suspicious of Him and His gifts? What makes us so determined to "go it alone?"

We're not really sure God is trustworthy! We'd rather rely on our <u>own</u> evaluation of life, of what's good and evil, and what will make us happy. We spin elaborate stories in our minds to dismiss Him, convincing ourselves He doesn't exist or that He doesn't care, so we can go our merry way, pursuing those things we hope will silence the raging storm inside.

It's pride that keeps us on the run, pride that makes us think we know better than God what we need. But when we've run our course and come up empty, Jesus will still be waiting—still offering God's gift.

If we'll humbly receive God's provision, we'll find it was what we were looking for all along. Why were we running away? What were we afraid of? Why did we fight Him for so long?

PONDER: Do I trust God? Really? Or am I still trying to handle things myself, as if, with enough discipline, effort, and determination, I could fix the brokenness of my life?

PRAYER: Jesus, I'm through running. I've found I cannot satisfy this deep thirst in my soul! I've tried. Please give me what You see I need.

December 2
Am I More Loving Than God?

"You parents—if your children ask for a loaf of bread, do you give them a stone instead? Or if they ask for a fish, do you give them a snake? Of course not! So if you sinful people know how to give good gifts to your children, how much more will your heavenly Father give good gifts to those who ask him?" Matthew 7:9-11

Jesus is talking about being persistent when asking God for what we need. He insists that we keep on asking, seeking, and knocking with the confident expectation that **God truly desires to give us good things**. Do we believe that about God?

We humans love to give <u>our</u> children what they ask for, if it is within our power and if we are sure it would be "good" for them, not harmful. Are we more loving than God, Jesus asks? The answer from Scripture is a resounding "No!"

PONDER: How do I see God? As a tyrant, doling out favors for good deeds and perfect performance, somehow enjoying my failures so He can keep His gifts to Himself?

Or do I presume upon Him, as if He were a doting Santa Claus who gives his gifts simply because I want them, regardless of their propriety or safety?

PRAYER: Lord God, forgive me for selling You so short! Help me believe in Your love. Help me trust in Your wisdom. Help me rest in Your goodness. And then, help me ask with confidence and perseverance.

December 3
Tired Of The Struggle?

"Do to others whatever you would like them to do to you. This is the essence of all that is taught in the law..." Matthew 7:12; "...You must love the Lord your God with all your heart, all your soul, and all your mind. This is the first and greatest commandment. A second is equally important: Love your neighbor as yourself. The entire law... [is] based on these two commandments." Matthew 22:37-39; "But the Holy Spirit produces this kind of fruit in our lives: love, joy, peace, patience, kindness, goodness, faithfulness, gentleness, and self-control. There is no law against these things!" Galatians 5:22,23

When the Apostle Paul tells us we are not under law but under grace, he's not saying we should disregard the law of God, as some would have us believe. No! He is saying, if we allow God to fill our hearts with Himself, God's love will inform and permeate everything we do.

Christ's love will NEVER violate a neighbor. He seeks ONLY what is good and right and true. Love never delights in wrongdoing.

Rather than struggling to obey a list of rules and religious duties (The Law), let us seek to be filled with God's Spirit. As He floods our hearts with His love, the violation of God's law will not even be an issue.

PONDER: Will I allow Christ to do "in me" what the law could never do? *Romans 8:3*

PRAYER: Lord, I surrender. I'm tired of striving. Jesus, take the wheel!

December 4

May I Ask Who's Calling?

"…May He give you the power to accomplish all the good things your faith prompts you to do. Then the name of our Lord Jesus will be honored because of the way you live…" II Thessalonians 1:11,12

Perhaps it's not possible to act on <u>every</u> good motivation we have, but I dare say, if the motivation is coming from the Lord Himself, there is a way to make it happen. He will see to that, if we'll simply act on what we **know** He is saying.

How do we discern God's voice? As humans, that can get tricky because we are dealing with an enemy who loves to use even our sincerity to somehow trip us up and condemn us.

Here are a couple of tips to help us:

1. Ask, "Is this something I would naturally think to do on my own?" Typically, when self-sacrifice, trust, or humility are involved, it isn't our idea (or the devil's).

2. Ask the Lord, "If this is Your voice, keep it strong and make it intensify, until I obey." If our hearts are truly willing to comply, we will welcome the continued insistence as His verification, rather than ignoring or resisting it.

PONDER: Is my heart open to the gentle whispers of the Holy Spirit? Do I live close enough to Him to even hear Him when He prompts me?

PRAYER: Lord, help me learn to discern Your voice. Help me recognize and do the "good things" You have planned for me.

December 5
What Makes God Laugh?

"...a group of Jews got together and bound themselves with an oath not to eat or drink until they had killed Paul." Acts 23:12

Scripture records numerous times when human beings adamantly declared their intentions, only to find they were up against the God of the Universe, Who had other plans for their intended victims. In this instance, the Lord allowed Paul's young nephew to overhear their plot.

Remember Jezebel's threat to Elijah, *"May the gods strike me and even kill me if by this time tomorrow, I have not killed you..." (I Kings 19:2)* God had other plans!

I love the story in *Matthew 26* of the Pharisees plotting when to kill Jesus. *"...Not during... Passover..."* they all agreed. Ha! God had already determined Jesus would be our Passover Lamb. And guess when they crucified Jesus!

The Psalmist reminds us, *"The wicked plot against the godly... but the Lord just laughs..." (Psalm 37:12,13); "...Why do they waste their time with futile plans... plot together against the Lord... the one who rules in Heaven laughs. The Lord scoffs at them..." Psalm 2:1,2,4*

For those who are surrendered to His will, God's purposes will **always** be accomplished. Whether we live or die is in **His** hands and no one else's! That truth should evoke **trust** and **hope** and **peace** in our hearts!

PONDER: Do I feel I'm at the mercy of circumstances, people, viruses, calamities?

PRAYER: Lord, I choose to put my life in **Your** Hands and trust **You** alone! Whom then shall I fear?

December 6

Gone Before We Know It!

"Lord, remind me how brief my time on earth will be. Remind me that my days are numbered…" Psalm 39:4

One of the hardest things to comprehend, especially for young people, is the brevity of life. We feel so vital, so invincible! In our <u>heads</u>, we know we will die someday, but it seems such a distant reality. In <u>this</u> moment, life looms large in front of us! Why spoil it by contemplating death?

Without occasional reminders, few of us would **ever** contemplate the necessity to prepare for death and eternity. God has many ways of reminding us of our transience. He often uses life's experiences to teach us what we otherwise might be tempted to overlook.

The loss of loved ones, bouts with illness and disease, the presence of evil and crime, accidents, forces of nature… these are but a few ways we're reminded we are mortal and life is uncertain.

Will we take heed and allow these "warnings" to motivate us to contemplate and prepare for that inevitable day? Or will we close our ears to God's reminders?

Even if we defy the odds and live longer than most, when viewed in the rearview mirror, we are shocked at how quickly life has passed. We all thought getting old would take longer!

PONDER: Do I avoid thoughts of death and dying, assuming I have plenty of time for that later?

PRAYER: Lord, I don't want that day to catch me by surprise. I want to be ready!

December 7
Run Toward The Darkness

"You are the light of the world... No one lights a lamp and then puts it under a basket. Instead, a lamp is placed on a stand, where it gives light to everyone..." Matthew 5:14,15

Jesus is the true Light of the world *(John 8:12)*. But, because God has placed His Spirit within our hearts, He declares we, too, are now bearers of God's Light. Our task? Simply shine God's Light into our dark world.

The way we **live** should be noticeably different, should stand out in an attractive, winsome way that draws people to the Source of Light that warms and loves through us.

Jesus warns us not to conceal our light, but to position it strategically where it will be most obvious, like a city on a hill. If our light is not being seen by those groping their way through the darkness, then one of God's purposes for placing His Light within us will have been negated.

Jesus says, **"Don't hide your Light!"** Don't huddle yourselves together inside the cover of your church or your own homes. Put yourselves "out there"—in the darkness!—and shine, as brightly as you can, for Jesus!

If people choose to reject Light, at least they saw it. Those looking for Light will receive God's gracious salvation.

PONDER: Do I avoid "darkness" or run toward it, with Light ablaze?

PRAYER: Lord, don't let it be said of me, *"Those who sat in great darkness never even caught a glimpse of her Light."*

December 8
When All Is Lost

"He [Jesus] saw that they were in serious trouble, rowing hard and struggling against the wind and waves... Jesus came toward them, walking on the water. He intended to go past them..." Mark 6:48

Jesus had seen from the shore how much trouble they were in. Why not calm the sea from there? Once on the water, why not just step into the boat? Why move past them as if he intended to keep going?

These were seasoned fishermen, self-reliant, familiar with sudden squalls on the sea. They knew what to do! As long as they thought they could handle the crisis, they would keep on trying.

Jesus could not save them until they **acknowledged** their **need** of Him. He must allow them to struggle to the point of utter helplessness. Only after having exhausted every skillset they'd ever used or depended on would they finally realize there was **nothing** they could do to save themselves. At that point, all they could do was scream in terror.

That's when Jesus stopped and spoke to them, *"Do not be afraid."* Even then, the storm did not die down until He actually stepped into the boat, but by then, the storm no longer terrified them.

PONDER: Where does my confidence lie? Is it in myself, my education, my experience, my money, my friends?

PRAYER: Bring me, Lord, to the end of all self-effort, to the awareness that, without Jesus, I am totally, utterly, and hopelessly lost. **You** are my only hope!

December 9
Do I ~~Always~~ Have To Be Right?

"…Let's not allow this conflict to come between us…" Genesis 13:8

Abram and Lot were close relatives, who found themselves locked in a dispute that threatened to destroy their relationship. Sound familiar?

The only way to avoid conflict is to live as a total recluse, avoiding people altogether. None of us is immune.

The secret to harmony in ANY relationship is for at least one of the persons involved to care more about the <u>relationship</u> than about being "right" or "having their own way." We don't arrive at that place easily. It takes a lot of grace to initiate, even more to sustain over the long haul.

Abram settled the dispute by allowing Lot to choose first. Lot chose the "best," and Abram ended up with the leftovers, which neither of them really wanted. We tend to feel sorry for Abram, like we feel sorry for ourselves in similar situations.

We forget, however, that, because the relationship mattered more to Abram than the land they were fighting over, Abram actually ended up with what he wanted most—a good rapport with his nephew. Then He <u>trusted the Lord</u> to provide whatever else he needed, which God did, in abundance.

PONDER: What matters more to me—being right or building relationships? Have I ever jeopardized a bond with a loved one, because I just couldn't let go…?

PRAYER: Lord, I want to let go of my need to be right, but I can't do it without Your grace and power!

December 10
Hope–Ful or Hope–less?

"…It is impossible for God to lie. Therefore, we who have fled to him for refuge can have great confidence as we hold to the hope that lies before us. This hope is a strong and trustworthy anchor for our souls…" Hebrews 6:18,19

We live in a time of great anxiety and insecurity. A global pandemic, political upheaval, racial tension, and terrorist threats provide a steady diet of uncertainty, fear, and depression. Sometimes, it feels like the whole world has gone mad. Nothing is as it should be.

But what if…?

What if God's people kept their focus on God's **Word**, His **Promises**, and His **Faithfulness**? What if Christ-followers allowed His peace to **rule** in their hearts, His hope to **dominate** their thoughts?

What if, instead of wringing our hands in despair and filling our conversations with negative, divisive words, we chose to obey Jesus and "**look up**"—confident that our redemption draws near?

When it seems the whole world is being tossed and torn apart, the thing that will keep us steady and confident will be our strong and trustworthy anchor! This **HOPE** we have in Christ will make us stand out like stars against a dark sky. (*Philippians 2:15*)

PONDER: Is my soul anchored in hope? Really? How would being "filled with hope" change my response to all that is going on around me?

PRAYER: Lord, You **alone** are my refuge. Help me hold on to the hope that lies within me as I **trust** in Christ Jesus!

December 11
I'm Tired, But Can't Seem To Stop!

"For the person who keeps all of the laws except one is as guilty as a person who has broken all of God's laws." James 2:10

You may be thinking, ***"I work very hard at being a good person. Surely God wouldn't lump me with people who sin all the time."***

But Jesus said, *"...you are to be perfect, even as your Father in heaven is perfect." Matthew 5:48*

It's an unattainable goal, but we set off to achieve it. We soon find out, though, that trying to please a perfect, holy God can be exhausting, like running on a never-ending treadmill. We don't dare get off, but we find ourselves struggling to keep up. We berate our weaknesses and vow to try even harder.

When will we finally acknowledge there's only **one** perfect person who's ever lived, and it isn't me or you? It's **Jesus Christ**.

He offers us His perfect righteousness in exchange for our sinfulness. *"My old self has been crucified with Christ. It is no longer I who live, but Christ lives in me." (Galatians 2:20)* God's not asking us to live **FOR** Him. He wants to live **IN** us.

PONDER: Am I still on the treadmill of trying to make myself acceptable to God?

PRAYER: Lord, relieve me from the burden of self-effort. You've already accomplished everything necessary for my salvation <u>and</u> my sanctification. I trust You to live Your perfect, sinless life in and through my body as I yield to Your control.

December 12

He Was Born To Die

Jesus is *"…the Lamb who was slaughtered before the world was made." (Revelation 13:8b)*

How many of us would be willing to "take a bullet" for another person? *Romans 5:7* affirms that *"most people would not be willing to die for an upright person, though someone might perhaps be willing to die for a person who is especially good."*

Would we die for our spouses… our kids… our loved ones? Perhaps we would. Even so, humans don't usually have long to anticipate such sacrifices, which, most often, take place in an instant, on loving impulse, without much time to think about it.

Jesus, however, knew, before He created the world, what God's plan of redemption would entail. He left Heaven, laid aside all His divine prerogatives and privileges, took on human flesh and dwelt among us to deliver us from Satan's grasp, knowing full well what would happen to Him.

How long after His birth did His <u>human</u> mind begin to comprehend the magnitude of the sacrifice He was to make? Was He still a child? A teenager? Such a long time to anticipate, to dread, to wrestle with the thought of enduring a prolonged, untold agony He Himself did not deserve! He would bear the horror of all our sin, taste Hell on <u>our</u> behalf, though He Himself had **<u>NEVER</u>** sinned. Yet He stayed the course.

PONDER: What kind of love would make Jesus **<u>CHOOSE</u>** to be born for undeserving sinners, knowing **<u>EXACTLY</u>** what it would cost Him?

PRAYER: Lord, I stand utterly amazed!

December 13
Who Doesn't Love A Baby?

"She gave birth to her first child, a son. She wrapped him snugly in strips of cloth and laid him in a manger..." Luke 2:7

We love the Christmas story and all the pageantry associated with it. There's something about the birth of a baby that evokes human joy and kindness within even the hardest hearts. Babies are just so cute, so innocent, so lovable! We can't help but be drawn to them.

And this story is even more poignant because this baby is no ordinary baby. This is God, in human flesh, born of a virgin. Wow! It blows our minds, but it's so inspiring, so breathtaking!

Some of us would like the Savior to stay right there in the manger—a sweet, beautiful, holy child—because, when Jesus grew up, He caused quite a stir! He made some incredible claims. *"I am the Way, the Truth, and the Life. No one can come to the Father except through me." John 14:6*

Jesus insisted it's our <u>hearts</u> God looks at, no matter how impressive our outward appearance. He calls us to humble ourselves and serve each other. He demands we love and forgive those who wound us. He declares, *"If any of you wants to be my follower, you must turn from your selfish ways, take up your cross and follow me." Matthew 16:24*

PONDER: Do I prefer honoring Jesus as a sweet "baby" rather than obeying Him as Lord?

PRAYER: Jesus, be the Lord of my Life!

December 14

Do I Have Any Room?

"...She… laid him in a manger, because there was no lodging available for them." Luke 2:7

The inns were just too crowded that night! With the influx of people ordered by Caesar Augustus to return to their ancestral towns for registry, the innkeepers of Bethlehem can hardly be blamed for turning away the young couple who begged them for a place to stay.

There was one who took pity on the young couple, but I wonder how he felt when he lay down in his comfy bed that night, knowing the young woman to whom he'd offered his stable was most likely in the throes of childbirth.

They could not have known that the baby born that night was the Messiah, God Himself, clothed in flesh, come to save the world. Would that have made a difference?

They didn't know who He was, but we do! Yet our lives, too, are so crowded, so busy, so full of "stuff," that it's difficult to find time or energy or emotion for the One born in Bethlehem that night.

PONDER: What have I allowed to become more important to me than Jesus? Are there people, things, dreams, and goals, that have slowly crowded my heart so full that I no longer have room for God?

PRAYER: Lord, help me recognize and reject any person or thing that crowds out the place in my heart that should be Yours alone!

December 15
Is That Even Possible?

"When Joseph woke up, he did as the angel of the Lord commanded and took Mary as his wife. But he did not have sexual relations with her until her son was born..." Matthew 1:24,25

This is an amazing statement! Joseph, a red-blooded, normal, adult male, with hormones raging, took Mary as his wife, lived with her for several months in the same house; no doubt he even slept in the same room, if not the same bed, yet chose <u>not</u> to have sexual relations with her until after her baby was born.

We aren't told this was a specific instruction given by the angel, but Joseph somehow knew that remaining sexually abstinent was important in fulfilling the Scripture from *Isaiah 7:14, "A virgin shall conceive and bear a son..."* and so, he chose to subordinate his own physical desires in order to honor God's Word.

That kind of self-discipline, that kind of commitment to God's revealed Word, is rarely found in our modern world, sadly, even among those calling themselves Christians.

We are so conditioned by our culture to believe that being chaste, waiting until marriage, saving ourselves until we have the blessing of God on our wedding day, is not only <u>unnecessary</u>, but absolutely <u>impossible</u>! Our media would have us believe <u>nobody</u> does that anymore, and nobody ever really did.

PONDER: Have we bought the lie that sexual purity is not possible or necessary?

PRAYER: Lord, help me make choices based on what Your Word says is not only <u>right</u>, but <u>possible</u>.

December 16

I Give Only What I've Received

"...who am I, and who are my people, that we could give anything to you? Everything we have has come from you, and we give you only what you first gave us!" I Chronicles 29:14

Remember Christmastime when we were kids? We desperately wanted to buy a gift for Mom or Dad, but didn't have the money or legitimate means of earning it. Yet, when the day came for Christmas shopping, just being their son or daughter—fetching Dad's slippers, giving hugs and kisses, eating all our vegetables—had earned us a small sum we could then spend on the people we loved most in this world. To our adoring parents, those gifts were treasures.

I never realized what a life lesson that was, what a perfect illustration of our relationship with God. Even when we <u>think</u> we're pulling our own weight, earning our own way, God smiles knowingly. If He withheld the air He so mercifully allows us to breathe, even for a few minutes, we'd be "toast."

Health and strength, the capacity to think and create, the food that nourishes and sustains, the resources we utilize in our pursuits—God is the Source of them all! Yet He still delights in gifts offered from a heart of worship.

PONDER: Does gratitude to God express itself in a worshipful desire to give to and serve Him?

PRAYER: All that I am, all that I have, I give back to You, Lord. Take joy, my King!

December 17

What Was It Like For God To Be A Baby?

"Because God's children are human beings—made of flesh and blood—Jesus also became flesh and blood by being born in human form. For only as a human being could he die..." Hebrews 2:14

God... clothed in flesh... living among people! The One who created the universe and flung the stars in space, now looking up into the sky through human eyes! He who spoke the world into existence now reduced to the cries and babblings of a baby!

This is the Master of the Universe, who had tenderly formed mankind out of the dust of the earth, now helpless and tiny, totally dependent on created beings for His every need and desire!

No matter that only a few would recognize and welcome such sacrifice! God was on a mission here to redeem fallen humanity. His goal? To be reunited with mankind who had been alienated from Him because of sin.

And so, God reaches to us with His gift of love. *"...the free gift of God is eternal life through Christ Jesus our Lord." (Romans 6:23)*

Those who have received God's gift by faith should exclaim in eternal gratitude, *"Thanks be to God for His indescribable gift!" II Corinthians 9:15 NIV*

PONDER: Does the birth of Jesus stir me to worship? Is my heart filled with awe and wonder, thanksgiving and praise, as I contemplate what He gave up to be my Savior?

PRAYER: Lord Jesus, keep the glory of Christmas alive in my heart. May I never lose its wonder!

December 18

The Miracle And Mystery Of The Incarnation

"...The virgin will conceive a child! She will give birth to a son and will call him Immanuel [which means 'God is with us']." Isaiah 7:14

Imagine for a moment what it would be like to know you were carrying, inside your own body, the child of God? This babe, conceived by the Spirit of God, was no less than God Himself, clothed in human flesh!

How would it feel to be walking around, every day, knowing that God Himself was alive, right inside your body? What a privilege for Mary! What wonder she must have known as she felt His movements, sensed His presence.

But wait! You and I, if we've received God's unspeakable gift of Eternal Life through this Incarnate One, also have God living in <u>our</u> bodies. No need to try to imagine because it's a reality we can know and experience every single day of our lives! *"...we are the temple of the Living God..."* (II Corinthians 6:16b); *"...Christ lives in me..."* Gal. 2:20

And just as Jesus Christ burst forth from Mary's womb, so this Light and Life within us must blaze forth from our lives, bringing light and hope to people who grope in spiritual darkness.

PONDER: Is Christ living in me? If so, how mindful am I of His nearness? Do others sense His presence in my life?

PRAYER: Make me aware, Lord, of Your life within me. May others be aware of it as well and be drawn to You.

December 19

Only God Could Pull It Off!

"For unto us a child is born, unto us a son is given... his name shall be called Wonderful Counselor, The Mighty God, The Everlasting Father, The Prince of Peace." Isaiah 9:6 KJV

700 years before Christ's birth, God spoke through Isaiah to describe His Promised One, the child who would come to save the world. God doesn't usually hide things in plain sight. Rather, He invites us to ask and seek, as in a treasure hunt.

But here, in this verse, God gives a very obvious description of the One He will send. All but one of the Hebrew words used here to describe Jesus are reserved **only** for God. They're **never** used to describe man. Clearly, Isaiah is foretelling that **the coming Messiah will be God Himself**.

How could God accomplish that? You and I can't imagine it because we could never do it! But nothing is too difficult for God!

Why would He do it? Because He loved us, and He knew there was absolutely **NO OTHER WAY** to reconcile us back to Himself.

You've heard it said, *"I'd have given my life, if it would've saved my child/wife, etc."* That's just a "saying," because we humans can't pull it off.

But God could! And He did! ...because He is God! Hallelujah! Merry Christmas!

PONDER: Will I let my inability to imagine **how** God could do something keep me from experiencing **what** He has accomplished on my behalf?

PRAYER: Thank you, God, for loving me that much!

December 20

Why A Virgin?

"...Mary was engaged to be married to Joseph, but before the marriage took place, while she was still a virgin, she became pregnant through the power of the Holy Spirit." Matthew 1:18

Have you ever wondered why it was necessary that Jesus be born of a **virgin**? Is that essential to the plan of redemption?

At Creation, the Lord gave Adam and Eve dominion over the earth. Their sin forfeited that authority to Satan, and every human, since then, has been born with a sinful nature that succumbs to Satan's domination.

God promised to redeem His children and restore the earth. However, because it was humans who'd been given, and then relinquished, its dominion, God Himself could not just "take it back" on their behalf. Only a perfect, sinless **human** would qualify to redeem mankind. And NONE could be found.

But God had a plan. A child would be born, His mother, human and a virgin, His Father, God Himself. This baby would be fully human, but also fully divine.

Stripped of all the "privileges" of divinity that humans don't have access to, He must live and die without ever once committing sin. If successful, He would overcome sin and the grave, rise triumphantly from death, and deliver from Satan's power **anyone** who put their trust in Him.

PONDER: Is Jesus's birth the centerpiece of all my Christmas celebrations? Have I allowed anything else to take center stage this season?

PRAYER: Fill me anew, Lord, with awe and wonder at the incredible story of Your Incarnation.

December 21
Do With Me What You Will

"…be it unto me according to thy word…" Luke 1:38 KJV

Mary is a very young, teenage girl who has just been given the news that she will mother the Messiah. This had been the dream of every Hebrew woman since the promise was given. Yet none had likely considered the "burden" that honor would carry with it.

In a culture and religion in which, most often, promiscuous women were shunned, even stoned to death, how was Mary to convince people that the impossible had just happened, that she **was** still a **virgin**, even though her belly was swollen with child?

As the angel's words penetrated Mary's mind, no doubt such thoughts assailed her. She'd witnessed the cruel justice demanded by the "keepers of the law." The wagging tongues had not escaped her young ears. And now, she herself would be the subject of their condemnation.

Yet Mary chose to trust God's wisdom, yielding her body to be used in His magnificent plan, no matter how costly it might become in the days ahead.

PONDER: When God's will takes me where, in my humanness, I'd rather not go, where I am misunderstood or forsaken, where my own dreams and plans might be altered or abandoned, what is my response? Can I say, with Mary, ***"Do whatever you want with my life?"***

PRAYER: That's my prayer, Lord, even though I fear You'll have to help me live it out: here I am— *"be it unto me according to Your will."*

December 22

Whose Birthday Is This Anyway?

"Glory to God in the highest Heaven… the Savior—yes, the Messiah, the Lord—has been born tonight in Bethlehem…!" Luke 2:14a,11a

Birthdays are fun to celebrate, aren't they? We decorate with streamers and balloons, serve ice cream and cake, give gifts to the birthday boy/girl. It's our way of acknowledging the worth of the one we love. Each of us has felt the validation of such celebrations.

Picture with me a party on <u>your</u> birthday. When the guests arrive, they walk <u>past</u> you, some ignoring you completely, others acknowledging you with only a slight tip of the head.

At this party, birthday presents are given to everyone <u>except</u> you. Partygoers are certainly celebrating; they're just focused on each other. Birthday songs are sung, candles lit, and goodies served, but everyone seems totally unaware of <u>your</u> presence in the room, completely preoccupied with the excitement of the party itself.

Thankfully, few humans will ever be called on to endure such a disappointment. But sadly, we subject our Savior to that kind of party every year and somehow expect Him to feel honored by our celebrations.

PONDER: Who or what consumes me this time of year?

PRAYER: Oh, Lord Jesus, forgive me for making the holidays more about me and mine than about You and the unspeakable gift You came to provide. Forgive me for allowing my heart to grow complacent to the old, old story of Your Incarnation. Help me know how to truly honor You on Your birthday, and always.

December 23
Extravagance Wasted On Shepherds?

"...some shepherds were in the fields... guarding their flocks of sheep. Suddenly, an angel of the Lord appeared among them... joined by a vast host of others—the armies of Heaven—praising God." Luke 2:8,13

This was the most extravagant heavenly display in human history! But then, of course, God can afford to be lavish. His resources are unlimited—totally inexhaustible! When He throws a party, He doesn't worry about the cost!

Does it seem strange to you, however, that the <u>only</u> ones who experienced this phenomenon were a small band of lowly shepherds?

We mortals would <u>never</u> waste such a display on a tiny group of insignificants. Our human "productions" are carefully planned and orchestrated to maximize the size, influence, and reciprocity of the audience.

Such an announcement certainly merited more "press." God chose, however, to reveal His plan only to those who would welcome and receive it. He's not impressed with the "labels" we pin on ourselves and others.

God knows that humble hearts are open to His message, and proud souls resist Him. Therefore, He is drawn to anyone humble enough to acknowledge his/her need, no matter their human condition.

PONDER: Do I tend to "qualify" those to whom I will reach out with the love of God? How generous am I with the "Good News" entrusted to my care?

PRAYER: Thank You, Lord, for being so wildly profuse in Your outpouring of love to me! Help me pass on that love with the same, indiscriminate extravagance!

December 24
Jesus— The Lamb Of God

"…the shepherds said to each other, "Let's go to Bethlehem! …They hurried to the village and found… the baby, lying in the manger." Luke 2:15,16

How appropriate that Jesus, **the Lamb of God**, would be born in a stable and laid in a manger, with shepherds His first visitors.

God quietly snuck into our world without pomp and circumstance. The Jews expected a king. God showed up as a "lamb." And hadn't He hinted as much in Scripture?

When Abraham assured young Isaac that God would *"provide Himself a lamb"* for their sacrifice, he could not have known he was describing the coming Messiah.

Again, in Egypt, when a perfect lamb was slain and its blood sprinkled over the doorposts of Israeli houses, how could they have imagined God was foretelling the One who would become the ultimate sacrifice for sin?

Isaiah portrayed the Messiah as a lamb being "led to the slaughter." John the Baptist declared Jesus to be *"The Lamb of God who takes away the sin of the world!"*

In the Revelation, Jesus is revealed as the Lamb who was slain from the foundations of the world. His redeemed ones overcome Satan by the blood of the Lamb and are invited to the Lamb's marriage supper.

PONDER: What response does God's intricate plan evoke in me? Does it inspire awe and gratitude in my heart?

PRAYER: Worthy is the Lamb who was slain to receive wisdom and power and glory and honor and strength forever and ever! Amen!

December 25
Too Brilliant To Look At

"...He [God] lives in light so brilliant that no human can approach him. No human eye has ever seen him, nor ever will..." I Timothy 6:16

That is why He clothed Himself in flesh and became a human.

"In the beginning the Word already existed. He was with God, and He was God. So the Word became human and lived here on earth among us... And we have seen His glory, the glory of the only Son of the Father." John 1:1,14

"The Son reflects God's own glory, and everything about him represents God exactly..." Hebrews 1:3

"For God, who said, 'Let there be light in the darkness,' has made us understand that this light is the brightness of the glory of God that is seen in the face of Jesus Christ." II Corinthians 4:6

"...Though he was God, he did not demand and cling to his rights as God. He made himself nothing; he... appeared in human form. And in human form he obediently humbled himself even further by dying a criminal's death on a cross." Philippians 2:6-8

"Because God's children are human beings—made of flesh and blood—Jesus also became flesh and blood by being born in human form. For only as a human being could he die, and only by dying could he break the power of the Devil, who had the power of death..." Hebrews 2:14

PONDER: Wow! How should I respond?

PRAYER: I worship You, Almighty God! There is none like You!

December 26

Christmas Is Over!

"I once thought all these things were so very important, but now I consider them worthless... Yes, everything else is worthless when compared with the priceless gain of knowing Christ Jesus my Lord." Philippians 3:7,8

Christmas has come and gone. No more packages under the tree. The living room is strewn with wrapping paper and boxes. We dare not voice the pathetic sense of disappointment we feel inside. After looking forward to this day with <u>such</u> anticipation, why do we feel so empty? Is there anything wrong with giving and receiving gifts at Christmastime?

Of course not!

Unfortunately, however, too many of us have subtly begun to equate happiness with the accumulation of "things." The media constantly entices us with all with "bigger and better" stuff.

Almost before the paint is dry, this year's craze is obsolete, yet we can't keep ourselves from wanting it. We spend money we can ill afford to get it. And once we possess it, we suddenly notice something else looks even more exciting. We must have that, too.

PONDER: Has anything I've accumulated to this point ever really filled the empty space in my heart? Do I ever hear myself thinking, *"If I could just have THAT, I could finally be content!"*?

PRAYER: Lord, nothing I have **ever** accumulated has truly satisfied my soul. I see now that my heart has always hungered for **You** and You alone. Forgive my futile longings and empty pursuits. Be to me the consuming passion of my life.

December 27

Secret To A Satisfied Life

"...be satisfied with what you have. For God has said, 'I will never fail you. I will never abandon you.'" Hebrews 13:5

As the sense of expectation, promised by beautifully wrapped presents under the Christmas tree, gives way to a vague sense of disappointment, now that the hoopla is over, we realize that all the "things" we thought would bring us joy and happiness have fallen woefully short of their anticipated results.

The Lord is asking us to simply *"be satisfied"* with what we have. It's an assignment we don't find easy to complete in a world where the "latest and greatest" is always clamoring for our attention and our affection.

God says the key to the satisfaction, that always seems to elude us, lies in comprehending that He, the Infinite, Holy God—the Creator of the world, the Almighty, Everlasting One—will never fail us or abandon us!

Once I comprehend the **wonder** of that truth, I will know for certain—beyond a shadow of doubt—even if I was stripped of all earthly possessions and positions, I would still have the **ONE** thing that truly matters for all eternity!

PONDER: If I lost every thing and every one dear to me, would God be enough? If not, I am destined to a life of always grasping for the newest, flashiest "thing," the next challenge or coveted title I have not yet taken possession of.

PRAYER: O, God, show me You are all I need. You are enough!

December 28

Am I Ever Really Alone?

"You know when I sit down or stand up. You know my thoughts… You see me when I travel and when I rest at home. You know everything I do… even in darkness I cannot hide from you…" Psalm 139:2,3,12

When we want to do something we know we shouldn't be doing, we go off by ourselves, don't we? We hide our actions from the eyes of anyone who might disapprove. Somehow, that feeling of being "alone," of not being seen, makes it easier for us to justify what we are about to do.

But are we ever really alone? God says not! If we read *Psalm 139* in its entirety, we will see that no matter where we may go, or what we may do, God sees us. He knows our actions, what we say, what we are thinking, even our motives. The truth is there is nothing, anywhere, anytime, that He does not see or know. And there is no place that He is NOT.

When I sit at my computer, when I'm parked in my car, when I'm behind closed doors at the office… God is THERE!

PONDER: Does that knowledge change anything for me? Can remembering God's all-seeing, all-knowing watchfulness protect me from that which beckons to me from "the shadows?"

PRAYER: Oh, God, thank You that nothing is hidden from your sight. Help me always remember that. May the awareness of Your continual Presence protect me from myself, my flesh, the world's allure, and the devil's schemes.

December 29
Peace In The Face Of Loss

"'If the Lord sees fit,' David said, 'He will bring me back... But if he is through with me, then let him do what seems best to him.'"
II Samuel 15: 25,26

King David's crown has been usurped by his son Absalom. He is fleeing for his life. As He leaves Jerusalem, the priests want to follow with the Ark of the Covenant to assure David's success against his enemies. He sends them back to the Tabernacle with those words.

Years earlier, King Saul, David's predecessor, was filled with jealous rage and suspicion when told he would forfeit <u>his</u> crown because of his stubborn and rebellious heart. Tragically, even at the end of his pathetic life, he was still grasping for what God had taken away.

David sinned as well, but when confronted with <u>his</u> sin, David humbled himself. Though he deserved condemnation, he received mercy instead. After that, He lived in continual, grateful awareness of God's amazing grace!

Now, it seems, the kingdom is being stripped from David as well. But notice <u>his</u> response. With quiet resignation to <u>whatever</u> God decides is <u>best</u>, David expresses deep confidence in the Lord's wisdom and mercy. His words reveal uncommon yieldedness to the will of God in the face of great, personal loss.

PONDER: How do <u>I</u> handle loss... especially when it seems untimely, unfair, and undeserved?

PRAYER: Lord, give me Your heart and Your perspective, so I, like David, may be at peace, fully surrendered to whatever You determine is best.

December 30
What Will People Remember About Me?

"Jehoram was 32 years old when he became king, and he reigned in Jerusalem eight years. No one was sorry when he died…" 2 Chronicles 21:20

What a sad memorial! Surely there was <u>someone</u> in all of Judah who mourned his death. After all, he was the king!

But Scripture tells us that <u>no</u> <u>one</u> grieved when he died. *"His people did not build a great funeral fire to honor him as they had done for his ancestors." (v. 19)* He was an evil king who had abandoned the Lord and done what was wicked in God's sight.

What a contrast to the death of Dorcas in Acts chapter nine. She was just a simple, relatively unknown woman who went about doing good in the name of her Savior Jesus.

When she died, Peter was called to her house where *"the room was filled with widows who were weeping and showing him the coats and other clothes Dorcas had made for them."* Acts 9:39

PONDER: What kind of legacy am I leaving the people in my life? If, at the conclusion of my days, the words on my tombstone summarized my life in one sentence, what would it say? Am I allowing God to shape me into the kind of person whose life adds value to those around me? If not, why not?

PRAYER: O God, change me, <u>deep within my heart</u>, so that what flows from my life will be blessing and encouragement to all those you've placed around me.

December 31

Out With The Old — In With The New!

"...those who become Christians become new persons. They are not the same anymore, for the old life is gone. A new life has begun."
II Corinthians 5:17

A new year is about to dawn. For many, however, the thought of closing out one year and beginning another brings a heightened sense of guilt and regret.

Every January, people make New Year's resolutions, which they seldom keep. There are those, of course (perhaps even you), who, through sheer willpower, have broken bad habits and brought about huge changes in their lives. But when it's all said and done, no amount of effort on our part ever changes what's really true about us deep inside our hearts. Only God can do that.

He has a solution for the "sin" we try to deny and hide from. It's called repentance, and it brings forgiveness, peace, and transformation. That's what Jesus paid for on the cross, when He spilled His blood for our redemption.

"'Come now...' says the Lord. 'No matter how deep the stain of your sins, I can remove it. I can make you as clean as freshly fallen snow...'" Isaiah 1:18

What a great way to begin a new year!

PONDER: Do I long to be new and different... on the inside?

PRAYER: I repent, Lord, of the sin and self-centeredness of my heart, of my efforts to run my own life and be my own "savior." You're the only One who can truly make me new. Change my heart, O God.

Made in the USA
Monee, IL
01 May 2025

020d6e0b-6e1a-4277-a5ea-5d52a6216e27R01